FROM CAPTIVITY TO FREEDOM: THEMES IN ANCIENT AND MODERN SLAVERY

FROM CAPTIVITY TO FREEDOM: THEMES IN ANCIENT AND MODERN SLAVERY

Constantina Katsari
Enrico Dal Lago

© Copyright individual authors 2008

ISBN 978–0–9560179–0–1

Published by the
School of Archaeology & Ancient History,
University of Leicester

All rights reserved. No part of this publication may be reproduced, stored in a retrieval system or transmitted in any form or by any means, electronic, mechanical, photocopying, recording or otherwise, without prior permission

Front cover: Crater 4th century BC Antikensammlung, Staatliche Museen zu Berlin. Inv.F3043

Typeset and printed by
4word Ltd, Bristol

Table of Contents:

Acknowledgements   vii
The Authors   ix

Diachronic Slavery
1) World Slavery and Comparative Slavery: Diachronic Approaches   1
   Introduction by Constantina Katsari and Enrico Dal Lago

Captives and Slaves
2) Enslavement and Death: the Third Macedonian War   19
   Constantina Katsari
3) Enslavement of Native Americans during Queen Anne's War   41
   Rebecca M. Seaman

Female Slaves
4) On the Moregine *ancilla* or Slavery and Prostitution at Pompei   57
   Giovanni Salmeri
5) From Slaves to Sergipanos: Gender, Labour and Family in Brazil's Cacao Area, 1870–1920   71
   Mary Ann Mahony

Slave Rebellions
6) Rewriting Slave Rebellions   93
   Theresa Urbainczyk
7) Denying the Evidence: Slave Rebelliousness and the Denmark Vesey Debate   107
   Douglas R. Egerton

Freedom after Slavery
8) 'Independent' Slaves in Classical Athens and the Ideology of Slavery   121
   Nick Fisher
9) The Abolition of Slavery and Plans for Freedom in Late Nineteenth Century Brazil.   147
   Walter Fraga Filho

Index   167

Acknowledgements

We wish to thank the contributors to the international conference on "Slave Systems, Ancient and Modern", held at the Centre for the Study of Human Settlement and Historical Change, National University, Galway, on November 24th–26th, 2004. Several of the papers included in this volume were presented in an early form, while others were added later.

In particular, we wish to thank the Director of the Centre for the Study of Human Settlement and Historical Change, Nicholas Canny, and the Centre's Secretary, Marta Shaughnessy, for their help and availability. Also, the conference would not have been possible without the financial help of the President's Office at the National University of Ireland and of the university's History Department; we wish to thank wholeheartedly both the former President, Ignoid O' Muircheartaigh and Professor Stephen Ellis, Head of the History Department. Finally, we wish to thank those who contributed in different ways, offering their enthusiastic help at difficult junctures in the enterprise of organizing the conference, and especially Professor Gearoid O'Tuathaigh and Sonia Guilhe. We own also many thanks to Mary Ann Mahony who kindly translated Walter Fraga Filho's article in English.

In addition, this volume would not have seen the light without the crucial help of our publisher or the helpful comments of the anonymous reader.

The Authors

Enrico Dal Lago is Lecturer in American History in the History Department of the National University of Ireland, Galway. He is the author of *Agrarian Elites* (Baton Rouge, LA 2005). He also co-edited the books *Slave Systems: Ancient and Modern* (Cambridge 2008), *Slavery and Emancipation* (Oxford 2002) and *The American South and the Italian Mezzogiorno: Essays in Comparative History* (Basingstoke/ New York 2001).

Douglas R. Egerton is Professor in the Department of History in Le Moyne College. His publications include *Charles Fenton Mercer and Trial of National Conservatism* (1989), *Gabriel's Rebellion* (1993), *He Shall Go Out Free: The Lives of Denmark Vesey* (1999), *Rebels, Reformers and Revolutionaries* (2002) and *Atlantic World: A History 1400–1888* (2007). He has also written numerous essays and reviews regarding race in early America.

Nick Fisher is Professor of Ancient History in the Cardiff School of History and Archaeology, Cardiff University. He has written books on *Hybris* (Warminster 1992), *Slavery in Classical Greece* (London 1993), and a translation and commentary on *Aeschines: Against Timarchos* (Oxford 2001), as well as many articles on the political and social history of Athens and Sparta. His current project brings together the study of the Greek concepts of *charis* and the *Charites* and the advancement of social cohesion through festival participation in classical Greece.

Walter Fraga Filho is Adjunct Professor of Brazilian History at the State University of Bahia. He is the author of *Encruzilhadas da liberdade: Histórias de Escravos e Libertos na Bahia, 1870–1910* (São Paulo 2006). He studied extensively post-emancipation in Bahia, Brazil.

Constantina Katsari is Lecturer in Ancient History at the School of Ancient History and Archaeology at the University of Leicester. She co-edited two books, *Slave Systems: Ancient and Modern* (Cambridge 2008) and *Patterns in the Economy of Roman Asia Minor* (Swansea 2005), while she published several articles on both slavery and the ancient economy. She is currently preparing her forthcoming monograph on the Roman Monetary System.

The Authors

Mary Ann Mahony is Associate Professor of History at Central Connecticut State University. She is the author of several articles on Brazilian history and is working on a book entitled *Color, Class and Conflict in a Brazilian Agricultural Region* (2007–2008).

Giovanni Salmeri is Professor of Latin Epigraphy at the University of Pisa. His many publications concentrate on the history of the Greek world under the Roman Empire and the history of classical scholarship. Since 2000 he is director of the Cilicia Survey Project.

Rebecca M. Seaman is Associate Professor in History in Elizabeth City State University. She is an expert of the enslavement of Indians in Colonial America.

Theresa Urbainczyk is Senior Lecturer in the School of Classics, University College Dublin. Her main interest is in the way people write history, both now and in antiquity. Her first two books were on the struggle between church and state for the history of the early Christians (*Socrates of Constantinople*, University of Michigan Press 1997 and *Theodoret of Cyrrhus*, University of Michigan Press 2002) and more recently she has turned her attention to the way another group of rebels have been written about, those involved in slave revolts in antiquity (*Spartacus*, Duckworth 2004 and *Slave Revolts in Antiquity*, Acumen 2008).

Part 1

Diachronic Slavery

World Slavery and Comparative Slavery: Diachronic Approaches

Introduction by
Constantina Katsari and Enrico Dal Lago

Comparison has lately become one of the most popular, albeit difficult, methods for the study of ancient and modern history. In accord with current trends in contemporary historiography, we organised an International Conference on 'Slave Systems: Ancient and Modern' at the Moore Institute, National University of Ireland, Galway, in November 2004. The subject was broad enough to allow the study of several themes on the 'peculiar institution' of slavery, and we decided to publish a selection of papers in this edited volume. The topics in the contributions range from the fate of captives in ancient Rome and the United States of America, to the lives of female slaves in the Roman world and modern Brazil, slave revolts in Roman Italy, slavery in the Antebellum American South and other parts of the modern world and 'independent' slaves in Classical Athens and freedmen in Bahia. All of the papers are presented in different sections of the book according to the topic.

Originally, comparison was a method widely employed by social sciences other than history. In fact, between the end of the nineteenth century and early twentieth century it became popular among anthropologists, linguists and sociologists.[1] The German sociologist Max Weber was the first who applied the comparative method to history; throughout his work, Weber analysed the characteristics of western society and culture in a historical perspective and compared them with the high civilisations of the Far East.[2] However, the first historian to write about the methodology of comparative history was Marc Bloch, the co-founder, with Lucien Febvre, of the Annales School. In 1928, Bloch wrote a seminal paper entitled 'Toward a comparative history of European societies', in which he stated that the general requirements for historical comparison are two: 1) a certain similarity between the facts

---

[1] Among them the most prominent was Emile Durkheim, the father of modern sociology. See Burke, 1992, pp. 22–23.
[2] See Weber, (transl. of 1905 German version) 2002.

observed, and 2) certain dissimilarities between situations in which they have arisen.[3] Since Bloch's article, historians and sociologists have often held discordant views on how to write comparative history. Responding to the need to update Marc Bloch's methodological essay and taking into account recent developments in comparative historical studies, Theda Skocpol and Margaret Somers wrote a seminal article on comparative method which appeared in the 1980 issue of *Comparative Studies in Society and History*.[4] In their article, Skocpol and Somers outlined three different methods of comparison and distinguished between works that use comparison in order to find out general explanations of historical processes and works that use comparison to highlight similarities and differences between the historical paths followed by two or more societies. The first category of works implements what Skocpol and Somers called 'Macro-Causal Analysis'; these works analyse the historical evidence and, through comparison between different case studies, build a general model or theory of history. The second category of works implements either one or the other of what Skocpol and Somers termed 'Parallel Demonstration Theory' and 'Contrast of Contexts': while the former seeks to prove that *"a given hypothesis, based on similarities between the two cases, can repeatedly prove its usefulness"*, the latter seeks *"to bring out the unique features of each particular case... and to show how these unique features affect the working out of putatively general social processes"*.[5] If we were to analyse the most important studies of comparative history written in the past fifty years, we would discover that virtually each and every one of them implements a method which falls along one or more of the three categories described by Skocpol and Somers in 1980.

It is no coincidence that many comparative studies focus on issues related to either slavery or unfree labour. This historical field offers abundant opportunities for comparison across states or nations or even continents. George Fredrickson's *White Supremacy* (1982) and Peter Kolchin's *Unfree Labour* (1987) are probably the most important examples of such studies. Both employ a method, which is half way between the 'Parallel Demonstration Theory' and the 'Contrast of Contexts'. In *White Supremacy*, George Fredrickson takes two societies – the United States and South Africa – in which racism of whites towards blacks developed to the point of becoming an institutionalised state ideology and compares them in order to bring out the unique features of each of them. Fredrickson's focus is not on the discovery of a grand theory to explain the general workings of the historical process, but rather on the attention to the similarities and differences between the two case studies. Specifically, Fredrickson finds parallels between the United States and South Africa in

---

[3] See especially, Bloch, (transl. of 1924 article) 1973; and Bloch, (transl. of 1939–140 manuscript) 1961.
[4] Skocpol and Somers, 1980.
[5] Skocpol and Somers, 1980, p. 178.

the reliance on black slave labour as a means of diffusing class conflict in the white community; the two slave systems were essentially racial in character and drew a clear line between slavery and freedom based on skin colour. At the same time, Fredrickson is equally interested in the unique features which make American and South African racism so distinct from one another; this search leads him to the conclusion that the most important distinguishing feature between the two societies – one that had momentous consequences for the difference in the history of race relations in the two countries – is the absence of a real plantation system with widely diffused slave-holding in South Africa as opposed to the southern part of the United States.[6]

Another important comparative work is Peter Kolchin's book, *Unfree Labour*. Kolchin's interest lay in comparing the historical development of American Slavery and Russian Serfdom, especially in regard to issues related to labour relations and labour control and management. Like Fredrickson, he focuses on both similarities and differences between the two case studies and starts from general assumptions over the similarity in historical process, but ends up showing what makes each case different and unique. Kolchin's point of departure is the simultaneous appearance of slavery in the American colonies and the reappearance of serfdom in Russia around the seventeenth century. However different from one another the two systems were, they seem to have developed for largely similar reasons: shortage of labour combined with availability of land in economies undergoing rapid growth and transformation. Kolchin finds further similarities in an inherent contradiction between the two economic systems. On one hand, both American and Russian masters were commercially oriented and they participated in the capitalist economy from two peripheral areas, while, on the other hand, both slavery and serfdom have essentially a non-capitalist character. Kolchin also detected another major similarity; the fact that in both systems paternalism was the dominant ideology of the master class. Despite this fundamental similarity, he rightly expends much energy in showing the consequences of the different relationship between masters and their bondsmen in the two case studies.[7]

George Fredrickson's *White Supremacy* and Peter Kolchin's *Unfree Labour* are, thus, bright examples of the best kind of comparative history that historians and historical sociologists have become engaged in. However, we believe that, together with being interdisciplinary and cross-national, comparative history should be also strongly diachronic, not simply synchronic: it should conceive of the possibility of comparing societies across the entire breadth of world history. This approach could also be highly rewarding, if the focus were on comparison of specific issues characterising both the ancient and the modern worlds.

---

[6] See Fredrickson, 1982.
[7] Kolchin, 1987.

Important studies by some ancient historians have already moved in this direction. First and foremost among them is Moses Finley, the Cambridge historian who was involved in the founding of the journal *Slavery and Abolition* and remained a member of its editorial committee until the end of his life. Finley compared the ancient Greco-Roman systems with more recent slave systems, making distinctions between genuine 'slave societies' and 'societies with slaves'. In his 1968 study,[8] he claimed that a 'slave society' existed only when *"the economic and political elite depended primarily on slave labour for basic production"*, while a 'society with slaves' is exemplified by the existence of slavery affecting the economy in a limited way. Accordingly, he proposed that only Greece, Ancient Italy, Brazil, the US South and the Caribbean could be identified as 'slave societies' with more than one third of the population enslaved.[9] The common characteristics of societies that belonged to the first or the second groups justified Finley's undertaking of the comparison and highlighted the similarities between them. Other ancient historians followed in Finley's footsteps; namely Keith Bradley[10], Keith Hopkins,[11] Brent Shaw[12] and Ingomar Weiler[13]. All of the above studies may have focused on Roman slavery but they also offered hints, some more extensive than others, on the value of a comparative approach with several other 'slave societies'. However, they never developed into a full comparison of the type that Peter Kolchin's study represents. The exception to the rule is Walter Scheidel's work on the comparative history of Greece and Rome,[14] the Mediterranean and the Atlantic,[15] and more recently the Roman Empire and the Chinese Empire.[16] Scheidel manages to effectively compare and contrast slave systems of different societies across the globe, using a range of evidence coming from both ancient and modern contexts.

In fact, Scheidel's work reminds us of similar studies that may well fall into the discipline of 'World History' or 'Global History'. One emblematic study of this order is the 1982 book by Orlando Patterson, *Slavery and Social Death*;[17] a book that has influenced the writings of both ancient and modern historians until today. Its value lies in the fact that Patterson attempted both diachronic and trans-regional comparisons between ancient and modern slavery in sixty six slave-holding societies from the Greco-Roman world to nineteenth century Americas. The author used a large body of evidence, which, combined with

---

[8] Finley, 1968.
[9] Finley, 1985, p. 71.
[10] Bradley, 1987; Bradley,
[11] Hopkins, 1978.
[12] Shaw, 2001 in his introduction.
[13] Weiler, 2003.
[14] Scheidel, 2005.
[15] Scheidel, 1996.
[16] Scheidel, 2008.
[17] Patterson, 1982.

the use of sociological, anthropological and historical theories, helped him to demonstrate that 'the peculiar institution' of slavery remained largely comparable across space and time. He eventually arrived to the conclusion that *"slavery is the permanent violent domination of natally alienated and generally dishonoured persons"*.[18] Even if his idea is not considered by every scholar a universal truth, it still may be applied to a number of slave societies across time and space. The comparable nature of the condition of slaves in some of these societies remains a fertile ground, from a historical point of view, for the growth of comparative studies on ancient and modern slavery.

Since Patterson published *Slavery and Social Death* in 1982, there have been many studies – especially, but not only – by specialists in African slavery that have refined, extended, and sometimes even contradicted his famous definition. Among them particularly important are Claude Meillassoux's *The Anthropology of Slavery: The Womb of Iron and Gold* (1991) and Paul Lovejoy's *Transformations in Slavery: A History of Slavery in Africa* (2000, 2nd ed.). Besides works on slavery in comparative perspective, there have been constant attempts in the past decade or so to catalogue and describe in a systematic way all the possible types of slavery in world history. Particularly valuable in this respect are *A Historical Guide to World Slavery* edited by Stanley Engerman and Seymour Drescher,[19] *The Historical Encyclopedia of World Slavery* edited by Junius Rodriguez,[20] also Paul Finkelman and Joseph C. Miller, eds., *The Macmillan Encyclopedia of World Slavery*,[21] and the two volumes of *Slavery and Slaving in World History* by Joseph C. Miller, which included 14,241 entries.[22] These reference books not only provide an overview of a very complex topic but they also look at specific slavery themes through the prism of global history.

The value of the historical treatises we mentioned, so far, is undeniable. However, such studies present us with a series of problems that should be eventually resolved in a more systematic fashion. In a recent book on *Comparison and History: Europe in Cross-National Perspective* the editors, Deborah Cohen and Maura O' Connor, are forced to acknowledge several of the disadvantages of comparative history. Specifically, they claim that *"comparison takes longer, offers more room for mistakes, may be poorly received by specialists in the field"*.[23] We also fully recognise the problems arising from the use of comparative methodologies, and especially the attempts to compare and contrast two or more 'slave societies', or else 'societies with slaves', in a direct way. However, we insist that this is also a method that allows modern researchers to acquaint

---

[18] Patterson, 1982, p. 13.
[19] Drescher and Engerman, 1998.
[20] Rodriguez, 1997.
[21] Finkelman and Miller, 1999.
[22] Miller, 1993; Miller, 1999.
[23] Cohen and O' Connor, 2004b, p. xvi.

themselves with data from other civilisations, societies or regions, that can fundamentally enhance their understanding, first of all, of world history and, secondly, of the era or region they are most interested in. The fact that most historians tend to specialise on a specific period and/or country is a problem that can be overcome, if we allow more flexibility with regard to comparative methodology.

Until today *"the most prevalent form of explicit comparison"* seems to have been the juxtapositional method.[24] According to this method, editors may bring together in a forum specialised historians with the explicit aim to discuss their respective fields. Once the discussion takes place, the similarities and differences between slave societies across history may become evident to the audience and may give rise to constructive comparative analysis. Such studies have already been published with varying results. One of the most significant ones is *Serfdom and Slavery* edited by Michael L. Bush.[25] This is an edited book exploring legal definitions of the two systems of unfree labour and their structure in Europe and the New World from the ancient world until the modern era. Although most papers are structured chronologically, offering only sparse comparative observations, the focus of the volume as a whole remains comparative. Another book edited by Leon Archer[26] on *Slavery and other Forms of Unfree Labor* is probably the best example of a chronological survey of case-studies of unfree labor in Classical Greece, the Roman world, Latin America, Africa and the Antebellum American South; all the papers included in the collection provide an indispensable background on the different forms of servitude as they evolved through time. A similar publication was produced after a conference that was organized in 2001 by the Institute for the Study of Slavery at the University of Nottingham. The resulting volume, *The Faces of Freedom*,[27] brings together several papers on manumission and emancipation from both the ancient and the modern world. In the introduction the editor, Marc Kleijwegt, successfully clarifies similarities and differences between them, while he attempts to construct a new theoretical diachronic model.

Bearing in mind such examples of comparative studies that employ the juxtapositional method, we brought together papers written by specialists of either the ancient or the modern worlds to tackle sets of defined themes related to slavery. In our volume, scholars of ancient and modern history addressed similar topics within the field of slavery, from their different chronological and geographical perspectives. We hope that these individual studies will help historians to address in the future some of the more complicated issues of

---

[24] Green, 2004, p. 48.
[25] Bush, 1996.
[26] Archer, 2002.
[27] Kleijwegt, 2006.

comparative slavery and that they will start a dialogue between experts on several themes related to slavery across time and space.

In the first section of the present book, the contributors explore the theme of warfare as a crucial source for the capture of slaves in the ancient world and the early modern era. Specifically, the authors of the two chapters in the section are interested in the capture of enemy soldiers and their subsequent enslavement and exploitation. Although Orlando Patterson claimed that captives commonly are not the main source of slaves in any society,[28] his assertions do not apply to the case of Republican Rome, to which Constantina Katsari's chapter refers, while they are seemingly confirmed by Rebecca Seaman's chapter on the seventeenth-century American colonies.

In her chapter, Katsari explores this issue in the context of the Macedonian Wars; it is entitled 'Enslavement and Death in the Third Macedonian War'. During the wars that Rome conducted against the kingdom of Macedonia in the third and second centuries BC, hundreds of thousands of captive Macedonians found their way as slaves into the large estates of the Italian peninsula.[29] This labour force, in turn, changed the Roman agriculturally-based economy into a 'slave system'. The new economic conditions allowed the mass production of crops destined for the markets and, eventually, facilitated the enrichment of the slaveholders/estate owners in Italy. In this chapter, Katsari does not focus on the much debated topic of the impact of the new slaves on the Italian peninsula. Instead, she pays attention to the economic conditions resulting from the enslavement of large numbers of free men back in their country of origin, namely Greece. It seems that the men that the Romans captured in Hellenistic Greece were so many that their move to Italy would have certainly left their previous homeland partly depopulated. A devastated workforce would, in turn, have led to a reduced agricultural production and a resulting negative economic growth. Effectively, the population that remained in Macedonia may have suffered from impoverishment and famines that in pre-industrial societies usually led to debt-servitude.

As Rebecca Seaman rightly states in the introduction of her chapter, 'Enslavement of Native Americans during Queen Anne's War', the practice of enslaving war captives also occurred repeatedly during the modern era. Especially in the case of the American colonial south-east during the seventeenth and the early eighteenth century, the European powers (Spanish, English and French), who were fighting for the control of the area, profited from the captivity and subsequent enslavement of Native Americans. These newly enslaved people became the predominant labour force on plantations and in

---
[28] Patterson, 1982, p. 107–112.
[29] Hopkins, 1978, chapter 1.

households alike, while a number of them served their masters as craftsmen. Nevertheless, unlike the captives from the Third Macedonian War, who were citizens of the Macedonian or the Epirotean kingdoms and had an underlying Greek identity, the captives of Queen Anne's War came from a variety of Indian tribes; these tribes sometimes participated actively in the slave trade, either directly or indirectly, in an attempt to reduce their traditional enemies (other Native Americans) and expand their territories. In the eyes of the Europeans (English, Spanish and French), though, all the Native Americans were in need of Christianizing and civilising,[30] and this offers stark contrast with the attitude of the educated Romans who admired the defeated Greeks and revered Greek culture.

Comparison between the two case studies shows that the underlying racism that defined modern slavery, absent in the ancient world, affected the infrastructure of slavery as well as the methods of enslavement. Another significant difference between the two case studies is the fact that the Native Americans were not forcibly removed to distant lands in order to boost a foreign economy with the fruits of their labour. Unlike the case of the captivity of the Macedonians that led to the depopulation of Greece and the enrichment of Italy, the American Indians remained in the Americas and contributed to the enhancement of a co-dependent economy that relied on the increasing trade relations between Europeans and Native American tribes.[31] This difference probably has its roots in the individual economic needs of the two societies. On one hand, the creation of colonies in the New World caused a demand for more labourers that would have served the new masters. On the other hand, since the Romans chose not to colonise Greece, they transported the necessary labour force to their own estates back in Italy.

In doing diachronic comparative history, two of the greatest challenges are a) the quantification and b) the qualification of existing data. With regard to the study of the ancient world, we encounter a further major challenge: the scantiness of written historical sources, or else the total lack of them. Consequently, ancient historians use extensively the accessible archaeological material, modern linguistic studies, and the philological assessment of all written sources in order to acquire more information, which would facilitate the examination of themes such as the development of slavery. Still, even though scholars employ all available disciplines, their picture of antiquity remains rather impressionistic because of the lack of adequate sources. Among the disciplines used for the reconstruction of the past, archaeology remains one of the most useful. Comparative archaeological studies have provided a range of significant works relating to

---

[30] See Seaman's chapter in this volume.
[31] White, 1983.

slavery in the ancient Mediterranean and the New World.[32] Nevertheless, modern historians have to face the difficult task of uncovering, categorising and analysing a vast (to the eyes of the ancient historian) range of historical material. Consequently, the majority of historians of modern slavery, with a few exceptions, prefer to set aside all archaeological material in favour of the written sources, unlike the historians of the ancient world. The limitations and the methodological differences in the study of ancient and modern slavery can be easily grasped by reading the chapters by Giovanni Salmeri and Mary Ann Mahony, who both try to assess the contribution of slave women in past economies, in the following section of the present book.

In his chapter entitled 'On the Moregine *Ancilla* or Slavery and Prostitution at Pompeii', Salmeri explores the role of slave women in the sex 'industry' of the Roman city of Pompeii, as well as, more broadly, in the domestic sphere. Archaeological excavations have allowed archaeologists to identify several brothels, one of which contained the remains of a woman wearing an inscribed *armilla* (bracelet), a sign of prostitution. Taking this inscription as a point of departure, Salmeri explores the possibility of slave women working side by side with free-born women in the brothels of Pompeii. The largest part of their earnings would have undoubtedly ended up in the pockets of their masters, although part of it may have contributed to the *peculium* (a sum of money or other property that the master gave to the slave for his own use) of the prostitute – what ultimately would have enabled her to buy her freedom. If, on the other hand, the *armilla* was not a sign of prostitution but signified the affection of the master towards his slave,[33] then we may assume that the woman worked within the domestic space and, consequently, was legally protected from becoming part of the sex industry. It is worth noting that Pompeii is unique in its quality and quantity of dated archaeological evidence and, thus, enables us to open a slightly wider window into slave society in the Roman period.

In the case of the slaves of nineteenth-century Bahia, Mahony discusses in her chapter 'Gender, Labor and Family in Brazil's Cacao Area, 1870–1920' enslaved women, who were largely involved in the agricultural activities alongside male slave labour. The low price of slave women, their higher numbers and their perceived docility made them especially attractive to profit-seeking masters and increased their employability in the fields. At the same time, they contributed with their labour to the economy of the domestic space as well as the sex 'industry'. However, unlike the female slaves in the Roman empire, Brazilian women who worked in the households or in the fields, or both, were not protected by law from being sold into prostitution. Despite the

---

[32] For modern slavery see Hall, 2000. For archaeological comparisons between ancient and modern slavery see, Carandini, 1985 on Italian villas and Webster, 2005.
[33] Costabile, 2001, pp. 447–74; Costabile, 2005, pp. 43–50.

differences between the two case studies, a point of comparison that should be examined more extensively is the existence of the *peculium* (see above) in the Roman world and the *rocas* (permission for the slaves to plant things on certain days that were their own) in nineteenth-century Bahia. In both cases, the master allowed the slave to 'own' property, even though this permission could only have been a legal fiction, since the slave herself/ himself was considered property. Still, despite the inconsistencies and contradictions of the law, once the slave managed to profit from his/her *peculium* or *rocas*, s/he could trade it for his/her freedom or the freedom of his/her family.

Nevertheless, the comparison becomes more complicated when we wish to explore the gradual path towards the abolition of slavery that the Brazilian government followed, a development that is not encountered anywhere in the ancient or medieval worlds. As in every other case, we notice similarities as well as differences between slave women of Rome and Bahia. In the Roman empire slave and free-born women worked side by side in brothels on almost equal terms. Similarly, the *Law of the Free Womb* in 1871 (guaranteeing that no more slave children would be born in Brazil) blurred the divisions between slavery and freedom in the fields of Bahia; so, both slave and free women were employed in the same roles. Particularly important, in regard to the differences between the two slave societies, is the fact that the Roman slave system lasted for centuries and seems to have been enforced continuously until the rise of the medieval kingdoms. On the other hand, the rise of capitalism and the need of modernisation led to the rise of an increasingly strong movement for the abolition of slavery in nineteenth century Brazil, which, in turn, promoted the replacement of slavery with different types of unfree labour, leading to a momentous transformation in labour relations between the upper classes and the workforce.

Recently, a major theme that has filled the pages of increasingly larger numbers of books and articles on slavery is that of slave rebellions/revolts (and, at least in one case, revolutions), the subject of the next section in the present book. To be sure, revolts or rebellions were only some of the choices that slaves had in terms of altering their condition permanently. In fact, drastic measures, such as large scale insurrections of the magnitude of the Roman Slave Wars, occurred comparatively rarely in ancient and modern societies, while the outcome of these actions rarely guaranteed the eventual freedom of the slaves. On the contrary, most of these revolts/rebellions were doomed to failure even before they started, and afterwards the surviving slaves had to face the unavoidable consequences arising from their audacity. Thus, we should conclude that the most effective ways to exit the slave condition were probably the ones sanctioned by law.[34] Although such legal ways differ from

---

[34] Petre-Grenouilleau, 2008.

one society to the next and from one chronological period to another, they have some common characteristics, among which, especially the elaborate aspect of the legal process and its ultimate outcome in the eventual incorporation of the freedman in the existing social structure.

First, in her chapter, Theresa Urbainczyk focuses on slave rebellions and endeavours to analyse the views of modern historiography on the Roman Slave Wars that took place during the second and first centuries BC in southern Italy and Sicily. Over the past few decades the term 'slave wars' has been seriously contested in favour of other terms such as 'historical accidents',[35] in an attempt to diminish their political, social and economic significance. Urbainczyk questions these characterisations and brings forward a series of comparative examples from both the ancient and the modern worlds; examples include the rebellion of Aristonicus (132–129 BC), the helot wars against Sparta (especially in the 5th century BC), the revolution of Saint Domingue (1791–1803), and the American slave revolts occurred between the eighteenth and the first half of the nineteenth century. In all of these cases, the author detects a tendency in modern western European scholarship to treat widespread uprisings with hostility or denial. On the other hand, eastern European researchers accept slave revolts as events of extraordinary importance, probably because of the Marxist tradition that has formed them.

Ideally linking his contribution with Urbainczyk's, in his chapter entitled 'Denying the Evidence: Slave Rebelliousness and the Denmark Vesey Debate', Douglas Egerton further examines the insistence of modern scholars on denying the existence or significance of slave rebellions, focusing, in particular, on the antebellum American South. Egerton's specific study on the historiography of the aborted rebellion of Denmark Vesey (1822) brings him to the conclusion that most researchers (with the exception of a few bright examples such as Herbert Aptheker[36]) *'erase black agency so that the conduct of the enslaved better fits the most recent model of labour culture'*, thus, failing to assess accurately the wealth of documentation that indicates the large scale and importance of slave rebellions in the antebellum American South. Seen in comparative perspective, then, both Egerton and Urbainczyk are clearly highly critical of contemporary historiography on ancient and modern slave rebellions; both argue that future scholarship needs to accept the existence of widespread slave insurrections as well as the ability of the slaves to organise them in a way that threatened (albeit mostly unsuccessfully) the socio-economic systems within which they lived.

Focusing on an altogether different topic, although one very much related to the discussion on the slaves' actual chances of breaking out of their

---

[35] See especially Bradley, 1989.
[36] Aptheker, 1943.

condition of enslavement – whether in a violent or a in a legal way – in his chapter on '"Independent" Slaves in Classical Athens and the Ideology of Slavery' Nick Fisher studies the first step towards freedom. According to Fisher, Athenian law during the fifth and the fourth centuries BC recognised the economic importance of 'independent' slaves and freedmen, especially in money-related sectors, such as commerce and banking; hence, these 'independent' slaves were indistinguishable in appearance from the free, whilst they conducted business. Despite the precariousness of their social situation, some of these slaves developed personal friendships with their masters, while others accumulated enough wealth that, in the end, helped them buy their own freedom, become citizens or acquire some political power. In a comparable way, in the Roman world, slaveholders were in favour of the manumission of their slaves, although the government tried to curb this attitude through the introduction of laws that reduced the numbers of slaves who could be freed during the Augustan period.[37] Society's fears with regard to 'independent' or freed slaves existed also in classical Athens; however, in both cases, manumission became a widespread practice among slaveholders, an action that perpetuated the established slave system, according to some researchers.[38] These similarities, though, should not deceive us into believing that the incorporation of freedmen into society was exactly the same across the Classical world.

Despite the widespread practice of manumission of slaves in antiquity, the ancient world has never witnessed an abolitionist movement of any kind and the existence of slavery has never been seriously contested. The movement for the abolition of slavery is a uniquely modern phenomenon made possible by a combination of factors. On one hand, the influence of the Enlightenment with its doctrine of natural rights and, on the other hand, the creation of the discipline of political economy, according to which slavery violated the tenets of classical capitalism, led to the acknowledgement that slavery was a coerced and violent institution. Partly for this reason, slavery started to be seen as inefficient and unproductive. More important still was the rise of a reformist and partly radical public opinion. In this case, the abolitionist attitude took ideas from the Enlightenment to their logical consequences. At the same time, attempts sprang up directly from the strength of Evangelical and other religious movements – the Quakers especially – which swept through the English speaking world in successive waves to morally reform society, by claiming that slavery was an inherent evil that corrupted slaveholders and caused unspeakable suffering to the slaves. Once legislation was passed in both Britain and the United States at the beginning of the nineteenth century, aiming initially at the end of the international slave trade, the institution of slavery underwent

---

[37] Gardner, 1991, pp. 27–29 and 37.
[38] Findlay, 1975.

a gradual or abrupt decline, the speed of which, then, depended entirely on the individual case. Such decline may have been marked by the enforcement of law, as in the case of Great Britain in 1833, or in one case occurred by abolition through Civil War, as the antebellum American South in 1863.

In his chapter, entitled 'The Abolition of Slavery and Plans from Freedom in Late Nineteenth-Century Brazil', Walter Fraga Filho deals with a case-study of legal abolition of slavery – similar, in this case, to Britain – and precisely with emancipation in Brazil in 1888. As a consequence of emancipation, the lives of hundreds of thousands of slaves in Brazil changed overnight, much to the dismay of the Brazilian slaveholders, who watched the slaves celebrate their new freedom and defy their direct orders. Although some of the experiences of the newly freed people in Brazil may have resembled the experiences of freedmen in antiquity, it is important to remember that the traumatic experience of the Brazilian masters who witnessed the abolition of slavery had nothing in common with the conscious choice of ancient masters to free their slaves, and this difference shows well how the abolition of slavery is a distinct phenomenon that highlights the overwhelming differences between modern and pre-industrial societies.

Still, future comparative studies could help us understand better the reasons that forced modern masters to follow – for the first time in history – entirely different paths from the ones of their predecessors in antiquity. Doubtless, such reasons had much to do with a momentous change in the common perception of slavery and in the making of a radical public opinion against it, and also with the idea that systems of 'free labour' were much better fit for the type of economic performance required in a world economy driven by industrial capitalism. Thus, once the movement for abolition became widespread and slavery became increasingly rare, new institutions of labour – most only partly 'free' – replaced slavery globally. Our wish for a future comparative study of these new systems of 'free' and 'unfree' labour replacing slavery is thus both a fitting way to end the description of the content of the present volume and also a hope that future research on these topics may characterize the work of comparative scholars working on the ancient and modern worlds.

In conclusion, we would like to stress again that the purpose of this volume was to bring together specialists of ancient and modern slavery in order to discuss in comparative perspective topics relevant to the sources of slaves, their experience, instances of resistance, rebellion or revolts and their eventual freedom. We hope that scholars will take the opportunity to expand on these themes and approaches and that they will venture into the in-depth study of slavery both diachronically and synchronically. Although comparative history is not devoid of problems, the simple methodological approach of the juxtaposition of papers included here may go some way toward solving some of them and open scholars' eyes to the value of such methodology. In doing this we hope that it may lead us to a better understanding of ancient and modern societies.

Bibliography

Aptheker, H. (1943), *American Negro Slave Revolts*, New York.
Archer, L. (2002), *Slavery and Other Forms of Unfree Labour*, London.
Bloch, M. (1961), *Feudal Society* (translation of 1939–40 manuscript), Chicago.
Bloch, M. (1973), *The Royal Touch: Sacred Monarchy and Scrofula in England and France*, (transl. of 1924 article), London.
Bradley, K. (1987), *Masters and Slaves in the Roman Empire: A Study in Social Control*, Oxford.
Bradley, K. (1989), *Slavery and Rebellion in the Roman World, 140BC–70BC*, London.
Bradley, K. (1994), *Slavery and Society at Rome*, Cambridge.
Burke, P. (1992), *History and Social Theory*, Cambridge.
Bush, M.L. (ed.) (1996), *Serfdom and Slavery: Studies in Legal Bondage*, London.
Carandini, A (1985), *Settefinestre: una villa schiavistica nell'Etruria romana*, Modena.
Cohen, D. and M. O' Connor (eds.) (2004a), *Comparison and History: Europe in Cross-National Perspective*, London/New York.
Cohen, D. and M. O' Connor (2004b), 'Introduction: Comparative history, cross-national history, transnational history – Definitions', in D. Cohen and M. O' Connor (eds.), *Comparison and History: Europe in Cross-National Perspective*, London/New York, pp. ix-xxiv.
Costabile, F. (2001), '*Ancilla domini*. Una nuova dedica su armilla aurea da Pompei', *Minima Epigraphica et Papyrologica*, 4.6, pp. 447–474.
Costabile, F. (2005), '*Contra meretricium ancillae domni*', in V. Scarano Issani (ed.), *Moregine, Suburbio 'portuale' di Pompei*, Naples, pp. 43–50.
Drescher, S. and Engerman, S.L. (eds.) (1998), *A Historical Guide to World Slavery*, New York.
Findlay, R. (1975), 'Slavery, incentives and manumission: A theoretical model', *The Journal of Political Economy*, 83.5, pp. 923–934.
Finkelman, P. and Miller, J.C. (eds.) (1999), *The Macmillan Encyclopedia of World Slavery*, Macmillan.
Finley, M.I. (1968), 'Slavery', *International Encyclopedia of the Social Sciences*, vol. 14, David L. Sills (ed.), New York, pp. 307–313.
Finley, M.I. (1985), *The Ancient Economy*, Cambridge (first published 1972).
Fredrickson, G.M. (1982), *White Supremacy: A Comparative Study of American and South African History*, Oxford.
Gardner, J. (1991), 'The purpose of the *Lex Fufia Caninia*', *Echos du Monde Classique*, 35, pp. 21–39.
Green, N.L. (2004), 'Forms of comparison', in D. Cohen and M. O' Connor (eds.), *Comparison and History: Europe in Cross-National Perspective*, London/New York, pp. 41–56.
Hall, M. (2000), *Archaeology and the Modern World: Colonial Transcripts in South Africa and the Chesapeake*, London.
Hopkins, K. (1978), *Conquerors and Slaves*, Cambridge.
Kleijwegt, M. (ed.) (2006), *The Faces of Freedom: The Manumission and Emancipation of Slaves in Old World and New World Slavery*, Leiden.
Kolchin, P. (1987), *Unfree Labor: American Slavery and Russian Serfdom*, Cambridge Mass.

Lovejoy, P. (2000), *Transformations in Slavery: A History of Slavery in Africa*, 2nd ed., New York.
Meillassoux, C. (1991), *The Anthropology of Slavery: The Womb of Iron and Gold*, Chicago.
Miller, J.C. (1993), *Slavery and Slaving in World History: A Bibliography, 1900–1991*, Millwood NY.
Miller, J.C. (1999), *Slavery and Slaving in World History: A Bibliography – Vol. 2, 1992–96*, Armonk NY.
Patterson, O. (1982), *Slavery and Social Death. A Comparative Study*, Cambridge Mass.
Petre-Grenouilleau, O. (2008), 'Processes of exiting slave systems: A typology', in E. Dal Lago and C. Katsari, (eds.), *Slave Systems: Ancient and Modern*, Cambridge, pp. 233–264.
Rodriguez, J. (ed.) (1997), *The Historical Encyclopedia of World Slavery*, ABC-CLIO.
Shaw, B. (2001), *Spartacus and the Slave Wars: A Brief History with Documents*, Boston.
Scheidel, W. (1996), 'Reflections on the differential valuation of slaves in Diocletian's price edict and in the United States', in: *Münstersche Beiträge zur antiken Handelsgeschichte*, 15, 1, pp. 67–79.
Scheidel, W. (2005), 'Real slave prices and the relative cost of slave labor in the Greco-Roman world', *Ancient Society*, 35, pp. 1–17.
Scheidel, W. (2008), 'The divergent evolution of coinage in eastern and western Eurasia', in W. V. Harris (ed.), *The Monetary Systems of the Greeks and Romans*, Oxford, pp. 267–286.
Skocpol, T. and Somers, M. (1980), 'The use of comparative history in macro-social enquiry', *Comparative Studies in Society and History*, 22.2, pp. 174–197.
Weber, M. (2002), *The Protestant Ethic and the Spirit of Capitalism* (translation of 1905 German version), London.
Webster, J. (2005), 'Archaeologies of slavery and servitude: bringing 'New World' perspectives to Roman Britain, *Journal of Roman Archaeology*, 18.1, pp. 161–179.
Weiler, I. (2003), *Die Beendigung des Sklavenstatus im Altertum: Ein Beitrag zur vergleichenden Sozialgeschichte*, Stuttgart.
White, R. (1983), *Roots of Dependency: Subsistence, Environment and Social Change among the Choctaws, Pawnees and Navajos*, Lincoln.

Part 2

Captives and Slaves

ENSLAVEMENT AND DEATH: THE THIRD MACEDONIAN WAR[1]

Constantina Katsari

Introduction

The expansion of the Romans in the East stumbled over the armies of the powerful Hellenistic kingdoms, which were established in Greece, Egypt, Asia Minor and Syria after the death of Alexander the Great. When Rome decided its military intervention in these areas, the continuous wars that lasted for more than a century – especially the ones against the Macedonian kings – were bound to be fierce. The First Macedonian War between Rome and Macedon started as part of an alliance between Philip V and Hannibal against Rome and ended in 205 BC with terms favourable to Macedonia. The Second Macedonian War began only five years later in 200 BC and lasted for four years until 196 BC. Despite the fact that Rome was still exhausted from its fight against Carthage, the Romans declared war against the king Philip V, who provoked Roman anger by moving against some of the (friendly to Rome) Greek city-states. As a result of the Second Macedonian War, Macedonia acknowledged the nominal autonomy of the Achaean and Aetolian Leagues; an autonomy that was, in turn, suppressed by the indirect Roman rule of the areas in question. Almost 25 years later, in 171 BC, the Third Macedonian War finally took place. Perseus, the son of Philip V, lost the battle of Pydna and consequently the war against the Romans in 168 BC. Following this battle, Perseus and his family were sent to Rome in order to become the main spectacle of a celebrated triumph, while the kingdom of Macedonia was divided in four semi-autonomous parts that paid annual tribute to Rome. This nominal independence finally came to an end in 148 BC for Macedonia and in 146 BC for the rest of Greece. At this point Rome officially annexed the Greek lands, while, later, two provinces (Macedonia and Achaea) were created; these provinces were under the command of Roman governors and, consequently, they were directly ruled by the Roman State.

---

[1] I am obliged to Graham Shipley who looked at an early draft of this paper and offered invaluable comments.

Instances of the unavoidable impact of the Macedonian wars on Greek soil and their effects on the Greek people are mentioned in the writings of a contemporary Greek historian, Polybius. A Roman historian, Livy, who wrote his History in the first century BC, is considered also a valuable source. Although, both of these writers acknowledge the political, military and moral superiority of Rome, they do not hesitate to describe the most shocking part of ancient warfare and its impact on the lives (and death) of local inhabitants. Nevertheless, their references on slavery and/or un-free labour are scanty at best. In this paper I will use the available material to analyse the effects of the massive enslavements and the rise of the death toll in both the rural countryside and the urban centers during the Third Macedonian War until the conclusion of the peace in 167 BC. I will also focus on the economic and administrative regulations Rome imposed on Macedonia and their impact on the structure of the local workforce and the livelihood of the inhabitants. The social and economic effects of this war seem to have lasted until 146 BC, when the annexation of Macedonia was completed. At this point in time (during the middle of the second century BC) Rome made a decisive turn from a hegemonial towards annexationist imperialism,[2] a fact that probably made the lives of the conquered peoples more tolerable, since the region entered an era of political stability and, consequently, the opportunities for economic development multiplied.

Before the War

Although the Third Macedonian War started in 171 BC, the preparations commenced much earlier. The agreement of new alliances with neighbouring kingdoms, the financial security necessary for a struggle of that scale and the training of the existing army were complemented with a series of measures to ensure the compliance of the local population. Long before the final battle took place, Philip V, the architect of the Roman-Macedonian conflict, decided

> *"to deport with their whole families from the principal cities and from those on the coast all men who took part in politics, and transfer them to the country now called Emathia and formerly Paeonia, filling the cities with Thracians and barbarians whose fidelity to him would be surer in the season of danger".*[3]

Because of their ethnic origin, the Thracians and the other barbarians living in northern Greece were not considered loyal to the Macedonian king.

---

[2] It seems that the Senate was very reluctant to annex new territories during the third century and the first half of the second centuries BC, probably because of the administrative burden it would have caused. For more details see Badian, 1968, p. 4.
[3] Polybius 23.10.4.

Consequently the Macedonian authorities entertained the idea that these ethnic groups could have turned against the king in case of war, in an attempt to gain their 'independence'. Consequently, the removal of their leaders and other political figures along with their families to distant areas became imperative. However, such an action justifiably caused uproar amidst the population; an uproar that needed to be suppressed anew.

> *"While this project was being executed, and the men were being deported, there arose such mourning and such commotion that one would have said the whole country was being led into captivity. And in consequence were heard curses and imprecations against that king uttered no longer in secret but openly. In the next place, wishing to tolerate no disaffection and to leave no hostile element in his kingdom, he wrote to the officers in whose charge the cities were, to search for the sons and daughters of the Macedonians he had killed and imprison them."*[4]

It is possible that the stripping of the northern tribes of their political (and economic) elites would have affected both the administration of the region and the management of the estates and other sources of wealth.

On top of the attempts to reduce the power of local political leaders, the Macedonian kings had also to face the results of regional social struggles. Specifically, after the defeat of Philip V at Cynoscephalae, the Romans favoured the establishment of federal oligarchic constitutions in Thessaly, Magnesia and Euboea. These constitutions were similar to the Italian mode of political administration and, therefore, may have been considered friendly towards Rome.[5] Whether the second century Greek aristocrats sided with Rome[6] or whether the majority of the population expressed anti-Roman feelings[7] is not an issue that will be explored in detail in the course of this paper.[8] What matters is that in 170s[9] the Thessalian aristocrats, who assumed the power invested to them by Rome, attempted to enrich themselves at the expense of their fellow citizens. This attitude led to the impoverishment of the region and a widespread debt crisis was followed by social disorder in the cities.[10] Similar events took place in Aetolia that also suffered during the first and the second Macedonian wars. In fact, modern historians claim that the economic crisis in Aetolia was directly connected to the war indemnities,[11] the

---
[4] Polybius 23.10.4.
[5] Larsen, 1968, pp. 284–285; de Ste. Croix, 1981, p. 525.
[6] De Sanctis, 1969, pp. 94–95, 109–110, 263–264; Frank, 1914, pp. 201–203; Errington, 1971, p. 202.
[7] Deiniger, 1971, pp. 159–164.
[8] Although Erich Gruen (1976, pp. 29–60) considers such class preferences unlikely, there is a possibility that the underlying economic differences between the rich and the poor were aggravated by the contemporary political climate.
[9] For the latest study on the exact date see, Walsh, 2000, pp. 300–303.
[10] Diodorus 29.33.
[11] Gruen, 1976, p. 35.

Roman plundering[12] and, last but not least, the possible irregular payments and consequent unemployment of the Aetolian mercenaries.[13] At the same time, the serious shortages of grain that occurred in the first half of the second century BC[14] could also have had their origin in the increasing demands of the passing armies and the lack of adequate agricultural labour. All in all, the political problems Macedonia was facing had a negative impact on the populations within and outside the kingdom, while the recurring social and economic problems did not seem to have been resolved before the beginning of the Third Macedonian war.

Battles, Massacres and Enslavements

Once the war started, large scale massacres awaited the population of the Greek cities that resisted the invasion. Following standard Roman military practices, the massacre of the defeated citizens aimed at destroying all potential resistance coming from the sacked city. According to the Greek historian Polybius[15], in the first instance, the Romans attacked the inhabitants *"with orders to kill all they encountered, sparing none, and not to start pillaging until the signal was given"*. The outcome of such practices is that not only humans but also domestic animals borne the wrath of the conquerors. In theory, the looting followed only when the massacre was completed, for obvious security reasons. Once the booty was collected in the market or another open space, it was distributed to the troops in perfect order. Again, theoretically speaking, this practice should have been applied only to cities that were captured by assault; nevertheless, the fact is that *direptio* just as well took place in the cities, which opened their gates willingly to the besiegers.[16] According to another ancient account, the fate of the politically and socially inconsequential individuals – women and children – followed the same fate, as described above by Polybius. Livy refers to men of military age as the main victims of the soldiers' swords.[17]

Some authors suggested that the massacres in the Roman world resembled ritual sacrifices that took place in other societies; thus, they served a religious purpose rather than a socio-economic one.[18] It is true that the sacrifice of prisoners was not unknown in Republican Rome, since the Senate issued a decree in order to forbid them only in 97 BC, while the emperor Hadrian may have

---

[12] Rostoftzeff, 1941, pp. 616–617.
[13] Gruen, 1976, p. 35.
[14] Walsh, 2000 pp. 301–302.
[15] Polybius 10.15.4–16.9.
[16] Ziolkowski, 1992, p. 77.
[17] Livy 31.27.4; 31.23.8.
[18] Patterson, 1982, p. 107.

renewed this prohibition three centuries later.[19] However, there is a strong possibility that the otherwise ritualized killing of the captives was serving practical reasons. The massacre of captive citizens seems entirely sensible, if we take into consideration that the male adults were the most probable source of political and military opposition. Let us not forget that men not only fought in the wars but they also run civic institutions, they voted for their magistrates and they controlled the wealth of the country. On the other hand, women and children were deemed powerless, since they did not participate actively in the political life of their cities and/or the kingdom, while they had limited control over their finances; the occasional abuse of these powerless inhabitants could only be seen as acts of unnecessary violence or collateral damage. The attempt to control Greek politics has been a long term worry for the Romans; so their attempts to eliminate all possible opposition by killing their main adversaries are perfectly justified under the circumstances.

Accordingly, in the Third Macedonian War Haliartus and Thebes, two Boeotian cities, were sacked by Gaius Lucretius Gallus and were pillaged.

> *"In the first confusion of the captured city the old men and boys whom they chanced to meet were killed. The combatants took shelter in the citadel, and as all hope was now lost they surrendered, and were sold as slaves. There were about 2500 of them. The adornments of the city, the statues and paintings and all the valuable plunder were placed on shipboard and the place was razed to its foundations. From there the army marched to Thebes, which was captured without any fighting, and the consul handed the city over to the refugees and the Roman party. The households and property of the other party, who had worked in the interests of the king and were Macedonian sympathisers, were sold."*[20]

In another instance, the city of Abdera was sacked and its magistrates were beheaded, while the rest of the population was sold into slavery, as a result of the actions of undisciplined Roman soldiers.[21] In other cases, the commanders disregarded the moral code that should have been followed when a city opened its gates to the enemy. A well known example is the pillaging of the friendly city of Chalcis by the praetor Lucretius who allowed his soldiers to despoil the temples and sell the citizens into slavery, while they plundered both public and private properties.[22] The above examples, though, are not nearly as extreme as the case of the city of Oreus, where the Romans put to the sword indiscriminately all the women and children as well as the adult

---

[19] The existence of ritual sacrifice has been noticed early in the 20th century when Edward A. Westermack published his treatise on The Origin and Development of the Moral Ideas in Two volumes (Westermack, 1912, p.434). His assertions were later repeated and may be found in Palmer, 1974, pp. 154–171.
[20] Livy 42.63.
[21] Livy 43.4.7.
[22] Livy 43.7.

males.[23] The extensive pillaging of properties and the massacres of the inhabitants was probably the final stage of a process that started as early as the First Macedonian War. Since the beginning of the conflict between Rome and Macedonia several Greek cities were despoiled and the citizens were forced to pay contributions or were sold into slavery; otherwise they were killed and their properties were utterly destroyed.[24]

The first obvious impact from these massacres and enslavements could have been the depopulation of some of the cities or of several regions in Greece. We should not forget that the citizens who died during the Roman incursion were also the labour force of the Greek city-states and the Macedonian kingdom. During the siege, usually both the urban population as well as the farmers living in the surrounding villages gathered within the walls for protection. Once the slaughter started, the conquerors did not distinguish between the higher social classes administering the city and the poor individuals that found refuge behind the walls. The day after the distribution of the spoils left the countryside deserted, the crops destroyed by the Roman troops and most able-bodied Greek citizens killed or enslaved. The surviving women, children and old men scarcely had any means of survival, while the economy suffered a crushing blow. The apparent inability of the conquered peoples to reconstruct their destroyed fatherlands was not of any consequence to the decisions of the Romans. After all, the Romans were only interested in the despoliation of the Greek cities that would have brought them immediate profits; they were not interested in the reconstruction of the subjugated lands. Such a mentality is clearly shown in the treaty signed between the Romans and the Aetolians during the First Macedonian War, according to which the Aetolians would occupy all the lands, buildings and walls of captured cities, while Rome would own all persons as well as personal property.[25] This agreement allowed Rome to carry warfare of pillage, destruction and enslavement without taking heed of the long-term economic consequences. The same policy was probably followed also during the Third Macedonian War, since Rome did not seem to be interested in the direct administration or systematic economic exploitation of the newly conquered lands. Despite the negative impact of Roman pillaging on individual cities, we cannot claim that all of Greece was despoiled, since, in all likelihood, this type of destruction remained geographically restricted.

---

[23] Livy 43.19.
[24] Polybius 9.39.2; Livy 26.26.3; Pausanias 7.7.9; Livy 32.22.10; Pausanias 7.17.5; Polybius 22.8.9; Livy 28.7.4–5; Livy 29.8. 5 ff.
[25] Livy 26.24.8–14: "*The conditions were that the Aetolians should immediately make war on Philip by land, in which the Romans should assist with not less than 25 quinqueremes, that the site and buildings, together with the walls and lands, of all the cities as far as Corcyra, should become the property of the Aetolians, every other kind of booty, of the Romans*". Polybius 9.5.5.

The possible partial depopulation of the Greek soil[26] that followed the massacres was further complemented by the enslavement of an unusually large numbers of civilians. It is a well-known fact that when the hostilities of the Third Macedonian War were over, Aemilius Paulus systematically annihilated around seventy cities in the region of Epirus, which had revolted and followed Perseus, despite the official Roman declarations that the Epiroteans should be '*freed*' like the Macedonians. Specifically, after settling the affairs in Macedonia Paulus sent his troops to plunder the part of Illyria that rebelled against the Romans. On their way to that region, the army dispatched centurions to Epirus with explicit instructions for the ten leading citizens of each city to dispatch all the available gold and silver to a public place in order to be collected by the Romans. One morning, in a synchronised attack throughout Epirus, the soldiers seized the treasure and sacked the cities. One hundred and fifty thousand Epirotes were sold into slavery, while the leaders of the opposition were ordered to appear in front of the senate in Rome.[27] Thus, the Roman army left the region of Epirus "*for the most part a wilderness with here and there a decaying village*"[28] This situation was not remedied and no positive financial measures were taken until the early empire, after two Roman colonies (Nicopolis and Bouthroton) were founded in the area.

The hypothesis that a huge number of war captives were brought to Italy as slaves is not amply evident in the ancient sources but it is widely assumed as true by most modern historians. Keith Hopkins was the scholar who managed to gather the scattered evidence in a single monograph and attempted to establish a clear connection between the Republican wars, the booty, the formation of large *latifundia* and the development of a slave based agricultural economy.[29] The importation of vast numbers of captive slaves in Italy destined to work in the newly formed large estates would have caused radical changes in the economic system of Rome and would have contributed to the re-organization of the labour force.[30] The slaves, destined for work especially in the *latifundia* but also in villas, wealthy houses and in other environments, were a cheap, non specialized workforce. In all likelihood, the most important development that demanded the use of slaves was the fact that the upper classes needed to exploit fully the newly acquired lands of the Italian Peninsula that came recently under their control either after they dispossessed the owners or,

---

[26] Although there is no direct evidence for this depopulation, there are strong indications towards this direction. In another context Polybius talks of a decline in population because of willful childlessness on Macedon under Roman rule (Polybius 36.17.5).
[27] Polybius 30.16; Strabo 7.7.3; Livy 45.34.1–7; Plutarch, *Aem.* 29.
[28] Strabo 7.7.6.
[29] Hopkins, 1978.
[30] Finley, 1980.

in some instances, after they purchased the fields.[31] The relocation of the slaves in the west was nothing less than the transfusion of new blood in the labour force of the Roman Republic. The ancient sources describe enslavement as one of the consequences of the Third Samnite War,[32] the First[33] and Second Punic Wars,[34] the attack against Acragas in Sicily[35] and, of course, the episode in Epirus between 201 and 167 BC. According to Walter Scheidel the total of 700,000 slaves captured during these wars fails to portray the full scale of war enslavements. He further suggests that, even if some of these may have been bought up by merchants in situ or ransomed by their own relatives or transferred to other areas, the majority would have been transferred to Italy.[36] Keith Bradley, also, claims that enslavement during Republican wars was the most important source of slaves for Rome, while breeding became the principle source during the empire.[37] The interrelation of captivity and slavery is further attested during the Principate, although its importance was diminished; both William Harris and Walter Scheidel affirm the existence of imported slaves (some of which may have been captives).[38] In effect, the use of captives as slaves in Italy was probably the main reason for the enslavement of the population of Greece during the second century BC. Even if some researchers may disagree with the existence of a grand plan (namely the provision of slaves for the new *latifundia*), we may be certain that at least the enslavement of the Epirotes was not caused by the actions of a single '*villain*', as Scullard suggested.[39]

There is a secondary but equally pragmatic reason for the transportation of new slaves to an area far away from their country of origin. As Orlando Patterson suggested,[40] if the indigenous people were sold locally as slaves, they may not have been '*natally alienated*', because the Romans (master class) were, in actual fact, the intruders in the conquered lands. The native population would have shown undue solidarity towards the enslaved and, consequently, there may have been social unrest. For example, if the new slaves decided to escape or rebel, their actions may have been successful, since they still lived and worked in familiar lands. The comparative case of the unsuccessful attempts to enslave all Native Americans may further illustrate the point that

---

[31] Crawford, 1977, p. 50.
[32] Welwei, 2000, pp. 42–48.
[33] Welwei, 2000, pp. 65–81.
[34] Welwei, 2000, pp. 88–131.
[35] Diodorus, 23.9.1.
[36] Scheidel, *CAH*, table 2.
[37] Bradley, 1987, p. 59.
[38] Harris, 1980. For a revision of Harris's article see Scheidel, 1997, pp. 156–169. For a revision of Scheidel's article see Harris, 1999.
[39] Scullard, 1945, pp. 59–64.
[40] Patterson, 1981, pp. 111–2.

Patterson made. In an article written by Beccie Seaman for this collection,[41] it seems that the use of Native American slaves by Europeans reached its peak in the Americas during Queen Anne's War. Only later, though, these slaves were substituted in the local markets by African Americans. It is possible that the natally alienated African American slaves did not threaten (through acts of resistance or rebellions) the slave system, in the way the indigenous Indians did; a threat that, in effect, resulted to the genocide of these native Indian peoples. Although the Romans could not have even imagined the failed attempts to enslave the entire Indian population, they probably were aware of the dangers arising from similar situations and they followed a different path. Specifically, one of the reasons for transporting the captives far from their own homeland to distant Italy would have been in order to control them more efficiently as well as profit from their labour.

However, we should not exclude the possibility that some of the Epirotes and Macedonians in question were ransomed locally by the commanders or the soldiers that received the immediate profits. The possible '*purchasers*' were either the relatives of the unfortunate slaves or slave traders that conducted their business with the blessings of Rome.[42] According to Orlando Patterson the majority of captives in most pre-industrial societies were not brought back to the country of their captors in chains but they were ransomed locally by their relatives. This view has some merit (though it is not universally true), if we take into account the problems arising from having a large number of prisoners that would have followed the soldiers back home.[43] The ancient sources inform us that Hannibal seemed to have been convinced that the Romans would have accepted ransom for their prisoners,[44] while he kept his prisoners from Trebia and Trasimene with him, hoping for a future exchange.[45] However, in our case and in view of the fact that most of the gold and silver of Epirus has already been gathered by the Romans in a swift move, it seems that the Epirotes had no other solution but being led to Italy and being used there as slaves in the large agricultural estates. Although we are not aware of the logistics of transporting such a large number of slaves, we should not dismiss this possibility. Besides, the transportation of captives over long distances was not only possible but it also flourished during other historical periods. Let us not forget that eleven to thirteen million slaves, as spoils of wars, were transferred from the west coast of Africa to the Americas between the fifteenth and until the end of the eighteenth centuries. Certainly, it is true that the

---

[41] See relevant chapter in this volume.
[42] Millar, 1984, p. 10.
[43] Patterson, 1982.
[44] Polybius 6.58.13; Livy 22.56.3; 22.58.1–6.
[45] Polybius 3.77.3–7 and 3.85.1–5.

From Captivity to Freedom

warfare conducted by Europeans which resulted in the direct enslavement of the African people lasted for only a century.[46] Nevertheless, the European forces relied on local wars conducted by African rulers for the supply of slaves.[47] These wars and raids often resulted to the sale and transport of captives abroad, records of which were left by the slave trading companies, such as the English Royal African Company and the Dutch West Indies Company. The organization of the transfer of so many captives/ slaves from one continent to another would have involved similar, if not more serious, logistical problems with the transportation problems that the Romans faced almost fifteen hundred years earlier; problems that seem to have been resolved in one way or another.

The devastating effect of the Macedonian Wars in Greece was not restricted to the immediate and violent death or social death (slavery) of the citizens but it was also followed by the destruction or seizure of the seasonal crops. According to ancient military practices, warfare took place during the late spring, summer and early autumn, at a time when corn is ready to be gathered or when the farmers are already in the process of turning it into flour. The movements of both the Macedonian and the Roman troops from one area to another demanded the immediate availability of food supplies, normally provided by the local inhabitants. In the first instance, Perseus occasionally collected the corn for his army, when he was in hostile territory within Greece.[48] Following the same practices, the Romans cut and carried off the corn from the fields and brought it in the camp. Subsequently, the soldiers participated actively in the food process, cutting off the ears with their sickles, so that they might rub the corn cleaner.[49] When necessary supplies were secured, both armies preferred destroying the remaining crops in their passage, thus, devastating the countryside and leaving the enemy devoid of resources.[50] Neither Livy nor Polybius provides detailed information on the manner of the destruction of the cities and/or their lands. However, the example of the utterly destroyed Carthage and its surroundings could give an indication with regard to the extent of the Roman vengeance and the effectiveness of their methods.[51] Again, the areas most likely to be devastated were the ones that lay directly on the military paths of either the Roman or the Macedonian army. Once the destructive forces left, the remaining local

---

[46] Birmingham, 1966.
[47] Thornton, 1999.
[48] Livy 42.54; 42.56. The areas of Mylae and Pherae are two of the examples.
[49] Livy 42.64. The same procedure probably took place in Crannon (Livy 42.65), although in other areas, such as Tempe, the corn may have already been processed (Livy 44.7).
[50] For example, the Macedonians devastated the fields of Pherae (Livy 42.56) and the Romans devastated the areas of Thessalonica and Aelia (Livy 44.10).
[51] Ridley, 1986, pp. 140–146.

population would most likely have starved during the winter, since famines were a regular and sometimes irreversible phenomenon in pre-industrial economies.[52]

Roman warfare was not only restricted to the destruction of life or property. The troops were also responsible for plundering cities and villages and carrying off with them all valuable artifacts that could be found. Specifically, the spoils of Aemilius Paulus that were exhibited in Rome during his three-day triumph after the battle of Pydna surpassed in value the sum of 210,000,000 *sestertii*.[53] In front of Roman eyes passed for the first time an unprecedented amount of wealth and artistic artifacts; the best that Greece could offer.[54] Furthermore, the Macedonian imperial treasury provided silver and gold that was estimated at 36,000,000 *denarii*.[55] On top of this we should add the revenues resulting from the expulsion of the Greek elite (around 250 people)[56] that used to be in the immediate service of king Perseus before the war. All of these magistrates accompanied by their sons were forced to follow the consul to Rome as people in exile. Since there was none left back in Greece to manage their property, the Romans undertook the task and made certain that the profits would end up into their own pockets.[57] This policy stripped the kingdom from its major revenues and did not allow the speedy recovery of its previous glory.

The degree of the effect of the Third Macedonian War in the region was, therefore, directly analogous to the death or captivity of the inhabitants and the parallel destruction of the crops. In the case of the death and/or enslavement of the men, it seems that the remaining population came to terms with three different alternatives: a) the areas with most of the losses in human lives could have been re-populated fairly fast, if people from densely inhabited neighbouring cities decided to move, b) women and old men could undertake the daily jobs that were performed by men until then or c) the inability to replace the skilled and unskilled labour force would have led to the undoubted economic impoverishment of the affected region. Similarly, the destruction of the crops could only have led to famines of different duration and extent, although we cannot exclude the possibility that the local authorities would have taken emergency measures in order to avoid such an outcome. The most widespread choice, in these cases, would have been the use of agricultural (or other) surplus in order to buy food from outside the community. Nevertheless,

---

[52] Garnsey, 2003.
[53] Hammond and Walbank, 1988, pp. 566–567.
[54] Livy 45.33.5–7; 45.35.2–8; 45.39.2–8; Plutarch, Aemilius Paulus, 28.7; 32.33; 38.1; Diodorus, 31.8.9–11.
[55] Polybius 18.35.4: πλείω των ἑξακισχιλίων ταλάντων.
[56] Diodorus 31.8.12.
[57] Livy 45.28.7. Σαρικάκης, 1962, pp. 110–111.

the Roman pillaging, the stripping of Greece from its treasures and the eventual decrease of Macedonian revenues would probably have left the area stripped from its monetary capacity to purchase large quantities of foodstuff.

Economic Annihilation and Debt-Bondage after the Battle of Pydna

The winter that followed the battle of Pydna in 168 BC was probably very difficult for the inhabitants of Macedonia, since they were left with scant supplies of food and a limited labour force. The Romans, on the other hand, did not want to undertake the burden of administering the newly acquired regions and, instead, preferred to assert themselves as a hegemonic power. This way they managed to reap the financial profits of an imperialistic war without sharing any of the responsibilities that usually follows the annihilation of another country. Although Rome was constantly interfering in the affairs of cities and kingdoms, it neither imposed a direct administrative system nor dispatched a permanent military force in the East; hence, the Romans limited themselves to diplomatic moves by weight of their authority.[58] Furthermore, the limited manpower they could employ in the second century BC (after the Hannibalic War) probably affected their prudent decision not to turn Macedonia into a province after their victory in 167 BC.[59] The administrative system they imposed on the region seemed to allow a greater degree of flexibility for the victorious power, while it gave a sense of freedom to the defeated party.[60] The Macedonians were allowed to keep their nominal independence along with their political institutions and their local legislative system.[61] However, the kingdom itself was broken up into four administrative divisions that did not communicate with each other either politically or economically;[62] consequently, reducing the possibility of reunification.[63]

The division of Macedonia and the imposition of a series of economic regulations affected deeply the well-being of the inhabitants who have already suffered during the prolonged wars. The measures that hit harder the livelihood of Greek inhabitants were probably the ones that targeted the freedom of trade and the accumulation of wealth. One of the first restrictions imposed on the Macedonians was the *jus conubii* or the ban of intermarriages between

---

[58] Rich, 1992, p. 48.
[59] Harris, 1979, pp. 144–145.
[60] Livy 45.29.4: *omnium primum liberos esse iubere Macedonas*.
[61] Livy 45.29.4: *habentis urbes easdem agrosque, utentes legibus suis, annuos creantis magistratus*.
[62] Livy 45.29.5–10.
[63] Gruen, 1984, p. 424.

the inhabitants of the four different districts of Macedonia.[64] As Gruen rightly claims, the aim of this law was probably to limit marriages-alliances between the wealthy families that could undertake the recreation of a strong central power in the future.[65] The Romans realized from the beginning the potential of a probable reunification of the four districts and did everything to limit the political and economic power of the people who could achieve such an aim. It was obvious that the merging of large properties through marriage would have facilitated the emergence of a rising powerful elite which, in turn, could have dominated the economic reconstruction of the area. As part of the same policy, the Romans did not allow the inhabitants of one district to buy land or buildings in another.[66] This way the Macedonians were forced to conduct all their property transactions either locally or through the Roman entrepreneurs who were willing to purchase land and houses in the region, of course, at lower prices in view of the limited demand.

With regard to the conduct of commercial transactions it is interesting to note that the Romans also prohibited the inter-regional trade in salt. This restriction may not have been crucial for the inhabitants of the first three districts, since they were close to the sea and could produce their own salt. The fourth district, though, was stretched on a piece of land away from the sea. Its position probably caused multiple problems, especially to the farmers who were breeding cattle and needed this product for the survival of their animals. In an attempt to solve a crisis even before it begun, Aemilius Paulus probably allowed the fourth district as well as the Dardanes, a northern tribe, to import salt from Stobi in Paionia (a part of the third district) at a specified price.[67] According to two different hypotheses the prohibitions in the trading of salt may[68] or may not[69] reflect a general prohibition of commerce between the four Macedonian districts. It seems preferable to accept the thesis that the restriction in the trading of salt was an exception and not the rule, since Livy would have certainly mentioned a general prohibition in trade, if such a prohibition was indeed imposed. The exact aim of this measure that resembles modern monopolies is not yet known; however, its impact on the lives of the people may have been limited by comparison.

Further measures that probably affected a large part of the population were those targeting the leasing of the use of the Macedonian woods, the mines and the royal lands. It is a well known fact that timber was one of the most important sources of wealth for the Macedonian kingdom and its citizens. A large

---

[64] Livy 45.29.10.
[65] The same policy was followed in Italy. For more information see Κανατσούλης, 1962, p. 108.
[66] Livy 45.29.10.
[67] Livy 45.29.11-13.
[68] Gruen, 1984, p. 424. Κανατσούλης, 1964, p. 89.
[69] Larsen, 1938, p. 299.

number of the inhabitants were probably employed in the cutting of woods and its subsequent process that ranged from the manufacture of furniture to shipbuilding. The Roman prohibition with regard to the cutting of woods[70] aimed specifically at the restriction of shipbuilding. Until then, Macedonia was a strong naval power in the Mediterranean. The new measures aimed at constraining the widespread phenomenon of piracy, in favour of imposing order and law in the seas. Since the Romans have not yet constructed a strong navy, it became evident that the continuation of shipbuilding in Macedonia would have been dangerous for the plans of Rome to expand in the East. Another reason for imposing such a prohibition was probably the wish to drive into bankruptcy the wealthy citizens that previously held leases for the exploitation of woods. The Macedonian timber was not used exclusively for the needs of the kingdom in fuel, domestic construction, furniture and shipbuilding but was also exported in other Greek cities, and especially Athens.[71] The revenues from such activities were especially large and provided Macedonia and the Macedonian elites with steady financial revenue throughout the centuries.

The elimination of all existing contracts for the operation of gold and silver mines in Macedonia[72] had the same or similar aims. The impact on the economy should have been substantial since neither the rich Macedonians nor the Roman *publicani* could lease the mines of Pangaion that used to be in operation since the fourth century BC and provided gold for the armies of Philip II and Alexander the Great. Only the mines of iron and bronze metals continued its operations throughout the Republican period,[73] probably in order to provide the local markets with coins of smaller denominations. The mining of silver metal was resumed in 158 BC, while there is a possibility that the mining of gold has been discontinued already before 167 BC due to its scanty presence.[74] This change in Roman economic policy was, in fact, the result of a conscious decision to provide the necessary bullion for the minting of silver *sestertii* in Rome.[75] The conquerors never took into consideration the financial distress of the people who until then earned their living through the working of the mines. There is also a possibility that these measures led to the partial demonetization of the Macedonian economy, since the circulation of silver coinages in the markets was probably reduced.[76] We cannot deny that the measures probably affected directly the Macedonian elite, since a) the workers

---

[70] Livy 45.29.14.
[71] Borza, E.N., 1987, pp. 32–52; MacDonald, 1981, pp. 141–146.
[72] Livy 45.18.3; 45.29.11; Diodorus 31.8.7.
[73] Livy 45.29.11.
[74] Larsen, 1938, pp. 328 and 487.
[75] Crawford, 1977, pp. 44–45.
[76] Touratsoglou, 1995.

Enslavement and Death

of the mines were mostly slaves, whose fate has not been attested in the sources and b) the use of silver coins was restricted in major transactions mainly carried out by wealthy people. However, an indirect effect on the poorer inhabitants probably arose from the reduced economic capacity of the wealthy that, until then, played the role of magnanimous benefactors and regular employers.

One of the harshest financial measures affecting the local economy and the living standards of the local inhabitants was the prohibition of leasing the royal Macedonian lands.[77] These lands became Roman property when Perseus and his family – the lawful proprietors – were eliminated; consequently, the *populus Romanus* had the legal option to undertake their administration and/or forbid their exploitation.[78] The tenants of the royal lands and their workers would have been forced to seek employment elsewhere in order to survive. Nevertheless, the opportunities of new employment in the already devastated lands of the kingdom were probably limited. This rather difficult situation probably lasted until 158 BC when these areas were leased to the Roman *censores*.[79] The profits were probably significant but this time they ended up in the hands of the wealthy Romans rather than the Macedonian elite. Despite the fact that the wealthy Macedonians would not have profited after 158 BC from the leasing of the lands, we should not disregard the fact that a substantial local labour force was probably employed in the cultivation of the fields and the tending of the cattle; thus, the financial pressures on the lower classes were alleviated.

Unfortunately the ancient sources do not give any information on the consequences of such policies especially with regard to the lives of the local population. Since the results remain a matter of conjecture rather than an undisputable fact, it will be better to abstain from any detailed hypotheses. There is, though, one point in connection to the economic developments of the Roman State that should be mentioned. The Romans demanded the payment of only half of the taxes paid until then to the Antigonids.[80] Plutarch reveals that the entire sum was no more than 100 talents for the four Macedonian districts. This sum was much smaller than the one imposed on the inhabitants of Carthage after the First Punic War (32,000 talents) and the Second Punic War (10,000 talents).[81] In the case of the Third Macedonian War we should not attribute the imposition of lower taxes to the magnanimity of the Romans. Instead, it is possible that the extensive looting of Macedonia

---

[77] Livy 45.18.3–5.
[78] Larsen, 1938, p. 312–3.
[79] Cicero, *De lege agraria* 2.51. Κανατσούλης, 1964, p. 89.
[80] Livy 45.18.7–8; 45.29.4.
[81] Abbott, 1926, p. 118.

and the subsequent economic measures completely drained the kingdom from its financial resources and inhibited its capacity to pay an annual tribute. On the other hand, the extent of the profits of the victors becomes evident if we take into consideration that in 167 BC the Romans stopped gathering the *tributum* (direct taxation) in Italy for almost a century.[82] At the same time, Roman authors started complaining about the moral decline of the Roman State marked by *luxuria* (self-indulgence) and *avaritia* (greed).[83] The amount of wealth that arrived in Italy was not the immediate outcome of the imposition of taxes but the result of extensive looting during the war and the subsequent restrictions on the use of the most important Macedonian resources.

Although the measures imposed by the Romans targeted mainly the wealthy Macedonian citizens, it is probable that the economic dysfunction that resulted would have affected the growth of the economy and the living standards of the rest of the population. Especially, the people who lived, until then, at subsistence level would have found it exceedingly difficult to find jobs in the deserted agricultural lands, enjoy the support of the civic benefactors who lost part or all of their income, pay their taxes and, in general, survive. In these cases, the only solution for some of these individuals was to sell themselves or members of their immediate family into slavery. This process is called debt-bondage and in economic terms it resembles other forms of slavery, although it remains fundamentally different in the sense that the status of the debtor is not inherited by the debtor's children.[84] Debt bondage is often attested in the Greek world by ancient historians, while similar evidence may be found on Greek inscriptions.[85] Usually it occurs during periods of subsistence crisis. Then poor people borrow from kinsmen or wealthy individuals, either in cash or in kind, promising as repayment a portion of the crop.[86] A well known instance is that of third century Amorgos, where a benefactor was honoured for lending money at an interest rate of 20% per annum to individuals who were buying his grain during a shortage period.[87] Such high interest rates in a time of crisis could only imply that the debt would have been exorbitant and may have led the debtors into bondage. Even though we do not have similar evidence from Macedonia after the battle of Pydna, we may assume that the process was still in existence and that the possibilities of debt-bondage would have multiplied after the imposition of the Roman measures.

---

[82] Gruen, 1984, p. 427.
[83] For more details on the economic profits of the wars see Harris, 1971, pp. 1371–1385.
[84] Finley, 1965.
[85] Lysias, *Speeches*, 12.98; Isocrates, *Against Platicus*, 14.48; Aristophanes, *Ploutos*, 147–184; Aristophanes, *Acarnanians*, 729–835; Meiggs and Lewis, 1969, no. 5.
[86] Gallant, 1989, pp. 404–5.
[87] Migeotte, 1984.

Conclusions

The general attitude of the Roman forces during and after the Third Macedonian War shows a disregard towards the lives and welfare of the northern Greek inhabitants. The destruction of the cities, the massacres or enslavement of the citizens, the annihilation of properties and the devastation of the fields provided the Romans with short term profits that enabled them to continue successfully their warfare of destruction. On one hand, the death of the adult male population and the widespread enslaving processes probably caused labour problems, especially in the fields. On the other hand, the enslavement of a substantial segment of the Epirote population and several of the inhabitants of the hostile Greek cities would have caused havoc, especially in the rural economy. The majority of these new slaves were relocated to Italy; hence, they left behind them a gap in the local workforce that could not have been replaced by the remaining women, children and old men. The short and long term effect of the partial depopulation of the region on the agricultural production could have been none other than local famines and/or the impoverishment of certain regions.

The problems did not cease when the Romans returned to Italy, mainly because of their attitude in the aftermath of the war. The economic measures that followed Perseus' defeat in the battle of Pydna did not ensure the collection of new profits, since Greece was not directly administered by the Roman State. On the contrary, these measures ensured the complete destruction of the Macedonian economic system and stripped the region from its most precious resources. The prohibition of exploiting the mines as well as the royal lands from 167 until 158 BC, and the lasting cessation of the exploitation of timber probably affected not only the Macedonian elite but also the poor individuals who until then earned their meager living from all kinds of jobs related to these sectors. Furthermore, the prohibition of *conubium* and the ban on the trade in properties did not allow the resurrection of powerful Macedonian elite that would have contested the Roman power. Although these measures seemed to aim at the economic capabilities of the wealthy inhabitants, the truth is that it also undermined the livelihood of the poorer classes that until then was employed in the fields, mines, woods and buildings of the upper class. It is possible that the poverty that followed the destruction of the Macedonian social system and infrastructures left the weakest members of the society destitute. In some of these cases the only alternative could have been selling ones' children or other members of the family into slavery in order to pay for the accumulated debts. Debt slavery was already in existence in the region and would have been an acceptable way to solve the problem. In fact, this was probably the only sensible solution; otherwise, starvation may have resulted to even more dire consequences. In effect, the inhabitants of

Greece may have witnessed a change in the structure of the local workforce. A wider participation of women and old men in professions otherwise held only by adult males may have been made possible by the relocation of the new slaves to Italy. In addition, parts of the remaining population would have been sold into slavery (debt-bondage), thus, augmenting the number of slaves in the Greek regions but decimating the group of free workers.

Bibliography

Abbott, F.F. and Johnson, A.C. (1926), *Municipal Administration in the Roman Empire*, Princeton.
Badian, E. (1968), *Roman Imperialism in the Late Republic*, 2nd ed., Oxford.
Birmingham, D. (1966), *Trade and Conquest in Angola: The Mbundu and the Neighbours and the Portuguese*, Oxford.
Borza, E.N. (1987), 'Timber and politics in the ancient world: Macedon and the Greeks', *Proceedings of the American Philosophical Society*, 131.1, pp. 32–52.
Bradley, K.R. (1987), 'On the Roman slave supply and slave breeding', in M.I. Finley (ed.), *Classical Slavery*, London, pp. 42–64.
Crawford, M.H. (1977), 'Rome and the Greek world: Economic relationships', *The Economic History Review*, 30.1, pp. 42–52.
De Sanctis, G. (1969), *Storia dei Romani*, 2nd ed., Turin.
de Ste. Croix, G.E.M. (1981), *The Class Struggle in the Ancient World*, London.
Deininger, J. (1971), *Der politische Widerstand gegen Rom in Griechenland, 217–86 v. Chr.*, Berlin.
Errington, R.M. (1971), *The Dawn of Empire: Rome's Rise to World Power*, London.
Finley, M. (1980), *Ancient Slavery and Modern Ideology*, New York.
Finley, M. (1980), 'La servitude pour dettes', *Revue historique de droit français et étranger*, 43, pp. 159–184.
Frank, T. (1914), *Roman Imperialism*, New York.
Gallant, T.W. (1989), 'Risk-buffering behaviour in Hellenistic communities', *Journal of Interdisciplinary History*, 19.3, pp. 393–413.
Garnsey, P. (2003), *Famine and Food Supply in the Greco-Roman World*, 2nd. ed., Cambridge.
Gruen, E. (1976), 'Class conflict and the Third Macedonian War', *American Journal of Ancient History*, 1, pp. 29–60.
Gruen, E.S. (1984), *The Hellenistic World and the Coming of Rome*, Berkeley.
Hammond, N.G.L. and Walbank, F.W. (1988), *History of Macedonia*, III, Oxford.
Harris, W.V. (1971), 'On war and greed in the second century BC', *The American Historical Review*, 76.5, pp. 1371–1385.
Harris, W.V. (1979), *War and Imperialism in Republican Rome 327–70 BC*, Oxford.
Harris, W.V. (1980), 'Towards a study of the Roman slave trade', in J.H. D' Arms and E.C. Koppf (eds.), *The Seaborne Commerce of Ancient Rome: Studies in Archaeology and History*, Rome, pp. 117–140.
Harris, W.V. (1999), 'Demography, geography and the sources of Roman slaves', *Journal of Roman Studies*, 89, pp. 62–75.
Hopkins, K. (1978), *Conquerors and Slaves*, Cambridge.
Larsen, J.A.O. (1938), 'Roman Greece', in T. Frank (ed.), *An Economic Survey of Ancient Rome*, IV, Baltimore.
Larsen, J.A.O. (1968), *Greek Federal States*, Oxford.

MacDonald, B.R. (1981), 'The Phanosthenes decree tax and timber in fifth-century Athens', *Hesperia*, 50, pp. 141–146.
Meiggs, R. and Lewis, D. (eds.) (1969), *A Selection of Greek Historical Inscriptions to the End of the Fifth Century BC*, Oxford.
Migeotte, L. (1984), *L' Emprunt public dans les cites Grecques: Recueil des documents et analyse critique*, Paris.
Millar, F. (1984), 'The Mediterranean and the Roman Revolution: Politics, War and the Economy', *Past and Present*, 102, pp. 3–24.
Palmer, R.E.A. (1974), *Roman Religion and Roman Empire: Five Essays*, Philadelphia, pp. 154–171.
Patterson, O. (1982), *Slavery and Social Death: A Comparative Study*, Cambridge Mass.
Rich, J. (1993), 'Fear, greed and glory: the causes of Roman war-making in the middle Republic', in J. Rich and G. Shipley (eds.), *War and Society in the Roman World*, London/New York, pp. 38–68.
Ridley, R.T. (1986), 'To be taken with a pinch of salt: The destruction of Carthage', *Classical Philology*, 81.2, pp. 140–146.
Rostoftzeff, M. (1941), *The Social and Economic History of the Hellenistic World*, vol. 2, Oxford.
Scheidel, W. (1997), 'Quantifying the sources of slaves in the Early Roman Empire', *Journal of Roman Studies*, 87, pp. 156–169.
Scheidel, W. (forthcoming), 'The Roman slave supply', in K. Bradley and P. Cartledge (eds.), *The Cambridge World History of Slavery, 1: The Ancient Mediterranean World*, Cambridge.
Scullard, H.H. (1945), 'Charops and Roman policy in Epirus', *Journal of Roman Studies* 35, pp. 59–64.
Thornton, J. (1999), *Warfare in Atlantic Africa, 1500–1800*, London.
Touratsoglou, Y. (1995), *Disjecta Membra: Two New Hellenistc Hoards from Greece*, Athens.
Walsh, J.J. (2000), 'The disorders of the 170s BC and Roman intervention in the class struggle in Greece', *The Classical Quarterly*, 50.1, pp. 300–303.
Welwei, K.W., (2000), *Sub corona vendere. Quellenkritische Studien zu Kriegsgefangenschaft und Sklaverei in Rom bis zum Ende des Hannibalkrieges*, Stuttgart.
Westermarck, E.A. (1912), *The Origin and Development of the Moral Ideas*, 2 vols., London.
Ziolkowski, S. (1992), 'Urbs direpta, or how the Romans sacked cities', in J. Rich and G. Shipley (eds.), *War and Society in the Roman World*, London/ New York, pp. 69–91.
Κανατσούλης, Α. (1964), *Ιστορία της Μακεδονίας μέχρι Μεγάλο Κωνσταυτίνο*, Thessalonica.
Σαρικάκς, Θ. (1962), *Αεύκιος Αμίλιος Παύλος. Συμβολή εις την Ιστορίαν του Γ'Μακεδονικού Πολέμου*, Athens.

ENSLAVEMENT OF NATIVE AMERICANS DURING QUEEN ANNE'S WAR

Rebecca M. Seaman

Wars in the ancient world often resulted in the capture of enemies and sale of captives into slavery. While states fought wars for expansion and control, participants profited from the wars through the sale of their captives to willing buyers. Early modern eras saw a continuation of these practices. Centuries of indigenous enslavement and slave trade with Islamic societies in the African continent expanded and transformed enslavement practices with the arrival of European traders along the western coastal regions of Africa. The dawn of New World colonization further heightened the practices and changed the policies of slavery in participating nations. In the Americas the methods of national expansion, via wars of conquest and the resulting sale of captives as slaves, greatly affected the invading Europeans as well as the American Indians. While these practices closely resembled enslavement systems of West Africa, certain characteristics made early eighteenth century enslavement of Native Americans in the colonial southeast distinct from its eastern Atlantic counterparts. The presence of three competing European powers, a multitude of rival Indian tribes and timing contributed to the distinctive character and extreme incidence of slave captures and sales in the American colonial southeast during "Queen Anne's War".[1]

The seventeenth century witnessed shifting alliances between many nations and peoples. In Africa, European nations tapped into the existing slave trade, stimulating the contemporary internal trade while simultaneously increasing the ownership of slaves locally.[2] In North America, relations between differing nations of Indians and colonists were also in flux. Determined to employ

---

[1] Throughout this article, when specific examples are related to a single tribe, the commonly used tribal names are applied. When multiple tribes are considered at once, more generic terms are necessary. Due to a lack of agreement upon a single generic title by scholars and among aboriginal peoples of North America, an attempt has been made to accommodate all and offend none by applying the three most commonly adopted generic titles: Native Americans, Indians and First Peoples.

[2] Thornton, 1998, pp. 73–4.

practices and policies that benefited their own people, the colonists and neighbouring tribes constantly jockeyed for positions of strength in trade, friendship and war. Into this competitive climate, the War of the Spanish Succession or Queen Anne's War for English colonial America intensified rivalries and amplified abuses. The war was the primary milieu for the drastically increased enslavement of Native Americans in the colonial southeast during the early 18th century. While studies of Indian enslavement among individual tribes, or the entire region over several decades, have come forth recently, no historical analysis exists that explores why Indian enslavement reached a peak during Queen Anne's War. Like the wars that took place during the Roman Republic[3], Queen Anne's War extended far beyond the mere acquisition of slaves for plantation labor. Yet the complexity of the southeastern region of North America in the early 18th century lent itself to a sharp rise of Indian enslavement not seen before or since in the region. Though not unique in the history of slavery, the extreme increase over such a brief period of time, especially in the midst of ongoing enslavement in West Africa, makes the sudden spike in Native American Enslavement exceptional and worthy of further examination. This study explores the major players and the complexity of factors that contributed to the distinctive surge in enslavement of Indians during this eleven-year period.

Slave systems have existed around the world across the ages. The Romans contributed greatly to early modern slave systems through the codified laws (Justinian) that medieval Europeans eventually integrated into their own legal codes. This classical style of slavery was similar to the later West African and North American practices of enslaving prisoners of war.[4] West African and Native American slavery differed in relation to the concept of private property. Historian John Thornton asserted, "*Slavery was widespread in Atlantic Africa because slaves were the only form of private, revenue-producing property recognized in African law.*" This contrasted to the European legal systems that, like classical Rome, saw land as the basis of private, revenue-producing property, and slavery as a minor, though interconnected revenue source.[5]

Contrary to popular belief, slavery was not new to the Indians of North America at the time of European arrival, but it differed from the classical form or that of West Africa. In the southeast, natives practiced temporary enslavement to pay off debts, usually the result of gambling. Long-term enslavement resulted from wars with neighbouring tribes but existed in small numbers. Captives typically experienced adoption or execution, with minor

---

[3] See Katsari's chapter in this volume.
[4] Phillips, Jr., 1985, pp. 16–7.
[5] Thornton, 1998, pp. 74–5.

numbers exchanged in trade deals, or exploited as slaves.[6] Surviving captives eventually merged into the society of their captors, marrying and leaving their slave status behind. This practice of adoption was necessary in a world with zero to negative population growth, as was the case in North American Indian tribes in the colonial era. The accompanying integration of differing tribal cultures created complex intertribal relations, but assisted in the survival of people in the midst of wars, diseases and famines. With European settlement, the flexible nature of the southeastern tribes contributed to their quick adaptation of their own slave practices to fit the new economics and politics of European colonization. However, with very limited native exploitation of slaves for agriculture as in the complex legal systems of West Africa, and with different views on property ownership as practiced in Europe, the First Peoples of the southeast adopted new slaving practices in keeping with tribal political and economic strategies.[7]

Europeans brought with them differing views on slavery as they came to America. The European powers involved in the struggle for colonizing North America in the early 1700s, included the Spanish, the French and the English. Prior to extensive colonization of the New World, slavery in these European nations more closely resembled serfdom. The Spanish wars of *Reconquista* gradually shifted slave practices, incorporating a strong element of racism and religious superiority. The English colonization of the Caribbean sugar islands drastically changed the serfdom practices of old England with regard to the interpretation of slaves as personal property, to be bought, sold, used and moved at will. The practice merged with English laws in the Caribbean and later was incorporated into Carolina's laws by the early Barbadian settlers. By the time of Queen Anne's War, chattel slavery was the norm for all three colonizing powers. The chattel concept replaced temporary enslavement for indebtedness practiced by First Peoples. This distinct difference in slave perceptions was in turn to create conflicts between Native Americans and the Europeans who bought, held, or captured slaves from the neighbouring tribes who, in turn, performed agricultural labor for their masters.

In Florida, the Spanish used *Indios* on their inland *haciendas* and at St. Augustine. There the *repartimiento* provided the cloak of morality for the actual practice of forced, involuntary labor. Following a series of violent uprisings by the Guale in 1597 and the Timucua in 1638, the Spanish implemented policy changes that attempted to keep the tribes submissive and unarmed. Indeed, Spanish trade with inland tribes forbade the exchange of guns or ammunition for goods. Yet the practice of involuntary labor or *servicio personal*,[8] continued,

---
[6] Swanton, 1964, p. 68; Lawson, 1967 [1708], pp. 287, 292; and MacLeod, 1925, pp. 375–6.
[7] Martin, 1994, p. 308.
[8] Villamarin and Villamarin, 1975, pp. 13, 149.

justified by rationales of maintaining a foothold in North America to protect Spanish territorial claims. Even as the Spanish felt the pincer movements of English and French colonization in the southeast in the late 1690s, trade in guns with the local tribes remained illegal while involuntary labor continued unchecked. Instead of maintaining a servile native populace, the Spanish refusal to trade in arms turned potential tribal allies to other sources of trade, namely the English and French.

The propensity of tribes to shift locations and alliances for their own benefits is similar to shifts in location and trade alliances that occurred in West Africa. There, peoples under attack by the well-armed nations of Bornu, Bagirmi and Adamawa often shifted from their traditional locations to mountains and other geographic places of refuge to escape raids and enslavement.[9] In the American southeast, tribes similarly relocated to avoid attacks by well-armed tribal enemies. In the late 16th and early 17th centuries, the Spanish of Florida incited raids upon neighbouring tribes to the north. Poorly equipped to resist well-armed Spanish soldiers and their Timucua allies, the Yamasee and Guale shifted further north. With the arrival of the English in Virginia and ensuing trade in guns for slaves with the Westo, the Yamasee and Guale shifted southward and resumed alliances with the Spanish. Spanish fears of tribal alliances with the English often resulted in better treatment of the allied tribes, to include enforcing proper implementation of the *repartimiento*.[10] With the start of Queen Anne's War and the increased targeting of Spanish missions by English-led slave raids, approximately 1400 Apalachee (allies with Spain since early 1600s), moved to Carolina to protect their people from further raids and to reap the benefits of English trade in cheaper goods and guns.

At other times, tribes broke their alliances, or held simultaneous conflicting alliances with opposing European powers. In the middle of the 17th century, Lower Creek villages vainly sought alliances with the Spanish, as increased raids by Westo and other English armed tribes threatened their survival. In 1679, the governor of Florida sent Fray Ocon to establish a long overdue mission among the Lower Creek at Sabacola. However, Creek shifts in trade, to benefit from English guns and other superior goods, resulted in the leading *cacique* of Coweta (leading Lower Creek town) ordering the monk to leave. Over the next few years, Governor Cabrera ordered soldiers under Antonio Matheos to capture English traders and goods, and compel the Lower Creek towns to return to Spanish control. While officially giving obeisance to Spanish

---

[9] Thierno Mouctar Bah, 2003, pp. 16–18.
[10] 'Real Cedula Que No Se Provea Encomienda en Persona Que Tuviere Pension, Madrid, 2 julio 1666', in *Coleccion de Documentos*, 1958, pp. 539–40.

authority and receiving aid to rebuild targeted towns, the Creek continued to protect their English traders and carried on trade in English goods.[11]

The French were relatively late arrivals in the colonial southeast. Earlier attempts to settle the region resulted in dismal failure. Determined to control vast territories of North America, Frenchmen such as La Salle continued to explore and claim territories down the Mississippi River in the mid to late 17th century. Rumors of French intentions to settle the Mississippi River abounded through the 1690s. Royal restrictions placed upon French *coureurs de bois* within areas of colonial French influence encouraged French traders to move into English territories. There, the French conducted trade with local tribes, contributing to the further spreading rumors and fears of French exploitation of enemy tribes.[12] By 1699, the French arrived in the Gulf to establish a permanent settlement under the leadership of Pierre Le Moyne d'Iberville. Initially, d'Iberville forbade the acquisition of Native American slaves and ordered the return of captives, should any be discovered.[13] However, shortly after d'Iberville left for France in 1702, the French captured and enslaved a group of Chitimachas near the Mississippi. Months later, the French conducted another raid upon the Alabama, a tribe then in amity with the English. The French never enslaved large numbers of local Indians, but did participate in the practice of capturing, selling, and using Native Americans as slaves. These slaves often performed duties as hunters, guides, concubines and household servants, since large-scale farming did not initially play a role in early Mobile.[14]

Unlike the Spanish, the French initiated trade in arms with the area tribes from the outset, noting guns were the best lure of French Indian allies.[15] D'Iberville sought to establish a peaceful alliance of all tribes in the region, one based on trade with, and respect for, the French. This *Pax Galicia* aimed to align the tribes with the French against the encroaching English. To accomplish this agenda, d'Iberville sought to provision allied tribes with weapons and form a broad inter-tribal alliance. The lack of financial support from France undercut the goals of the *Pax Galicia*. The French depended heavily on their aligned tribes for trade and protection. The appearance of prosperity and power remained the best guarantee of continued French authority in the

---

[11] de Barcia, 1970, p. 32; Juricek, 1962, p. 148.

[12] 'Ordinance for maintaining the Frontenac, Missilimakinac and St. Joseph of the Miamis posts, by Louis XIV, April 28, 1697', in Peyser, 1992, pp. 61–2; McWilliams, 1981, p. 166; and 'Letter from Sauvole to Pontchartrain, 4 Aug, 1701', *MPA: FD*, 1929, p. 15.

[13] McWilliams, 1981, p. 173.

[14] The French use of Native American slaves in Louisiana closely resembles the Muslim use of slaves from Africa, resulting in a similar targeting of females as slaves. Phillips, 1985, p. 85.

[15] Jean Baptiste Le Moyne de Bienville, 'Le Sieur de Bienville, Extrait des Lettres, 28 juilles 1706', Archives de Nationales de France, New Orleans Historical Collection, Série C, C13A, reel 1, 530–1 (Cited hereafter as AC, C13A).

region. As early as 1702, the French proved incapable of maintaining consistent, adequate provisions to assure tribal allies of French superiority. The wishes of d'Iberville to cement an alliance that also prohibited Indian slave trade collapsed, as Frenchmen and local tribes conducted slave raids and traded slaves for goods. Simultaneously, the English colonists implemented their own policy of inciting Indian raids on tribes in alliance with the French. In return, the English provided low priced superior trade goods.[16]

The English southeastern colonies dominated the trade with Native Americans in the early 1700s. Despite an early Spanish presence in the region and French interests in friendly relations, the English ability to extend credit to traders, superiority of English trade goods, and willingness to trade in weapons and other desired goods shifted the balance of trade in England's favor. Simultaneously, English colonial trade restrictions and excessive costs resulted in only a few African slaves living in the southeastern region prior to the 1690s. Once King William III took the throne of England, that balance began to shift. Nonetheless, at the turn of the century, the slaves owned by the English colonists were of Native American origin, being readily available and less expensive than African slaves.[17] These forced native laborers served as household servants, farm laborers, as well as craftsmen. Additionally, the trade and export of First Peoples to Caribbean and other North American colonies increased. Groups of English traders and factors (or intermediaries) focused on two primary sources of profit in trade with tribes: deerskins and Indian slaves. Traders, their investors, and land hungry settlers did not take into consideration proprietary concerns arising from the slave trade; thus, inciting local wars. Friendly tribes were encouraged to raid enemy tribes for slaves and skins, and received guns and ammunition in return. The arrival of the French in the region and the alignment of France with Spain upon the death of Charles II, added incentives for English colonists to encourage allied tribes to target French and Spanish Indian allies.[18] On the eve of Queen Anne's War, the stage was set to expand the slave trade of Native Americans in the colonial southeast.

One should not be too quick to assume that the tribes of the southeast were pawns in the European colonial struggle. Too often historians dealing with Native Americans portray the tribes as *"noble savages"* who passively acquiesced to the greater European powers. Frank Klingberg, Herbert Bolton, Mary Ross, and Mark Boyd painted the image of a one-sided European manipulation of tribes in the practice of Indian slave trading. Nothing could be further from the

---

[16] Bienville, 1:515–6, 531–2, AC, C13A, 2:5–6; and Higginbotham, 1991, pp. 113, 117–19, 242–3.
[17] Seaman, 2001, p. 55.
[18] McWilliams, 1988, p. 159; and Martin, 1994, p. 312.

truth. Southeastern tribes sought out alliances with European nations for their own tribal purposes. The Westo, strongest tribe in the southeast when Carolina was first settled, actually used trade with the Virginia and Carolina colonies as a means of leveraging for the best trade deals in furs, skins and slaves.[19] From the moment of first contact, European diseases disrupted tribal stability and power, forcing the formation of new alliances and political structures among the regional tribes. Weak tribes assimilated into stronger tribes, and individual and tribal coalitions aligned with colonial governments. Following the devastating affects of the Westo War in the 1680s, the remaining Westoes and a neighbouring tribe of Winyahs fled to the Creek villages for protection from further raids. The smallpox epidemics of the late 1690s completely devastated some tribes, forcing remaining families to merge with other tribes within the same region.[20] Writing about the absorption of the Ouachas, the Chaouachas, and the Quinipissas by the Bayogoulas and the Mougoulashas of Louisiana, historian Daniel Usner said *"village consolidation and intertribal assimilation . . . was a rational response to the disruption of life being caused by epidemics and wars."*[21] These coalitions and alliances emerged from tribal needs and perceptions, often to maintain tribal independence, much like the previously mentioned migrations of interior African peoples in the wake of increased raids upon their communities.[22]

Trade exchanges with Europeans brought distinct changes to West Africans and North American Indians. In Africa, the '*"gun-slave cycle"* or *"horse-slave cycle"*' drove trade. Without these commodities, communities had no ability to defend themselves from enemies. With these commodities, the same communities could capture slaves and increase in wealth.[23] In America, slave trade brought warriors *"a whole estate at once, one slave brings a Gun, ammunition, horse, hatchet and a suit of cloathes."*[24] Every tribe that participated in the slave trade, directly or indirectly, became dependent upon guns, ammunition and other hardware items available only from Europeans. Without continued supplies of these items, the tribes risked defeat and destruction at the hands of their better-armed neighbours. The first tribes to acquire guns sought to immediately reduce their enemies and expand their territories. Dependence on European trade goods augmented the war and slave traditions of the southeastern tribes, while simultaneously affecting their ability to avoid consequential disasters. Historian Richard White's[25] dependency theory helps illustrate the entangled

---

[19] J. Leitch Wright, 1981, p. 107.
[20] Waddell, 1980, p. 2–6; Swanton, 1979, p. 145.
[21] Usner, 1992, pp. 44–5.
[22] Axtell, 1997, p. 6; Fausz, 1985, p. 232, 234; Martin, 1994, p. 308; and Saunt, 1998, p. 158.
[23] Thornton, 1998, p. 98.
[24] Nairne, 1988, pp. 47–8.
[25] White, 1983, passim.

web of economic reliance that grew with the increased trade relations of Europeans and Indians. Of equal value on this topic is Stephen Van Hoek's *Untangling the Roots of Dependency: Choctaw Economies*. Van Hoek's work clearly explains how the Choctaw successfully manipulated the trade economy of the southeast for over a century.[26]

Despite aggressive attempts by Native American leaders to maintain regional dominance, entire villages and tribes fell victim to the concentrated efforts of colonial agendas, wartime politics, and inter-tribal rivalries. Queen Anne's War exacerbated this complex series of events and entangled relations. The presence of three European powers in the region, along with the shifting tribal affiliations, prompted the targeting of certain borderland tribes for wartime raids. Repeated raids by the English and their allies resulted in the capture and sale of thousands of native slaves from 1702–1713. Increased enslavement raised the risk of local Indian wars. Additionally, Native American slaves escaped easily to their tribal villages. To counter this trend, and to increase profits, Carolina exported most native slaves to other colonies in North America or the West Indies. Jean-Baptiste Le Moyne de Bienville, governor of Louisiana, acknowledged the efficiency of First Peoples in cultivating crops, but requested permission to sell native slaves in the Caribbean in exchange for African slaves because the captive Indians *"deserted too easily."* Bienville's request was denied, specifically to avoid the *"disorder and animosity"* apparent between the First Peoples and the English in Carolina.[27]

The advent of Queen Anne's War in the southeast resulted in changes to colonial policies regarding the inciting of inter-tribal warfare and the practice of Native American slave trade. The French of Louisiana quickly abandoned d'Iberville's instructions prohibiting enslavement of local tribes and waged war on the Alabama and Chickasaw tribes, selling captives as slaves. French tribal allies also made war and took hostages, exchanging their captured slaves for guns and ammunition. This human barter system encouraged tribes to conduct raids for slaves on distant rival tribes.[28] The Choctaw, enemies of the Chickasaw, needed little encouragement to accelerate their attacks on their English backed neighbouring tribe.

D'Iberville encouraged the Spanish in Pensacola to use their Apalachee allies to strike a blow at the English. (France was an ally of Spain, but one regarded with great suspicion). The English thwarted the invasion by

---

[26] Van Hoek, 1999, p. 113. A Great example of Choctaw manipulation is their contriving to get the French into a conflict with the Chickasaw. This conflict helped restore old inter-tribal orders and also created a source for guns through the slave trade.
[27] Daniel Usner, 1997, p. 146.
[28] McWilliams, 1981, pp. 145, 171–3, 175; Higginbotham, 1991, p. 85.
[29] Crane, 1919, p. 385.

countering with a raid comprised of English, Alabama and other tribes.[29] Because of this disastrous advice, the Spanish rejected further French council, choosing to remain at Pensacola, primarily out of fear that the French would colonize the Spanish Gulf Coast. The Spanish Apalachee allies in the region depended upon Spain's protection, due to the refusal of the Spanish to arm their native allies.[30] That policy changed in Florida following the devastating Carolinian raids of 1704 upon Apalachee villages and Spanish forts.

English policy changes triggered the greatest devastation of certain southeastern tribes. Proprietary Carolina originally extended protections to tribes of the region.[31] In 1680, the Proprietors cautioned the colony *"not to suffer any Indian in League or friendly with us and lives within 200 miles to be made slaves or sent away without special instruction."*[32] This restriction attempted to prevent enslavement of tribes in amity with the English. As late as 1698, the proprietors of Carolina directed the Attorney General for the colony, Nicholas Trott, to

> *"enquire into the Indian trade and remarke what abuses are committed in the same, and to propose to the assembly such act or acts to be past by them as shall effectually prevent the said abuses . . ."*[33]

The new Fundamental Constitutions, devised that same year of 1698, dropped these protections. By 1700, the proprietors and the English Board of Trade authorized the extension of trade in order to establish firm control of lands and tribes in the southeast. The rumored arrival of the French in the southeast generated a rush to prevent French trade influence. The proprietors, concerned for the economic stability and survival of their colony, turned their attention from restricting the abuses of the Indian slave trade to allowing enslavement and exportation of Indian slaves as a means of securing the borders from the French. The distraction gave rise to trade abuses and a corresponding increase of inter-tribal confederations.[34] Contrary to the implication of historian William Ramsey, local tribes began forming alliances against the English early in Queen Anne's War, even without the encouragement of other European nations.[35] Carolina's Commons House of Assembly responded to the increasing alignments of disaffected tribes by appointing a commission to regulate trade and reduce the threat of attacks by alienated tribes and in

---

[30] de la Harpe, 1851, p. 379.
[31] Cheves, 1897, p. 120.
[32] 'Instructions for the Commissioners appointed to hear and determine differences between the Christians and Indians, 17 May 1680', BPRO, 1, p. 99.
[33] 'Letters of Bienville to Pontchartrain', MPA: FD, 1929, 2, p. 22; and 'Instructions for Nicholas Trott, Attorney General for Carolina from proprietors, 8 Mar., 1698', in Salley, 1947, 4, p. 13.
[34] 'Letter from proprietors to Andrew Percival, 18 Oct. 1690', in Rivers, 1846, pp. 412–14; 'Letter from Lord Lexington, Mr. Hill, and Mr. Lock', in Salley, 1947, 4, p. 97.
[35] Ramsey, 1999, pp. 65–66.

From Captivity to Freedom

response to the new French presence. This commission initially possessed no real authority.[36]

With the announcement of Queen Anne's War in 1702, the door opened to trader abuses. Verner Crane, noted historian of this era, correctly pointed out that the great Carolinian Assemblymen, Council members, and governors at this time were often affluent Indian traders. James Moore, Thomas Nairne, Joseph Blake and others profited from the trade in skins and slaves generated by inciting tribes in amity with the English to raid the Spanish and French traders and Indians.[37] The proprietors informed the capitalistic Carolinian government that

> "*we doe therefore order and direct you to declare war accordingly against France and Spaine and that you doe your dutyes in your severall stations to annoy the subjects of France and Spaine and to preserver and defend our colony from the enemy.*"[38]

Under the pretense of securing the frontier from advancing French and Spanish, the Carolinians outfitted the Chickasaw, Arkansas, Cherokee, Alabama, Creek, Yamasee and other tribes with guns and ammunition.[39] Thomas Nairne, first Indian agent for South Carolina, commented on the potential threat of French armed tribes, asserting that "*. . .only by trading and other management can [we] put a check to them . . . .*"[40]

"*Other management*" included English led raids against Spanish, French and their native allies. In 1702, Governor James Moore organized an expedition, again of tribal allies and Carolinians, against the town and fort at St. Augustine. The town was devastated, the Spanish tribal allies captured and enslaved, but the fort remained intact. Historian Verner Crane credited Moore with envisioning the real imperial threat posed to English Carolina by the French, and setting the stage for the inter-colonial contest to control the region of the Gulf and the Mississippi.[41] Indeed, there was some consternation on the part of the Carolinians about the French-Spanish union and presence along the Carolina frontier. However, reports by Nairne and friendly tribes regarding the French and Spanish state of affairs portrayed poorly provisioned opponents, weak in numbers, and easily surpassed in trade.[42]

---

[36] 'Letter of October 1, 1700 to Lords', Register of the Province of South Carolina, in Records of the States of the United States of America, 1949, Section E.3, Reel 2. A more complex system of "*protected*" and unprotected status of peoples existed in West Africa as a means of safeguarding specific privileged groups from enslavement along coastal regions. Lovejoy and Richardson, 2003, p. 102.

[37] Crane, 1919, p. 380.

[38] 'Letter from Proprietors of Carolina, 8 May 1702, to Carolina, St. James' in Salley, 1947, 5, p. 76.

[39] McWilliams, 1981, p. 144.

[40] 'Letter of 10 July 1708 to Proprietors from Thomas Nairne', in Salley, 1947, 5, pp. 195–8.

[41] Crane, 1919, p. 386.

[42] Nairne in Salley, 1947.

In May 1703, Governor Nathaniel Johnson received instructions from the Lord Proprietors to use South Carolina tribes as a defense and protection against France and Spain.[43] Carolina targeted the French in a raid led by Nairne and joined by the Alabama. The successful ambush resulted in Jean Baptiste Bienville (younger brother to d'Iberville) lashing out at the disloyal Alabama, using French and allied tribes to attack and enslave the Alabama. Captive Native American slaves, sold at Fort Louis (Mobile), saw their use on farms, as personal servants, and as French concubines.[44] Bienville's retaliation served to push the Alabama into closer alignment with the English for trade in guns and ammunition. Eager for better quality English arms, the Alabama increased their raids on Spanish and French Indians, reaping stored skins and slaves as bounty.[45]

In December 1703, James Moore and some Native American allies set out against the Spanish Indians at Apalachee. The English captured six or seven thousand Apalachee prisoners, and then sold several to pay for the cost of waging war on the Spanish and French neighbours. Additionally, 1400 Apalachee relocated to Carolina, eager to escape attack and to profit from relations with the English. The Apalachee relocation generated Native American allies for Carolina's fight against the Spanish and French and exposed the Spanish settlements at Pensacola.[46] The tribe's relocation also removed the Apalachee as a target of English aggression, while simultaneously increasing tribal trade opportunities and eliminating abusive *repartimiento* practices.

The Spanish colonies of Florida lacked the necessary numbers to hold territories, and possessed insufficient financing to bind the local tribes through trade. First Peoples, targeted by English led Indian raids, either migrated into English territories, or sought French protection and traded in guns and ammunition. Bienville reported in 1706 that the remaining Apalachee and Chatot of the Florida panhandle had relocated near Mobile.

English raids targeted tribes in amity with both the Spanish and French. By 1708, Native American slaves in Carolina accounted for 1,400 of the 5,500 people held in bondage. Additionally, Carolinians shipped another 10,000 to 12,000 Native American slaves to other English colonies in North America and in the West Indies.[47] In Louisiana that same year, Native American slaves comprised the majority of slaves, not Africans, and even outnumbered the

---

[43] 'Governor's Instructions for Nathaniel Johnson, by Lds. Proprietors, 1702', Records of the States of the United States of America, 1949, Section E.3, Reel 1, Unit 4.
[44] Seaman, 2001, p. 194.
[45] McWilliams, 1988, pp. 64–6; Higginbotham, 1991, pp. 124–5; and Bienville, 'Bienville to Pontchartrain, 6 Sept. 1704' Mississippi Provincial Archives: French Dominion, 1929, 3, pp. 21–2.
[46] Bienville, 'Bienville to Pontchartrain, 6 Sept. 1704', Mississippi Provincial Archives: French Dominion, 1929, 3, pp. 26–7.
[47] Haan, 1982, p. 345.

French settlers in the colony.[48] As African slaves increased in the southeastern colonies, native slaves initially labored alongside. However, perceptions of lesser value for Indian slaves, as well as increased fears of tribal insurrections and costs of runaways, encouraged the exportation of native slaves.[49]

Beleaguered tribes impacted by Carolina slave raids during Queen Anne's War included the Apalachee, the Yuchis (both of northern Florida), the Choctaws, Mobilians, and Tohomes. Though France was the primary threat, the ease of raiding southward into Florida encouraged English traders and First People allies to focus upon poorly defended tribes of the peninsula. By 1707, John Archdale of Charlestown reported that South Carolina had few enemies left along its borders.[50] The following year, Indian Agent Nairne reported that no decent Indian village remained from Charles Town to Mobile, or as far as the Florida Keys.[51]

Internal colonial squabbles resurfaced as Carolina secured its southern frontier. Diminished profits from raids on French and Spanish tribal allies for skins and slaves led to seeking profit elsewhere. Acts to regulate trade with the tribes of South Carolina, passed in 1707, charged a £8 license fee, available only in Charlestown, in an attempt to exclude profiteering by Virginia traders and to control trade abuses. This act quickly came under use by Carolina traders to justify seizing trade goods and slaves from Virginia traders. Even when the proprietors forbid the levying of duties on Virginia traders, South Carolina ignored the instructions and continued seizing all goods for payment of the license.[52]

During the early years of the war, the old divisions among the Carolinians, their government, and the proprietors appeared to ease. However, as the threats to the frontier receded, internal dissension increased. Local tribes in amity with Carolina often fell victim to profit seeking traders and debt-ridden tribesmen. Much like the experiences in West Africa, the shifting policies and alliances in the later years of Queen Anne's War resulted in the "*predators*" becoming the "*prey*" of slave catchers.[53] Fears of disaffected local tribes prompted renewed calls for trade reforms. Governor Johnson and the Council resisted the pressures for reform. Journal entries for the Commons indicate a clear power struggle between the Commons and the Governor and his Council. The conflict was resolved only when the Commons realized Johnson saw

---

[48] Usner, 1995, p. 146.
[49] Salley, 1940. Journal of the Commons House of Assembly of South Carolina, Session of June 5, 1707 – Jul 19, 1707, LAC 16521.
[50] Archdale, 1911, p. 285; and Perdue, 1984, p. 18–9.
[51] Nairne in Salley, 1947, 5, p. 197.
[52] 'Lds Proprietors to Lord Commissioners of Trade and Plantations, Aug 8, 1709', in Salley, 1947, 5, p. 290; and Robinson, 1964, p. 26.
[53] Klein, 2003, p. 64.

the reform as interfering with his "*Indian presents,*" totaling approximately £100 annually. Once the Commons agreed to reimburse the governor for his losses, reform passed, giving the Commons more direct control over Indian trade through the creation of a more powerful Board of Indian Trade.[54]

Despite provisions for reform, the lack of easy targets to raid for skins and slaves by 1708 resulted in increased internal abuses of allied tribes. Accusations of fraud in trade deals, illegal seizure of friendly free Indians for sale as slaves, and the pitting of trading allies against each other appeared regularly before the Commissioners of Indian trade. Apalachee, Ellcombee, Yamasee, Pocotallago, Pallachocola, Alabama, Chickasaw, Tallapoosa, Altimahaw, Santa Elena, Cherokee, and Savannah are just a few of the tribes that levied complaints of trade abuse and forced enslavement in the latter years of Queen Anne's War.

To redirect rising animosity, Indian traders, like James Moore, involved various Creek and Yamasee warriors in further raids during the 1711–1713 Tuscarora Wars. This time the targets were Tuscarora, Meherrin, Coree and other northeastern North Carolinian tribes, rather than the decimated peoples of Spanish Florida. The Tuscarora Wars are often treated separately from the slave raids typifying Queen Anne's War on the southern frontier. This distinction is usually made because the wars involved attacks by tribes in amity with the English. Additionally, the wars resulted in the use of English and Native American forces from one English colony against tribes of a neighbouring English colony. Nonetheless, assertions that the French encouraged the Tuscarora and their allies to attack North Carolina provided ample rationale for South Carolina assist North Carolina in fighting the Tuscarora. Evidence sustains a more primary argument for South Carolinian involvement. South Carolina sought to recover trade lost to North Carolinian traders encroaching on trade with South Carolinian tribes.[55] Carolinian traders encouraged tribes heavily in debt to recoup trade losses by raiding for, and selling captives from, the Tuscarora Wars. No longer able to obtain easy captives to the south, and needing English goods to maintain tribal security and status, the heavily indebted Yamasee and Creek elected to join the march against the Tuscarora.

The Tuscarora Wars turned out to be the last great raids of Queen Anne's War. Large numbers of resisting Tuscarora, Coree, and others fell captive to the English-led invading force of South Carolina tribes. In possession of valuable captives, the attacking Yamasee and Creek deserted their Carolinian allies in order to trade captives as slaves and reduce their debt. Sales of new captives helped reduce the tribal debts temporarily, but did not address the abuses and competition that produced the debts.

---

[54] Salley, 1940, pp. 50–1, 63, 65, 68–9, 77, 78, 93–5 and Friedlander, 1975, pp. 22–3.
[55] Saunders, 1993, p. 691.

Queen Anne's War, and the Tuscarora conflict, concluded in 1713. Further justification for raids against tribes aligned with the French and Spanish ended as well. Tribes continued to seek positions of strength in trade and status among their neighbours, native and European. The English continued to seek means to control trade, land, wealth and power in the southeast. Colonial Carolina had viewed a policy of attacking and enslaving large inland tribes as an *"acceptable defense"* against the Spanish and French, but these inland nations no longer posed an immediate threat. Additionally, the English, Spanish and French had used the enslavement of Indians as a means of Christianizing and civilizing the tribes. As Nairne so aptly put it, *"some men think it both serves to lessen their number before the French can arm them and it is a more effectual way of Civilizing and Instructing, then all the Efforts by the French Missionaries."*[56] The French and English asserted that enslaving and deporting Indians served as a means of clearing lands for settlement. Colonial practices clearly paralleled the English goals of securing lands against French and Spanish claims during Queen Anne's War. The conclusion of the war saw the French cede territorial lands and the Spanish threat fade. While the English were slow to adjust their attitudes, the blatant raids for slaves that marked Queen Anne's War ended.

West African slave trade in the 1700s experienced a different time line than the colonial southeast, in part due to changes in colonial labor and slave trade practices. The end of Queen Anne's War, and the ensuing disastrous Yamasee uprising of 1715, dramatically diminished the practice of enslaving Native Americans through wars, indebtedness and fraud. English colonies in North America and the Caribbean that previously received large numbers of First Peoples shipped as slaves from Carolina, feared uprisings along their own frontiers. Consequently, many colonies placed restrictions or bans on importations of Native American slaves. In the wake of these changes, West African slave traffic increased to fill the void and meet increasing demands of American colonists.

Without a Spanish and French menace, the powerful Indian tribes of the southeast lost their advantage to manipulate three European powers to meet tribal demands. Carolinian greed for land and profits increased as the deerskin market increased.[57] The rising use of African slaves reduced the need for Indian slaves. The market for Indian slaves in other colonies dropped due to fears of native uprisings like the Tuscarora Wars and later Yamasee War. Indian enslavement reached its peak during the midst of Queen Anne's War and collapsed in its wake. Further hostilities and enslavement occurred because of continued internal abuses and competition between the southeastern tribes

---

[56] Nairne in Salley, 1947, 5, p. 197.
[57] Braund, 1991, p. 606.

and the Carolinians. Yet, never again would the intensity and extent of slave raids and slave trade exist in North America for so long a time as during Queen Anne's War.

Bibliography

Archdale, J. (1911), 'A New Description of the Fertile and Pleasant Province of Carolina', *Narratives of Early Carolina, 1650–1708*, in Alexander Salley (ed.), *Original Narratives of Early American History Series*, New York, pp. 277–313.

Axtell, J. (1997), *The Indian's New South: Cultural Change in the Colonial Southeast*, Baton Rouge.

Bah, T. M. (2003), 'Slave-Raiding and Defensive Systems South of Lake Chad from the Sixteenth to the Nineteenth Century', Sylviane A. Diouf (ed.), *Fighting the Slave Trade: West African Strategies*, Athens, pp. 15–30.

Barcia, Andres Gonzalez de (ed.) (1970), *Barcia's Chronological History of the Continent of Florida*, trans. with an Introduction by Anthony Kerrigan, Introduction with a Foreword by Herbert E. Bolton, Westport.

Braund, K. H. (1991), 'The Creek Indians, Blacks and Slavery', *Journal of Southern History*, 57, pp. 601–636.

Cheves, L. (ed.) (1897), *The Shaftesbury Papers and Other Records Relating to Carolina and the First Settlement on the Ashley river Prior to the Year 1676*, 5, Charleston.

Crane, V. W. (1919), 'The Southern Frontier in Queen Anne's War', *American Historical Review*, 24, pp. 379–395.

Fausz, J. F. (1985), 'Patterns of Anglo-Indian Aggression and Accommodation Along the Mid-Atlantic Coast, 1584–1634', in W. W. Fitzhugh (ed.), *Cultures in Contact: The Impact of European Contacts on Native American Cultural Institutions, A.D. 1000–1800*, Washington, pp. 61–72.

Friedlander, A. (1975), *Indian Slavery in Proprietary South Carolina*, MA Thesis, Emory University.

Haan, R. L. (1982), 'The 'Trade Do's Not Flourish as Formerly': The Ecological Origins of the Yamasee War of 1715', *Ethnohistory*, 28.4, pp. 341–358.

de la Harpe, B. (1851), 'Account of the Journey of Bénard de la Harpe: Historical Journal of the Establishment of the French in Louisiana', in B. F. French (ed.), *Historical Collections of Louisiana, Embracing Translations of Many Rare and Valuable Documents Relating to the Natural, Civil and Political History of that State*, 3, New York, pp. 371–385.

Higginbotham, J. (1991), *Old Mobile: Fort Louis de la Louisiane, 1702–1711*, Tuscaloosa.

Juricek, John T. (1962), *Indian Policy in Proprietary Carolina, 1670–1693*, MA Thesis, University of Chicago.

Klein, M. (2003), 'Defensive Strategies: Wasulu, Masina, and the Slave Trade', Sylviane A. Diouf (ed.), *Fighting the Slave Trade: West African Strategies*, Athens, pp. 62–78.

Lawson, J. (1708), *A New Voyage to Carolina*, London.

Lovejoy, P. and Richardson, D. (2003), 'Anglo-Efik Relations and Protection against Illegal Enslavement at Old Calabar, 1740–1807', Sylviane A. Diouf (ed.), *Fighting the Slave Trade: West African Strategies*, Athens, pp. 101–118.

MacLeod, W. C. (1925), 'Debtor and Chattel Slavery in Aboriginal North America', *American Anthropologist*, 27, pp. 370–380.

Martin, J. (1994), 'Southeastern Indians and the English Trade in Skins and Slaves', in C. Hudson and C. C. Tesser (eds.), *The Forgotten Centuries: Indians and Europeans in the American South, 1521–1704*, Athens, Ga., pp. 304–324.

McWilliams, R. G. (ed.) (1981), *Iberville's Gulf Journals*, Tuscaloosa.

McWilliams, R. G. (ed.) (1988), *Fleur de Lys and Calumet: Being the Pénicaut Narrative of French Adventure in Louisiana*, Tuscaloosa. (1929), *Mississippi Provincial Archives: French Dominion MPA: FD*, 2, Jackson.
Nairne, T. (1988), *Nairne's Muskogean Journals: The 1708 Expedition to the Mississippi River*, Jackson.
Perdue, T. (1984), 'Red and Black in the Southern Appalachians', *Southern Exposure*, 12.6, pp. 17–24.
Peyser, J. L., (ed.) (1992), *Letters from New France: the Upper Country, 1686–1783*, Chicago.
Phillips, William, Jr. (1985), *Slavery from Roman Times to the Early Transatlantic Trade*, Minneapolis.
Ramsey, W. (1999), *"Heathenish Combination": The Natives of the North American Southeast During the Era of the Yamasee War*, Ph.D. Diss., Tulane University. (1958), 'Real Cedula Que No Se Provea Encomienda en Persona Que Tuviere Pension, Madrid, 2 julio 1666', *Coleccion de Documentos Para La Historia de la Formacion Social de Hispanoamerica, 1493–1810*, Madrid. (1949), *Records of the States of the United States of America* [*RUSA*], Washington.
Rivers, W. (ed.) (1846), *A Sketch of the History of South Carolina*, Charleston.
Robinson, S. (1964), 'Virginia and the Cherokees: Indian Policy from Spotswood to Dinwiddie', in D. B. Rutman (ed.), *The Old Dominion: Essays for Thomas Perkins Abernathy*, Charlottesville, pp. 21–40.
Sainsbury, Noel (ed.) (1928), *Records in the British Public Records Office Relating to South Carolina, 1663–84*, Indexed by Alexander S. Salley, Jr., 1:99, Atlanta.
Sainsbury, Noel (ed.) (1946), *Records in the British Public Records Office Relating to South Carolina, 1698–1700*, Indexed by Alexander S. Salley, Jr., 4.13, Columbia.
Salley, A. S. (ed.) (1940), *Journal of the Commons House of Assembly of South Carolina*, Session of June 5, 1707–Jul 19, 1707, Columbia.
Saunders, W. L. (ed.) (1993), *Colonial Records of North Carolina, 1662–1712*, Broadfort.
Saunt, C. (1998), 'The English has now a mind to make slaves of them all', *American Indian Quarterly*, 22.1/2, pp. 157–181.
Seaman, R. (2001), *Native American Enslavement in Proprietary Carolina: A Causality Study*, Ph.D. Thesis, Auburn University.
Swanton, J. (ed.) (1964), *An Early Account of the Choctaw Indians*, New York.
Swanton, J. (1979), *Indians of the Southeastern United States*, Washington, D.C.
Thornton, J.K. (1998), *Africa and Africans in the Formation of the Atlantic World, 1400–1680*, New York/London.
Usner, D. (1992), *Indians, Settlers, and Slaves in a Frontier Exchange Economy*, Chapel Hill.
Usner, D. (1997), 'Indian-Black Relations in Colonial and Antebellum Louisiana', *Slave Cultures and the Cultures of Slavery*, Knoxville, pp. 145–161.
Van Hoek, S. (1999), 'Untangling the Roots of Dependency: Choctaw Economies', *American Indian Quarterly*, 23.3/4, pp. 113–128.
Villamarin, J. A. and Villamarin, J. E. (1975), *Indian Labor in Mainland Colonial Spanish America*, Newark.
Waddell, G. (1980), *Indians of the South Carolina Low Country, 1562–1751*, Spartanburg.
White, R. (1983), *Roots of Dependency: Subsistence, Environment, and Social Change Among the Choctaws, Pawnees and Navajos*, Lincoln.
Wright, J. L. (1981), *The Only Land They Knew: The Tragic Story of the American Indians in the Old South*, New York.

Part 3

FEMALE SLAVES

ON THE MOREGINE *ANCILLA* or SLAVERY AND PROSTITUTION AT POMPEII

Giovanni Salmeri

1. In a very recent issue of the *Journal of Roman Archaeology*, Elisabeth Fentress starts her introduction to 'Five papers on Roman slave-traders and the buildings they used' by pointing out that: '*Although slavery is a recurring theme in Roman historical studies, the general consensus is that slavery is barely retrievable archaeologically*'.[1] And if this is the *communis opinio*, we find even more radical positions among certain historians like Walter Scheidel, who holds it quite '*unreasonable to expect archaeology to make a significant contribution to modern reconstruction of Greek and Roman slave-systems*'.[2] Indeed, he is convinced that archaeological excavations only seem to offer material illustrative of what we already know from other sources: they can neither contribute to furthering our knowledge nor provide new ideas for research.[3]

However, archaeologists display a rather more open approach to the subject than Scheidel and other historians. The excavations carried out by Andrea Carandini in the *villa* of Settefinestre in Etruria in the 1970s and early 80s,[4] on one hand triggered discussions among a group of Italian ancient historians and archaeologists[5] on Marxist analysis of ancient societies and the role of slavery, while, on the other hand, they brought new life to the study of slavery in the Roman period. Progress in the archaeology of slavery in North

---

[1] Fentress, 2005, p. 180.
[2] Scheidel, 2003, p. 581. Less radical appears to be the position of Bradley, 2003, who, reviewing Thompson, 2003, asserts that careful study of some museum pieces '*might well increase knowledge of the material lives of Greek and Roman slaves, knowledge of their relations with their masters, and knowledge of the place of slavery in ancient society at large*' (p. 576).
[3] Scheidel, 2003, reviewing Schumacher, 2001, writes that '*the antiquarian nature of much of the book fails to advance our understanding of Greek and Roman slavery in general*' (p. 580). A generally pessimistic view of the contribution archaeology can make to historical reconstruction is taken by Finley, 1975, but see Hodder, 1991, pp. 80–106 and, now, Hall and Silliman, 2006.
[4] Carandini and Settis, 1979; Carandini, 1985; Carandini, 1988.
[5] See Capogrossi, Giardina and Schiavone, 1978; Giardina and Schiavone, 1981.

and South America[6] and comparative studies of different slave societies[7] are opening up new perspectives in the investigation of ancient slavery. The exploration of archaeological sites associated with fugitive slaves in the New World[8] could, for example, serve as a model in studying some Sicilian settlements caught up in the two slave wars of the second half of the second century BC. And the investigation of the ruins of extant plantation buildings on Cuba with their prison-like structure[9] could likewise lead to new insights into the lay-out of the Roman *villa rustica*. In any case, it seems clear that archaeology is opening the way for a better understanding of the Greek and Roman slavery as a social and economic long-term phenomenon, but only very rarely allows for the reconstruction of exact events and the study of individuals without the help of other sources.[10]

But, what has this preamble to do with a paper which is supposed to be about slavery and prostitution? The answer is that the idea stems from an archaeological excavation. In November 2000, on the site of Moregine,[11] close to a prestigious building at first identified as an ex-*deversoria taberna* of the Emperor Nero,[12] a few hundred metres south-east of the walls of Pompeii, another and more modest building was brought to light which was identified as a *caupona*, that is, a tavern. Inside, in a small room, buried under the debris from the collapse of the floor above, the remains of two women and three youths were found. The younger of the two women, aged probably between thirty and thirty-five, wore two snake-shaped *armillae*, a ring on her left hand and perhaps a necklace. On her right side was found a small gold jewellery treasure in a *sacculus*, which consisted of four other *armillae* of various types, an intricate necklace with pendants, a lace of nearly two and a half metres in length and two rings. Two *aurei* of Vespasian and a *dupondius* of the same emperor were also present amongst these objects.[13] However, what makes this find interesting is that one of the *armillae* worn by the younger woman bears

---

[6] See especially the first issue of vol. 33 (2001) of *World Archaeology* devoted to *The Archaeology of Slavery* (P. Mitchell ed.).

[7] See, already in the 1980s, Carandini, 1985, i, pp. 187–206, and now Webster, 2005.

[8] Orser and Funari, 2001; Funari, 2006.

[9] Singleton, 2001.

[10] See Torelli, 2005, p. 110: '[...] *l'archeologia di norma non ci consente di fare storia evenemenziale, ma solo storia tipica; a noi archeologi solo raramente è consentito scrivere vicende individuali, ben sapendo che sovente, per non dire sempre, quando si fa questo si cammina su di un terreno vischiosissimo*'. See also Hodder, 1991, pp. 104–106.

[11] On the excavation, see Mastroroberto, 2001.

[12] Mastroroberto, 2002, pp. 69–72, *contra* Torelli, 2005, p. 136 who believes that the building housed the premises of an important *collegium*. For the use of *deversoriae tabernae* by Nero, see Suetonius, *Nero*, 27. 3. On the transference of the building into the hands of the Sulpicii in its final phase of life, before the eruption of Vesuvius in 79 AD, see Camodeca, 2005, pp. 28–35.

[13] For analysis of the woman's small treasure, see D'Ambrosio, 2001.

engraved the following words: *dom<i>nus ancillae suae*.[14] Short as the text is, it has fired debate and given rise to two completely contrasting interpretations ultimately based, notwithstanding the apparent wealth of the archaeological context, on ideological premises.[15]

2. In a paper published by the first editors of the text, Pier Giovanni Guzzo and Vincenzo Scarano Ussani,[16] the woman wearing the *armilla* is identified as a slave (*ancilla*) initiated into prostitution by her master (*dominus*); consequently, the object is considered a tool of the trade.

This interpretation appears to be in keeping with the reconstruction of Pompeii's 'erotic civilisation' in the work of the above mentioned authors, *Veneris figura: immagini di prostituzione e sfruttamento a Pompei*.[17] Guzzo and Scarano Ussani analyse the erotic, or rather pornographic, frescoes found at Pompeii and tend to present a city permeated by prostitution. In particular, on the assumption that the depiction of explicit sexual scenes was a characteristic of brothels and other places where sex was for sale, the authors draw up a list of prostitution centres throughout the entire area of the Vesuvian city.[18] They include *tout court* taverns and baths, and even the homes of some local notables, which, in their opinion, had areas set apart for this lucrative activity, such as the House of the Vettii. However, according to Thomas McGinn, it seems somewhat exaggerated to consider all inns, taverns and baths as actual brothels.[19] Finer discrimination is called for. As far as the homes of the local notables are concerned, the claim that in the rooms in which explicit sexual scenes were depicted – however secluded they were – prostitution in the strict sense of the term was practised,[20] cannot be easily justified, especially if we take into consideration the aspect of social respectability. These places were more likely to have been used as a kind of 'sex club' where sex was offered, perhaps even at a price, but in a private rather than public setting.[21] In other

---

[14] *AE* 2001, 803. For excellent photos and drawings of the inscribed *armilla*, see Scarano Ussani, 2005b, pp. 78–79, figs. 1–4 and Costabile, 2005, fig. 1.
[15] On the constant, intense ideological conditioning of modern study of slavery in ancient times, see Finley, 1980, pp. 11–66.
[16] Guzzo and Scarano Ussani, 2001.
[17] Guzzo and Scarano Ussani, 2000. See on the same subject, and from another point of view, Clarke, 1998, pp. 145–240.
[18] Guzzo and Scarano Ussani, 2000, pp. 66–67. The list needs some thinning out (*infra* n. 19), but it does suffice to rule out the hypothesis that a kind of moral zoning was practised at Pompeii, keeping prostitution centres in well-defined areas. See McGinn, 2004, pp. 78–84. In favour of moral zoning, see especially Wallace-Hadrill, 1995, pp. 51–54.
[19] McGinn, 2004, pp. 78–80, 232–239, 267–290; see also McGinn, 2002, pp. 11–13.
[20] As at least from the end of the first century BC prostitution was from the juridical point of view identified in the act of giving one's body *palam* (in public), even if no payment was requested: Guzzo and Scarano Ussani, 2001, pp. 994–995 and n. 55.
[21] McGinn, 2004, pp. 157–166.

words, local notables, who otherwise had no qualms about the presence of brothels in their properties,[22] preferred to take advantage from the sale of sex discreetly when it involved their homes.

Taking as background their image of Pompeii as city where prostitution reigned, Guzzo and Scarano Ussani base their interpretation of the Moregine find in the first place on the widespread belief that women practising prostitution in the Roman empire belonged essentially to the world of slaves.[23] In our authors the belief seems to stem from the static perspective of the Roman slave system, popular in the 1970s and early 80s among the Italian historians and archaeologists involved in the Marxist analysis of ancient societies. These scholars claimed that the slave system underwent no substantial change and was dominant – in Italy especially – between the second century BC and the end of the second century AD.[24] They were also convinced that the main sources of slaves in the imperial age continued to be wars and, to a yet greater extent, trade, piracy, and child exposure. The natural reproduction of slaves within the empire was given little or no attention at all.[25]

Adhering fully to this line of thought, Guzzo and Scarano Ussani believe that in Pompeii, and generally in the Roman empire, all, or almost all, of the prostitutes were slaves.[26] Proof that this was not actually the case may be found in various literary works, including, notably, some lines by Horace and several epigrams by Martial.[27] Moreover, the fact that in Rome the women citizens who practised prostitution had to declare so in advance before the *aediles*, as we learn from Tacitus,[28] indicates that the free women in this profession were by no means rare.[29] In addition to all this, the *cellae meretriciae* – small single rooms with direct access to the street for individual use in prostitution – found in excavations at Pompeii, represent fairly persuasive evidence that, especially in Italy, there were a certain number of prostitutes not dependent on pimps, quite possibly of free status.[30] Besides, we must not forget that in a province like Egypt some young women amassed their dowry

---

[22] *Dig.* 5. 3. 27. 1 (Ulp.): '*[...] in multorum honestorum virorum praediis lupanaria exercentur*'.

[23] See e.g. Flemming, 1999, pp. 40–41, 50–51, 56–61. At p. 59 the author seems to think that slaves accounted for 80 or 90% of the total of prostitutes in the Roman empire.

[24] On this, see Salmeri, 2005a, p. 145.

[25] See *infra* n. 50.

[26] The figure of the *hetaira*, active in classical Athens, is thought to be missing from the world of prostitution in the Roman empire by Flemming, 1999, p. 47. On *hetairai*, see Glazebrook, 2006. *Letters of courtesans* by Alciphron, an author datable between the second and third century AD, are of a highly literary nature, as has recently been demonstrated by Rosenmeyer, 2001, pp. 298–307.

[27] As for Horace, Treggiari, 1969, p. 142 says that he '*makes the* libertina *the mistress and harlot par excellence*'; for Martial, see especially Bradley, 2000, p. 469 n. 4.

[28] Tacitus., *Ann.*, 2. 85. 1, see Levick, 1983, p. 111.

[29] At any rate the profession generated *infamia* for them, see Edwards, 1997 and McGinn, 1998, pp. 20–69.

[30] See McGinn, 2004, pp. 216–217, *contra* Flemming, 1999, p. 46.

through prostitution;[31] and above all that many areas of the empire offer evidence of free women being forced to prostitution by their husbands and, even more, by the sheer poverty of their families.[32] Given such a variety of different cases, the link between prostitution and slavery in the Roman empire is not always justified, and there can be no excuse for automatically identifying the single prostitute as a slave in those cases where little or nothing else is known. Clearly, however, the sexual exploitation of free women was not different from that suffered by the slaves.

Guzzo and Scarano Ussani argue that the Moregine *ancilla* was a prostitute[33] also founding their interpretation on the gold objects the woman wore and carried with her. At the outset, the authors present these objects as part of the *peculium* of the *ancilla*,[34] given to her by her master or acquired through her activity as a prostitute. As for the *armilla*, they point out that the engraved inscription on it does not contain the name of the *ancilla*. Thus, they suggest that the piece of jewellery could have been previously given by the *dominus* to another slave,[35] and then passed on to ours, as if it were a tool of the trade belonging to the 'house'. The almost two and a half metre-length gold lace, designed to be wrapped around the nude body of a woman, is instead considered proof of the involvement of the *ancilla* in '*activities relating to sex*'.[36] Confirmation of this is found in the figure of a woman wearing a lace of the same kind depicted in one of the pornographic scenes in the House of the Vettii, as well as in the *apodyterium* of the suburban baths, which, again according to Guzzo and Scarano Ussani, were places where prostitution took place.[37]

In their interpretation of the jewellery found on and next to the Moregine *ancilla* as evidence of her condition as a prostitute, the two authors seem to have been prompted by the importance of gold ornaments in the construction of both the image and activity of a prostitute in the Roman world.[38] It is a pity that Guzzo and Scarano Ussani make only passing reference to this importance, failing even to quote a passage contained in the novel by

---

[31] Flemming, 1999, p. 42.

[32] See Lucian, *Dial. Meretricium*, 3. 3.

[33] Guzzo and Scarano Ussani, 2001, pp. 990–992. In any case, it is to be borne in mind that the term *ancilla* was used primarily to refer to female domestic slaves, not usually engaged in work outside the *domus*, see Garrido-Hory, 1997, p. 304 (with special attention to the literary language). For the small treasure of the *ancilla*, see *supra* n. 13.

[34] See now Scarano Ussani, 2005b, p. 88.

[35] According to Guzzo and Scarano Ussani, 2001, p. 989 so much can be conjectured also from the fact that the *armilla* seems to date back some decades before 79 AD. As for the inscription, it cannot be dated with precision. It might even have been engraved on the *armilla* some time after the object had been manufactured.

[36] Guzzo and Scarano Ussani, 2001, p. 992.

[37] See Guzzo and Scarano Ussani, 2001, pp. 993–994, and Scarano Ussani, 2005b, pp. 90–102 (with ample illustration).

[38] On the adornment of prostitutes, see McGinn, 2004, p. 53.

From Captivity to Freedom

Xenophon of Ephesus, *Ta Ephesiaka*, written towards the end of the first century AD,[39] which could bear out their point. Nor do they recall the figure of Fortunata, wife of Trimalchio, an ex-slave and almost certainly an ex-prostitute too, who in the *Satyricon*[40] arrives at the banquet and exhibits her jewellery, including two *armillae*, aware that all her prestige rests on this. Moreover, Guzzo and Scarano fail to consider the anthropological aspects of the phenomenon and, in particular, the symbolic value of gold in the context of prostitution.[41] But, even had the authors dealt with this aspect in detail, they would still have been in no position to state beyond doubt that – given the large amount of gold discovered on and next to her – the Moregine *ancilla* was a prostitute. This is a mere hypothesis which, whatever conclusions Guzzo and Scarano Ussani may draw, not even the presence of the long gold lace that lay beside the woman suffices to prove. Its use, in fact, perverse as it may seem, is attested by Pliny the Elder[42] as a characteristic of the Roman women of his times, and not specifically of prostitutes.

Summing up the various points made about the interpretation by Guzzo and Scarano Ussani of the Moregine find, it should be clear that there are no definite elements to maintain that the *ancilla* was initiated into prostitution by her *dominus*. This interpretation is, however, typical of the kind of approach, greatly influenced by ideological premises,[43] often adopted when dealing with objects connected with slavery. In short, the object takes on the value which best accords with the ideas of the scholar interpreting it. Thus, for Guzzo and Scarano Ussani, supporters of the image of a Roman empire characterised by all-pervasive slave economy and, at the same time, convinced that prostitution permeated life at Pompeii, the Moregine *armilla* is simply a tool of the trade and the relationship between the *dominus* and the *ancilla* of the inscription is based solely on the sexual exploitation of the latter.

3. The second interpretation of the Moregine find considered here is the one proposed by Felice Costabile.[44] He diametrically opposes Guzzo and Scarano Ussani, maintaining that the *ancilla* was loved by her master and so the *armilla* was a token of this sentiment. Basically, Costabile's reasoning follows on from

---

[39] Xenophon, *Ephesiaka*, 5. 7. 1: '*The brothel-keeper who had acquired Anthia, some time by then having gone by, forced her to put herself on display in front of the building. And having adorned her with a fine garment and much gold [...]*'. For the dating see Bowie, 2002, p. 57.

[40] Petronius, *Satyricon*, 67. On Fortunata's previous life as a prostitute, see Fornaciari, 1994, pp. 171–172. Gold had a prominent role also in the mentality and life of Trimalchio, an ex-slave: see Petronius, *Satyricon*, 32, 33, 71; on his figure, Veyne, 1961 remains fundamental. The insight into the mentality of slaves and masters afforded by Greek and Roman novels has rightly been stressed by Hopkins, 1993, pp. 6–7.

[41] In general on the symbolic value of gold, see Clark, 1986, pp. 50–57.

[42] Pliny, *Naturalis Historia*, 33. 12. 40, see Costabile, 2005, p. 49.

[43] See *supra* n. 15.

[44] Costabile, 2001; Costabile, 2005.

the interpretation of the inscription engraved on the *armilla*. In particular he holds that the adjective *suae* does not indicate possession, but rather the affection the master felt for his slave. In support of this, and of the existence of a relationship between the two, which would fall into the category of *servitium amoris*, Costabile quotes unconvincingly various Latin poets.[45] He goes so far as to suggest that the *dominus* might have married his slave after the gift of the *armilla* and, obviously, after her manumission *matrimonii causa*.[46] Finally, again in corroboration of his interpretation, the author points out that there is no proof that the room in the *caupona*, in which the *ancilla* was found, would have been used for the practice of prostitution as conjectured by Guzzo and Scarano Ussani. It is possible that the woman sought shelter there from the falling ash that would bury Pompeii, while fleeing towards the sea with her companions.[47]

Costabile de-sexualises and de-economizes the relationship between the *dominus* and the Moregine *ancilla* emphasising, in contrast, the emotional aspect. He does not take into consideration slavery in the Roman empire in terms of social and economic history,[48] and uses an antiquarian approach based on the separate analysis of single elements from the find or single words from the inscription. The risk the author runs with this approach is that of losing sight of the general context and proposing hazardous comparisons, such as when he invokes the *ancilla domini* from the gospel of Luke.[49] At the same time, Costabile fails to provide any definite proofs for his interpretation. Nevertheless he should be credited with the introduction of a new perspective in the study of the Moregine *armilla*, based on the evaluation of the relationship between *dominus* and *ancilla* in the Roman imperial period, not limited solely to the sphere of economic and sexual exploitation.

Some considerations in this respect will be now put forward, which – let it be said at the outset – are not enough to tip the scales in favour of Costabile's interpretation.

The *dominus/ancilla* relationship should be seen from the widest angle possible. Above all, we should not overlook the fact that, from the first century AD, of the various sources of slave supply natural reproduction acquired predominance.[50] The ensuing process of domestication of slavery was then the

---

[45] Costabile, 2001, pp. 463, 467–469. No reference here to Veyne, 1988, fundamental on Roman erotic elegy.
[46] Costabile, 2005, pp. 49–50. For the manumission – *matrimonii causa* – of an *ancilla*, see Gaius 1. 19.
[47] Costabile, 2001, p. 462, and also Costabile, 2005, p. 49.
[48] See for example Bradley, 1984; Veyne, 1987, pp. 51–69 and Hopkins, 1993.
[49] Lc. 1. 38, see Costabile, 2001, pp. 469–470.
[50] On this see especially Scheidel, 1997, *contra* Harris, 1999, who at any rate observes (p. 75) that the natural reproduction of slaves '*must in the end have imposed itself*' after the High Empire (first century AD?). See also Bradley, 1987.

real catalyst in the transformation of the living conditions of the group.[51] The master/slave relations became more harmonious and less violent in a domestic environment than they were in rural or industrial settings, where the turnover was faster.[52] Clearly all this happened in Rome not as a result of the masters' goodwill, deriving, for example, from their acceptance of ideals based on *humanitas*.[53] Rather, it was due to the particular patterns of behaviour that develop in the household and which are not comparable with those of a *villa rustica* with its *ergastulum*.

It is against such a background that we should reassess the relations between *dominus* and *ancilla* in the imperial age, starting from the clause *ne serva prostituatur* to be found in the slave sale contracts at least from the beginning of the first century AD.[54] Behind this 'restrictive covenant', which forbade the buyer to use the slave as a prostitute, threatening annulment of the sale, the Roman jurists identified the need to protect the *affectio* of the master.[55] Considering, above all, the legal and general context, this term cannot be translated with the common modern-day term 'affection'. It may better be translated as willingness, familiarity. The clause, then, was probably the result of the constant presence of slaves in the household and of the minimum sense of responsibility that this presence would induce in the masters.[56] It must have been on this basis, perhaps more than in consideration of the fact that the honour of the *dominus* could be marred by one of his ex-slaves being prostituted,[57] that the *ne prostituatur* clause was included in sale contracts, although obviously it did not change the woman's real situation.

We can, I believe, detect a more protective attitude towards the male and female slave in two imperial constitutions issued by Hadrian and Septimius Severus respectively.[58] The first forbade the sale of *servae* and *servi* to pimps or to *lanistae* without a valid reason. The second gave the *praefectus urbi* the *officium*

---

[51] See Hopkins, 1993, p. 7, and also Saller, 1998.
[52] There is an interesting reference in Dio Chrysostom 10. 9 to the care some masters took of their sick slaves. Seneca, moreover, in *De ira* (3. 24) sees in *familiaritas* a mitigating circumstance, which the master has to keep in mind in judging the misbehaviour of domestic slaves. In any case, closeness to the master exposed the slave to his outbursts of anger and whims. For this aspect see Hopkins, 1993, p. 7, and also Harris, 2001, pp. 323–329. Master/slave relations in the cacao growing section of the north-eastern Brazilian State of Bahia in the nineteenth century are given special attention in Mary Ann Mahony's contribution to this volume. The author highlights also the presence of structured families among the rural slaves of the Brazilian State, unlike the situation in Roman times.
[53] On this see especially Finley, 1980, p. 121 and Veyne, 1987, pp. 65–67. After Vogt, 1974, the notion of an improvement on a moralistic basis in master/slave relations in the High Empire is revived by Harris, 2001, pp. 317–336. *Contra* Bradley, 2003, p. 571.
[54] See McGinn, 1998, pp. 288–319, and also Sicari, 1991.
[55] And to avoid offence to his *verecundia*: *Dig.* 18. 7. 6 (Pap. 27 *quaest.*), see Licandro, 2005.
[56] See *supra* nn. 51–52.
[57] See McGinn, 1998, pp. 311–316.
[58] *Historia Augusta, Hadr.*, 18. 8, and *Dig.* 1. 12. 1. 8.

to ensure that the *mancipia* were not used as prostitutes. It is difficult to understand why these measures came into being. They do not seem to reflect a precise policy of the *princeps* in favour of the slaves,[59] and were probably the outcome of a long period of domestic slavery or continued contact between slaves and masters. This contact led to a change in the way the slave was viewed during the Principate: slightly more attention was paid to his/her moral and physical integrity.

Finally, in the closing decades of the first century AD some representatives of the empire's upper class began to display a new form of care of the inner person, as Michel Foucault convincingly demonstrated.[60] This attitude seems to have had some effect in the transformation of relations between the individual *dominus* and his *ancillae*, hitherto considered a reserve upon which he could freely draw to satisfy his sexual desires.[61] Particularly significant in this respect is the diatribe *Peri aphrodision* by Musonius Rufus, which contains an attack on those masters who have sex with their *doule* to satisfy their appetites.[62] From the wording of this attack it emerges that the stoic philosopher was not concerned with the protection of the slave but with the master, who should abstain from the pleasures he could gain from a woman in a servile condition in order to be in full control of himself.[63] Nevertheless, because of the need to avoid the *akrasia* (incontinence),[64] the slave's dominant role as object of the master's sexual desires may have begun to wane in the age of the '*souci de soi*', at least, in some upper class homes. Be that as it may, it is by no means certain that relations of affection or even love between *dominus* and *ancilla* were commonplace in the Roman empire, as Costabile appears to think.

4. In conclusion, the archaeological data alone cannot help us establish with certainty whether the Moregine *ancilla* was initiated into prostitution by her master or whether, more improbably, she was the object of his affection. Without a shadow of a doubt, however, in the period in which she lived (a) both slaves and free women were prostitutes and (b) in a few upper class homes female slaves were ceasing to be considered convenient means to satisfy their masters' sexual appetite.

---

[59] Harris, 2001, pp. 330–331, for example, holds that under Antoninus Pius '*the imperial court [...] had an active policy about the treatment of slaves*'. Against this perspective, see Bradley, 2000, pp. 471–475 and, more in general, Salmeri, 2005b.
[60] Foucault, 1986; Veyne, 1987; Veyne, 2005. See also Gaca, 2003.
[61] See Finley, 1980, pp. 95–96 and Bradley, 1984, p. 116.
[62] Musonius Rufus, *frag.* 12. 66H, see Foucault, 1986, pp. 172–173.
[63] Moreover, in the same text Musonius, like Seneca (*Ep.*, 94. 26; 95. 37; 123. 10), criticizes the conventional double standard, according to which a man might well have a slave mistress while women who had relations with slaves were censured; see Foucault, 1986, pp. 165–175 and also Saller, 1998, p. 89.
[64] This term is used by Musonius towards the end of the diatribe.

Bibliography

Bowie, E. (2002), 'The Chronology of the Earlier Greek Novels since B.E. Perry: Revisions and Precisions', *Ancient Narrative*, 2, pp. 47–63.
Bradley, K.R. (1984), *Slaves and Masters in the Roman Empire: A Study in Social Control*, Brussels.
Bradley, K.R. (1987), 'On the Roman Slave Supply and Slave Breeding', in M.I. Finley (ed.), *Classical Slavery*, Totowa, pp. 42–64.
Bradley, K.R. (2000), 'Prostitution, the Law of Rome, and Social Policy', rev. of McGinn, 1998, *Journal of Roman Archaeology*, 13, pp. 468–475.
Bradley, K.R. (2003), 'Slavery and Archaeology', rev. of Thompson, 2003, *Journal of Roman Archaeology*, 16, pp. 571–576.
Camodeca, G. (2005), 'Altre considerazioni sull'archivio dei Sulpicii e sull'edificio pompeiano di Moregine', in Scarano Ussani, 2005a, pp. 23–41.
Capogrossi, L., Giardina, A. and Schiavone, A. (eds.) (1978), *Analisi marxista e società antiche*, Roma.
Carandini, A. (ed.) (1985), *Settefinestre. Una villa schiavistica nell'Etruria romana*, i-iii, Modena.
Carandini, A. (1988), *Schiavi in Italia. Gli strumenti pensanti dei Romani fra tarda Repubblica e medio Impero*, Roma.
Carandini, A. and Settis, S. (1979), *Schiavi e padroni nell'Etruria romana. La villa di Settefinestre dallo scavo alla mostra*, Bari.
Clark, G. (1986), *Symbols of Excellence: Precious Materials as Expression of Status*, Cambridge.
Clarke, J.R. (1998), *Looking at Lovemaking: Constructions of Sexuality in Roman Art, 100 BC–AD 250*, Berkeley.
Costabile, F. (2001), '*Ancilla domini*. Una nuova dedica su armilla aurea da Pompei', *Minima Epigraphica et Papyrologica*, 4. 6, pp. 447–474.
Costabile, F. (2005), '*Contra meretricium ancillae domni*', in Scarano Ussani, 2005a, pp. 43–50.
D'Ambrosio, A. (2001), 'I monili dallo scavo di Moregine', *Melanges de l'Ecole Française de Rome*, 113. 2, pp. 967–980.
Edwards, C. (1997), 'Unspeakable Professions: Public Performance and Prostitution in Ancient Rome', in J.P. Hallet and M.P. Skinner (eds.), *Roman Sexualities*, Princeton, pp. 66–95.
Fentress, E. (2005), 'Selling People: Five papers on Roman Slave-Traders and the Buildings they Used. Introduction', *Journal of Roman Archaeology*, 18, p. 180.
Finley, M.I. (1975), *The Use and Abuse of History*, London.
Finley, M.I. (1980), *Ancient Slavery and Modern Ideology*, London.
Flemming, R. (1999), '*Quae corpore quaestum facit*: The Sexual Economy of Female Prostitution in the Roman Empire', *Journal of Roman Studies*, 89, pp. 38–61.
Fornaciari, E. (1994), '*Ambubaiae*: flautiste e non solo', *Studi Classici e Orientali*, 44, pp. 135–177.
Foucault, M. (1986), *The History of Sexuality*, iii: *The Care of the Self*, Eng. trans., New York.
Funari, P.P.A. (2006), 'Conquistadors, Plantations and Quilombo: Latin America in Historical Archaeological Context', in Hall and Silliman, 2006, pp. 209–229.
Gaca, K.L. (2003), *The Making of Fornication. Eros, Ethics, and Political Reform in Greek Philosophy and Early Christianity*, Berkeley.
Garrido-Hory, M. (1999), 'Femmes, femmes-esclaves et processus de feminisation dans les oeuvres de Martial et de Juvénal', in F. Reduzzi Merola and A. Storchi Marino (eds.), *Femmes-esclaves. Modèles d'interprétation anthropologique, économique, juridique*, Naples, pp. 303–313.
Giardina, A. and Schiavone, A. (eds.) (1981), *Società romana e produzione schiavistica*, i-iii, Roma-Bari.
Glazebrook, A. (2006), 'The Bad Girls of Athens: The Image and Function of *hetairai* in Judicial Oratory', in L.K. McClure and C.A. Faraone (eds.), *Prostitutes and Courtesans in the Ancient World*, Madison, Wisconsin, pp. 125–138.

Guzzo, P.G. and Scarano Ussani, V. (2000), Veneris figurae. *Immagini di prostituzione e sfruttamento a Pompei*, Naples.
Guzzo, P.G. and Scarano Ussani, V. (2001), 'La schiava di Moregine', *Melanges de l'Ecole Française de Rome*, 113. 2, pp. 981–997.
Hall, M. and Silliman, S.W. (eds.) (2006), *Historical Archaeology*, Oxford.
Harris, W.V. (1999), 'Demography, Geography and the Sources of Roman Slaves', *Journal of Roman Studies*, 89, pp. 62–75.
Harris, W.V. (2001), *Restraining Rage: The Ideology of Anger Control in Classical Antiquity*, Cambridge, Ma.
Hodder, I. (1991), *Reading the Past: Current Approaches to Interpretation in Archaeology*, 2nd ed., Cambridge.
Hopkins, K. (1993), 'Novel Evidence for Roman Slavery', *Past & Present*, 138, pp. 3–27.
Levick, B. (1983), 'The *Senatus Consultum* from Larinum', *Journal of Roman Studies*, 73, pp. 97–115.
Licandro, O. (2005), 'L'*armilla* di Moregine: segni di una *affectio domini*?', in Scarano Ussani, 2005a, pp. 139–142.
Mastroroberto, M. (2001), 'Il quartiere sul Sarno e i recenti rinvenimenti a Moregine', *Melanges de l'Ecole Française de Rome*, 113. 2, pp. 953–966.
Mastroroberto, M. (2002), 'Una visita di Nerone a Pompei: le *deversoriae tabernae* di Moregine', in P.G. Guzzo and M. Mastroroberto (eds.), *Pompei, le stanze dipinte*, Milan, pp. 35–87.
McGinn, T.A. (1998), *Prostitution, Sexuality, and the Law in Ancient Rome*, Oxford.
McGinn, T.A. (2002), 'Pompeian Brothels and Social History', in C. Stein and J.H. Humphrey (eds.), *Pompeian Brothels, Pompeii's Ancient History, Mirrors and Mysteries, Art and Nature at Oplontis, and the Herculaneum "Basilica"*, Portsmouth, Rh. I. (*Journal of Roman Archaeology* suppl. 47), pp. 7–46.
McGinn, T.A. (2004), *The Economy of Prostitution in the Roman World*, Ann Arbor.
Mitchell, P. (2001), *The Archaeology of Slavery* (= *World Archaeology* 33.1), London.
Orser, Ch.E. and Funari, P.P.A. (2001), 'Archaeology and Slave Resistance and Rebellion', in Mitchell, 2001, pp. 61–72.
Rosenmeyer, P.A. (2001), *Ancient Epistolary Fictions: The Letter in Greek Literature*, Cambridge.
Saller, R.P. (1998), 'Symbols of Gender and Status Hierarchies in the Roman Household', in S.R. Joshel and S. Murnaghan (eds.), *Women and Slaves in Greco-Roman Culture. Differential Equations*, London.
Salmeri, G. (2005a), 'Il contesto sociale', in Scarano Ussani, 2005a, pp. 143–148.
Salmeri, G. (2005b), 'Central Power Intervention and the Economy of the Provinces in the Roman Empire. The Case of Pontus and Bithynia', in S. Mitchell and C. Katsari (eds.), *Patterns in the Economy of Roman Asia Minor*, Swansea, pp. 187–206.
Scarano Ussani, V. (ed.) (2005a), *Moregine. Suburbio 'portuale' di Pompei*, Naples.
Scarano Ussani, V. (2005b), 'Un nuovo, significativo documento della condizione servile', in Scarano Ussani, 2005a, pp. 77–105.
Scheidel, W. (1997), 'Quantifying the Sources of Slaves in the Early Roman Empire', *Journal of Roman Studies*, 87, pp. 156–169.
Scheidel, W. (2003), 'The Archaeology of Ancient Slavery', rev. of Schumacher, 2001, *Journal of Roman Archaeology*, 16, pp. 577–581.
Schumacher, L. (2001), *Sklaverei in der Antike: Alltag und Schicksal der Unfreien*, Munich.
Sicari, A. (1991), *Prostituzione e tutela giuridica della schiava. Un problema di politica legislativa nell'impero romano*, Bari.
Singleton, T.A. (2001), 'Slavery and Spatial Dialectics on Cuban Coffee Plantations', in Mitchell, 2001, pp. 98–114.

Thompson, F.H. (2003), *The Archaeology of Greek and Roman Slavery*, London.
Torelli, M. (2005), 'Conclusioni', in Scarano Ussani, 2005a, pp. 107–136.
Treggiari, S. (1969), *Roman Freedmen during the Late Republic*, Oxford.
Veyne, P. (1961), 'Vie de Trimalcion', *Annales ESC*, 16, pp. 213–247.
Veyne, P. (1987), *The Roman Empire*, in id. (ed.), *A History of Private Life: From Rome to Byzantium*, Eng. trans., Cambridge, Ma, pp. 5–233.
Veyne, P. (1988), *Roman Erotic Elegy: Love, Poetry, and the West*, Eng. trans., Chicago.
Veyne, P. (2005), *Sexe et pouvoir à Rome*, Paris.
Vogt, J. (1974), *Ancient Slavery and the Ideal of Man*, Eng. trans., Oxford.
Wallace-Hadrill, A. (1995), 'Public Honour and Private Shame: The urban Texture of Pompeii', in T.J. Cornell and K. Lomas (eds.), *Urban Society in Roman Italy*, London, pp. 39–62.
Webster, J. (2005), 'Archaeologies of Slavery and Servitude: Bringing "New World" Perspectives to Roman Britain', *Journal of Roman Archaeology*, 18, pp. 161–179.

FROM SLAVES TO SERGIPANOS: GENDER, LABOUR AND FAMILY IN BRAZIL'S CACAO AREA, 1870–1920[1]

Mary Ann Mahony

In the town of Ilhéus, Brazil, in August of 1877 an enslaved man named José do Amparo jumped off the steamship bound for Rio de Janeiro. He was not attempting to commit suicide. Rather, he was trying to avoid being sold into the internal slave trade.[2] We don't know exactly what prompted him to risk death to do so, but the documents offer some clues. He had been born and raised in Ilhéus, a community with an enslaved labor force of extended families. On the day in question, he was in his mid-forties – the right age to have had strong emotional and even biological ties to any number of the other adults and children in the district. He was, therefore, being forcibly removed from people to whom he was emotionally attached and, this paper will argue, for whom he felt responsibility. Jumping off the boat was as much a response to separation from them as it was to enslavement.

José do Amparo's experiences point to the close ties that bound enslaved men, women and children to one another in the latter part of the nineteenth century in Brazil. For decades historians of slavery drew our attention to master-slave relations, including controversies over the possibility of sexual relations between female slaves and their male masters, such as those discussed in the chapter by Giovanni Salmeri elsewhere in this volume. Recently, however, they have also begun to explore the complex and difficult to ascertain connections between and among the enslaved themselves.

---

[1] I thank Joseph C. Miller, Alejandro de la Fuente, Susan O'Donovan, Walter Fraga Filho and the organizers and participants of the Conference on Slave Systems Ancient and Modern for insightful comments on previous versions of this paper.

[2] Arquivo Público do Estado da Bahia (Hereafter APEB), SH, 31 August 1877, Plínio de Sá Bittencourt Camara to the presidente da província, maço 2894; Classificação dos escravos para serem libertados pelo Fundo de Emancipação, Ilhéus, 1874–1884; Cúria de Ilhéus, Parochia de São Jorge dos Ilhéos (Hereafter CI-PSJI), Livro de Registro dos Batismos, 1823–1843 (hereafter Batismos I). Ilhéus was formerly spelled Ilhéos. For consistence, I have modernized the spelling in the text, but left it in the original in appropriate footnotes.

From Captivity to Freedom

This article tells the story of the efforts of enslaved men and women to maintain their family ties in the last two decades of slavery and how slave-owners reinforced these efforts prior to abolition and complicated them thereafter. Maintaining family ties always formed an essential part of the calculations that the enslaved and newly freed made, when deciding how to negotiate both enslavement and freedom. Ideas about gender influenced these decisions. Masters understood this and, indeed, prior to abolition used it to their advantage. After emancipation, however, gendered notions of family on the part of ex-slaves threatened ex-masters' efforts to administer their cacao properties as they wished.

This paper explores the ways in which gender shaped the constraints within which slaves and ex-slaves were required to live between about 1870 and about 1920.[3] It investigates the ways in which enslaved women and men might have attempted to shape their destinies within the constraining context of a system that they did not control, and how gender might have influenced both the constraints, which masters placed on them, and the options available to them.[4] Rather than look at this question through the lens of enslaved sex work – a form of labor that was not very common in nineteenth-century Brazil – or on romantic relationships between masters and their enslaved women – both known to exist and highly romanticized in Brazilian history – it focuses our attention on relationships between and among the enslaved – the most common and most important relationships slaves experienced.

---

[3] Bahia is a northeastern Brazilian state roughly the size of the European nation of France. Brazilians frequently use the term Bahia to refer to both the Brazilian state of that name and the city, Salvador da Bahia de Todos os Santos, which has been its capital since its founding in the sixteenth century. In this article, however, Bahia refers only to the state, and Salvador is used for the capital, in order to distinguish between the capital city and the interior communities under discussion here. Bahia and its counties, cities and towns went through extensive redistricting during the period covered by this article. Of most importance to readers of this text, the name Ilhéus referred to a wide variety of administrative districts over the course of the 500 years of Brazilian history. More specifically it refers to the town (city after 1882) of Ilhéus located on the Atlantic coast of Brazil at the confluence of the Engenho, Cachoeira and Fundão Rivers, in addition to varying amounts of settled and unsettled countryside to the north, west and south. In this text, Ilhéus refers both to the urban settlement on the coast and to the countryside that now forms part of the cities of Ilhéus, Itabuna, Uruçuca, Itajuipe, Lomanto Junior, and Buararema. Most of that territory was, however, unsettled forest during most of the period discussed in this article. It does not refer to the entirety of the territory called Ilhéus prior to 1850.

[4] Brazil went through significant political changes during the period covered in this chapter. Between 1822 and 1889, it was an empire and its major administrative districts were provinces run by presidents. After 1889, Brazil became a republic and its provinces became states run by governors. For the sake of continuity and clarity, in the text of this chapter the terms state and governor will be used, while the actual terminology will be used in the footnotes for ease of location, following common practices among historians of Brazil.

Enslaved Families on Cacao Plantations and Farms

In 1872, the enslaved population of Ilhéus included a relatively large number of women and children. Men between the ages of sixteen and fifty, the category that usually dominated enslaved groups of agricultural workers at the time, made up less than twenty five percent of the 1,051 enslaved persons living there.[5] Women and girls comprised fifty three percent of the enslaved population, outnumbering men and boys in each age category. Cut another way, forty one percent of the enslaved population was either under fifteen or over fifty.[6] In other words, the enslaved population in the town of Ilhéus in southern Bahia's emerging cacao region resembled a naturally occurring population rather than one constructed through the African slave trade.

Natural reproduction was an important factor in the construction of this labor force. The authorities of the Emancipation Fund in Ilhéus recorded the presence of more than 250 minor children and their mothers on Ilhéus properties in 1874, while between 1872 and 1887 the parish priest baptized at least 559 babies born to the enslaved mothers with whom they lived.[7] That meant that many of the women and children on the region's plantations and farms were related to one another. Most of the 18 enslaved people living on the Encarnação farm in 1863, for example, belonged to perhaps three extended families. Helena Cecília was living on the property with her two sons, Antonio and Jorge, while Martina lived with her son and daughter. Four adult women – Josepha, Luiza, Justina and Victória – were sisters, children of the deceased enslaved married couple, Custódio and Christina. Josepha, in turn, had two daughters among the enslaved on the property – Balbina and Laurinda – who knew their parents and aunts, and may have known their grandparents well.[8]

The partners and fathers of the women and children on the Encarnação plantation did not necessarily number among the eight enslaved men living there. Crossing property lines to find a spouse was not unusual among the enslaved in Ilhéus. Most Ilhéus plantations and farms were small or mid-sized and, therefore, few boasted labor forces large enough or balanced enough to allow captives to form families with other slaves on the same property. Sometimes that was because many of the enslaved residents were already related, as in the case of the Encarnação farm, or it was because the labor force was not particularly balanced, as in the case of the Saint Anthony of the Rocks plantation. In most cases, however, it was because the farms were very small.

---

[5] *Recenseamento*, 1872, 3:278–279.
[6] *Recenseamento*, 1872, 3:278–279.
[7] APEB, SH, Classificação dos escravos para serem libertados pelo Fundo de Emancipação, Ilhéus, 1874–1884; CI-PSJI, Registro dos nascimentos dos filho d'escravos que tiverem occorrido de 28 de septembro de 1871 em diante, conforme a lei 2040 d'aquella data. (hereafter Registro dos nascimentos).
[8] APEB, Inventory (Hereafter Inv.) No. 02/784/1251/02, Manuel da Encarnação, 1863.

Perhaps two thirds of those enslaved in Ilhéus lived on properties with ten or fewer slaves, only a few of whom might be adults.[9]

Enslaved men and women belonging to different owners could not live together. The law required that married slaves be allowed to share a home, but no law guaranteed the rights of men and women living in consensual unions to do so. Further, the enslaved could not marry without the owner's permission, but obtaining such permission was difficult in Ilhéus, since masters had no incentive to limit their authority over their enslaved laborers. In 1874, fewer than two dozen enslaved couples in Ilhéus had been married in Roman Catholic ceremonies – the only ones recognized as legal by the Brazilian state.[10] Other couples were joined in ceremonies overseen by owners, but those rituals had no legal validity and were not recorded in the parish register.[11] Most couples were joined only by their wish to be together. Officially, therefore, the enslaved children of Ilhéus had no fathers and the women had no husbands: in the eyes of the law, these were female headed households.

Although they enjoyed no legal status the consensual nature of these relationships did not mean that they were unimportant or brief. Rather, the ability of the enslaved to maintain ties despite significant upheaval suggests intense emotional attachments. Theresa and Pedro remained together for at least ten years and had five children together, despite having to cope with the fact that three of those children died very young and she moved to town and back to the countryside because she'd been sold twice. Even after she was dead, he recognized his paternity of their children.[12] Domingos Crispim Couto felt so strongly about his enslaved children and the freed woman with whom he lived consensually that he tried to guarantee their well being after his death.[13]

Whether based on legal or consensual unions, after 1871 these families included more and more freed people. In that year, legislators passed the Law

---

[9] Forum Epaminondas Berbert de Castro (Hereafter FEBC), Ilhéus, Primeiro Ofício da Vara Civil (hereafter POVC), Registro de Testamentos; Inv., Domingos José de Lemos, 1888; Aguiar, 1979, 266; APEB, SJ, Livros de Notas, Ilhéus, No. 14, 27/04/1854 a 10/11/1859, Hostílio Tulo de Albuquerque Melo; SJ, Inv., Salvador, No. 05/2177/2646/04, Testamenteiro, Pedro Cerqueira Lima, 1881; Invs., Ilhéus, No. 02/750/1216/09, Maria Bonim Lavigne, 1878; No. 03/1298/1767/08, Acrísio Januário Cardoso, 1887; No. 02/760/1226/04, José Lopes da Silva, 1888; No. 02/762/1228/12, João Carlos Hohlenwerger, 1886; No. 02/759/1225/3, Domingos Lopes da Silva, 1883; No. 02/761/1227/13, Joaquim Alves da Silva, 1885; No. 02/759/1225/6, Felícia Maria Abreu e Castro, 1883; No. 03/742/1207/03, Sofia Claudentina Batista, 1882; No. 03/762/1228/03, Maria Juliana Wense, 1885; No.03/742/1207/08, Agostino Antonio da Silva, 1868; CI-PSJI: Livro de Registro dos Batismos, part of a book, c. 1870–1876, (hereafter Baptismos, II); Registro dos Nascimentos.

[10] Robert Slenes found extensive formal intermarriage among slaves on the plantations of Campinas, São Paulo in the nineteenth century; see Slenes, 1999, pp. 163–4.

[11] Fernando Steiger took '*care that his slaves are married as soon as possible,*' in a ceremony over which he presided followed by a banquet attended by all the slaves; see Maximilian, 1868, III, p. 358.

[12] APEB, SJ, Processo Crime: No. 06/182/15, Homicídio, Diogo, escravo, 1887.

[13] APEB, SJ, Inv. No. 02/751/1217/03, Crispim Domingues Couto, 1878.

of the Free Womb guaranteeing that no more enslaved children would be born in Brazil. The law also set up an emancipation fund, which was intended to free slaves by compensating owners for the loss of their property. Finally, in 1886 the law freed all enslaved persons over the age of 60. [14]

These measures changed the legal status of many enslaved men, women and children, but did not change their day-to-day reality. Nearly 600 *ingenuo* children were born free under the 1871 Free Womb Law in Ilhéus. Nevertheless, they remained technically "wards" of their mothers' owner until age 21, or to age eight, if the master chose to emancipate them. Few did. Rather, masters tended to treat these children as slaves. They were listed as such in inventories and other documents, and transferred to heirs or new owners as though they remained enslaved. [15] Furthermore, the many elderly slaves freed under new emancipation laws also remained on the cacao plantations and farms. Unlike the *ingenuos*, they were allowed to leave the properties where they had been enslaved, but they were little more able to do so than their young counterparts. The law freed them at the same age that their ability to work was reduced. Without a network of support outside the plantations and farms, and little ability to earn a living, after a lifetime in slavery they had nowhere to go. By the 1880s, therefore, groups of free, freed and enslaved men and boys, women and girls could be found on many plantations and farms. Most of those free or freed people, however, were young children or elderly adults who were in no position to live independently.

Enslaved Families as Laborers

These enslaved families were almost completely inappropriate for growing large amounts of sugar – the crop for which Bahia was most famous in the nineteenth century. They were, however, quite well suited to cacao, a tree crop of increasing importance that was much less labor intensive than sugar and appropriate for any size plantation or farm.[16]

Women, children and the infirm could all be usefully employed on a cacao plantation. Census takers considered only 185 of the 1,051 enslaved men and women, boys and girls in Ilhéus to be "*without profession*," a figure that corresponds closely to the number of enslaved children between the ages of one and five years of age (116), and about half of those in the six to ten category

---

[14] On Brazil's Law of the Free Womb and gradual abolition see Viotti da Costa, 2000.
[15] See for example, APEB, SJ, Inv. No. 02/762/1228/15, Maria Margarida Ninck, 1886.
[16] On the colonial economy in southern Bahia see Ferreira da Câmara, 1789, pp. 304–350; Calmon du Pin e Almeida, 1904, Rodrigues de Souza, 1852; Schwartz, 1985; Barickman, 1999; Miller, 2000; Mahony, 2006, pp. 174–203 and Mahony, 1996.

(66.5).[17] In other words, somewhere between age six and ten, enslaved boys and girls went to work on the plantations and farms where they lived, and only death – not old age or infirmity – released them.

Physical capacity governed decisions about labor assignments. Masters sent enslaved men to carry out the tasks that required the most physical strength – clearing land for new groves, cutting the ripe fruit from the trees and transporting the processed cacao first to the plantation headquarters and then to the market. They assigned women and children to do most of the other tasks, from planting and weeding seedlings, to scooping ripe seeds from cacao pods, to putting the wet seeds in baskets, to finally turning the cacao over in the drying balconies.[18]

Southern Bahian cacao planters and farmers certainly understood the value of women, children, and older and injured slaves to their efforts to produce cacao for the world market. In 1860, for example, German cacao planter Franz Kahene sued cacao grower Guilhermina Wyrtzmun over control of an adult man, his wife, and 4 children of working age – in other words, an enslaved family.[19] In 1868, an enslaved woman, an enslaved child of 14 and an enslaved man with "*a chronic wound on his right leg*" were caring for the 2,500 cacao trees on the Bonim farm.[20] In 1882, Dona Paulina Kahene de Sá refused to sell, among other people, three children under 15 and four adults over 40, claiming that to do so would make it impossible for her to care for the family plantation.

By 1880, cacao growers' labor demands were also falling on the children born free under the *Law of the Free Womb*. In masters' views, these children owed them service in exchange for the room and board that they received. That meant that they should be put to work as their size and strength permitted. That was why eight-year-old *ingenuo* Alberto, was "*turning the cacao over in the drying balconies*" in 1887.[21] Hundreds of other *ingenuos* had been sharing Alberto's experience since at least 1880.

Separation and Sale

Masters' efforts to control the labor of entire families did not mean that the enslaved felt safe from forced separation in southern Bahia. Enslaved men and women, boys and girls knew that their precious but precariously formed families could be torn apart for many reasons. Owners might move and bring

---

[17] *Recenseamento*, 1872, 3:278–9.
[18] Calmon du Pin e Almeida, 1904; Rodrigues de Souza, 1852, p. 20 .
[19] APEB, SJ, Civil Suits, No. 3/7204, Franz Otto Kahene v. Dr. Gaspar Wyrtzmun and wife, 1860.
[20] APEB, SJ, Inv., 03/742/1207/02, João Pedro Bonim, 1868.
[21] APEB, SJ, Processo Crime, No. 06/182/15, Homicídio, Diogo, escravo, 1887.

their laborers with them. Or owners might die and the inheritance process that divided all property equitably between spouses and then among all of their heirs might send slaves to live far away. Someone in the masters' family might marry and they might be given as a gift or part of a dowry. The owner might go bankrupt and have to sell someone to raise funds. Or, owners might simply decide to sell someone whom he or she found irritating or dangerous.[22] Whether on large estates or small, enslaved partners, parents and children had good reason to fear separation.

Enslaved family members were in such difficulties because they were legally defined as property. By the last decades of slavery the law guaranteed some rights to enslaved married couples and after 1869 it became illegal to separate enslaved mothers from their children under age 15, later reduced to age 12. But no law guaranteed the rights of enslaved parents over their older children or recognized any legal relationship between the men in consensual relationships, their partners and their children. Masters customarily allowed mothers and children to stay together until the latter turned eight, but fathers enjoyed no such consideration.

The documents suggest that upheaval was common in enslaved families. José Pedro and Maria Calasans left four children behind in Sergipe when their new owners moved them to move to Ilhéus.[23] Theresa's mother, Maria Felícia, was able to bring her children with her when she was transferred to Ilhéus from the Recôncavo, but the documents do not say whether or not her parents, siblings and partner accompanied her as well. She may well have been required to leave them behind. She certainly left behind friends.[24] Once in Ilhéus she was required to tolerate further separation: First, her only son was sent to live in the owner's mansion in Salvador, a minimum of two days' journey away. Then she was sold to another local farmer and separated from her three daughters, the eldest of whom was about 16. Her middle daughter, Theresa, reacted so badly to the sale of her mother that the owner sold her – although thankfully only to a member of his extended family who lived in town. The two other daughters were able to remain on the plantation where the youngest had been born, so perhaps they were able to live near her father – but they may have been completely separated from their parents. Theresa was eventually sold again, and returned to the district where her mother and her sisters were enslaved, but in 1887 when she died, her mother was living in town.[25]

---

[22] APEB, SJ, Livro de Notas, Ilhéus, Escriptura de troca da escrava Teresa, 09/11/1872; APEB, SH, Juízes, Ilhéus, 20 December 1871, Antônio Gomes Vilhaça, juiz de direito to the presidente da província, maço 2402.
[23] APEB, SH, 19 August 1889, José Pedro Calasans to the presidente da província of Bahia, maço 5025.
[24] APEB, SJ, Livro de Notas No. 20, Ilhéus, Escriptura de troca, 09/11/1872.
[25] APEB, SJ, Inv., 02/749/1215/01, Manuel Antonio Vianna, 1875.

From Captivity to Freedom

Other families experienced similar traumas. Januária was somewhere between age 7 and 10 when she was sold the first time and found herself living in a household with an enslaved adult man of forty five and a boy of twelve. Three years later, either at age 10 or 13, she was sold again – this time at public auction.[26] Archangela's eldest daughter had the same experience when she was 16, or at least that is how old her owner said that she was. She also seems to have been sold locally, but she never again appears to have lived with her mother or siblings. Several years later her mother and two younger siblings were sold as well, as a group, but that probably did not last long.

By all accounts older women and young girls were frequently sold. The distances involved in these sales, however, were usually short and thus the resulting separations were difficult but not necessarily permanent. Friends and family members might expect to see one another from time since the buyers and sellers tended to live within the region. Young men, on the other hand, were sold less frequently, but those sales were more threatening. Young enslaved men could find themselves shipped to Rio de Janeiro, gateway to the expanding coffee region. Should they be sold, therefore, the separation from family and friends was usually permanent. Such events were relatively unusual in Ilhéus, but they occurred frequently enough that the enslaved nonetheless felt the constant threat that they represented.

Enslaved men and women, boys and girls reacted powerfully and emotionally to separation. Maria and José Pedro Calasans could not forget the children they left behind, nor apparently could those children forget them. Maria Felicia's daughter Theresa exhibited some kind of reprehensible behavior after her mother was sold – to the point that her owner said that he was "*well, fed up with her*".[27] Although she was unable to live with them, Maria Felicia kept watch over her children to the best of her ability, forcing the authorities to investigate her daughter's death in 1887 – 15 years after they were separated.[28] João Gomes, an unmarried African enslaved on Saint Anthony of the Rocks, may have confessed to a crime he did not commit, at least in part to keep an enslaved man young enough to be his son from being sold away. As we saw in the introduction to this chapter, José do Amparo was so desperate to remain in Ilhéus that he jumped off the steamship taking him to Rio de Janeiro.[29]

---

[26] APEB, SJ, Inv., 02/737/1202/18, Manuel Francisco Dunda, 1873.
[27] APEB, SJ, Livro de Notas, Ilhéus, No. 20, Escriptura de troca da escrava Theresa, 09/11/1872.
[28] APEB, SJ, Processo Crime: No. 06/182/15, Homicídio, Diogo, escravo, 1887, APEB, SH, 19 August, 1889, José Pedro Calasans to the presidente da província of Bahia, Maço 5025.
[29] APEB, SH, 31 August 1877, Plínio de Sá Bittencourt Camara to the presidente da província, maço 2894; Classificação dos escravos; CI-PSJI, Batismos I.

Enslaved Family Strategies for Freedom

Enslaved parents and children did not accept their situations passively, although few fled or openly rebelled against their owners. Rather, they relied on the "*internal economy of slavery*," frequently referred to as the "*peasant breach in slavery*" in the literature on Brazil. As elsewhere in the Americas, the "*internal economy of slavery*" allowed enslaved men and women to grow crops, raise chickens or make household items which they might use themselves or sell in local markets. The practice was very common in Ilhéus.[30]

Growing crops on small pieces of land on or near the owner's property was the predominant way in which enslaved men and women in Ilhéus participated in this internal economy. It allowed enslaved men and women to supplement the limited rations provided them by owners and to earn small amounts of money. Without going into the extensive debate over whether or not Brazilian planters and farmers required their enslaved men and women to feed themselves with their *roças*, we can nonetheless assert that slaves considered their farm plots to be vital elements of their lives under slavery. Indeed, Ilhéus was the site of the most famous example of slaves' efforts to defend and protect their access to *roças*. In 1791, the escaped slaves of the Santanna Plantation in Ilhéus demanded "*more time to work in their roças and greater freedom to choose where they would clear ground to plant food crops*" when they agreed to return to the plantation after two years in the surrounding forests.[31]

By the nineteenth century, however, all Ilhéus *roças* were not provision grounds, or at least not solely provision grounds. While most slaves planted some food crops like cassava, and many harvested piassava palms from wild trees, increasingly they were growing cacao as well. These groves were planted on land belonging to the slaveowners, but the trees themselves belonged to the slaves, by custom if not by law. When German immigrant João Segismundo Cordier died, among the improvements on his land were 84, ten-year-old cacao trees, belonging "*to the slave João of that same fazenda.*"[32] In the 1860s, Sabino was tending a new cacao grove in which he had planted corn and beans to shade his young cacao trees.[33] In the 1870s Jorge, an African slave belonging to Felipe Wense, and the slave Fortunato da Encarnação, both had groves of cacao.[34] José do Amparo may have refused to go to Rio de Janeiro because he had such a grove.

---

[30] APEB, SJ, Inv., 03/1270/1739, José Francisco de Abreu, 1863.
[31] Barickman, 1994, p. 664.
[32] APEB, SJ, Inv., 02/754/1220/14, João Segismundo Cordier, 1849.
[33] APEB, SH, 20 December 1871, Antonio Gomes Vilhaça juiz de direito to the presidente da província, maço 2402.
[34] APEB, SJ, Livro de Notas No. 27.

Whenever possible these *roças* were family projects. The more people in the family who could work, the more cacao the family could plant, tend and harvest. Women and children played the same role on their own cacao *roça* that they played on their owner's. They helped to plant the seedlings, and then weeded them and tended the cassava that grew in the rows between them. Harvesting was best done by at least two people, and slaves, whether single, married or engaged in a consensual union, and their children worked their *roças* together. That was why Pedro from Almada wanted his eight-year-old son Alberto to live with him. That was also why freed African Crispim Domingos Couto thanked his companion, the ex-slave woman Antonia, for helping "him to work with all the constancy and affection possible."[35]

These cacao *roças* were more than family subsistence plots. The owners of these *roças* were growing cacao for the international market – something which brought enslaved farmers into direct contact with the area's larger merchants and planters. Only a few local growers or merchants had direct connections to the outside world, and slaves – like their small farming free counterparts – had no choice but to work with them to sell their crop. Dozens of enslaved men and women sold their cacao to Aristides Francisco Vasconcellos Gusmão. Among them were six men and women "*belonging to Juca Sá*," Diogo and Taurino belonging to João Theodoro Farias, Antonio belonging to Dona Roza and four men and women belonging to Evaristo [Mello e Sá].[36]

Some slaves earned enough with their *roças* to purchase their freedom in the last two decades of slavery.[37] As one owner stated, they bought themselves "*with the product of [their] labor and [their] economies...*"[38] Others traded a well-tended cacao *roça* in production for their freedom.[39] The value of the *roças* was not necessarily enough to win freedom for an enslaved man, but it might be enough to purchase another relative whose estimated value was much lower.

Enslaved men and women saw these *roças* as the key to freedom, either for themselves or for members of their family. Chispim Domingos Couto made that particularly clear when he made out his death bed will, leaving one third of his *roça* to his partner Antonia and the rest to his three enslaved daughters. He was not legally obliged to do so. He and Antonia had never married and he was not registered as his children's father in the parish baptismal register. Yet, as he lay dying, he prepared a will that acknowledged his connections to them

---

[35] APEB, SJ, Inv., Ilhéus, 02/751/1217/03, Crispim Domingues Couto, 1878.
[36] APEB, SJ, Inv., Ilhéus, No.02/762/1228/9, Aristides Francisco Vasconcellos Gusmão, 1886.
[37] APEB, SJ, Invs., No. 02/760/1226/04, José Lopes da Silva, 1888; No. 03/749/1215/06, Antonio Alves Cerqueira, 1876, No. 03/1270/1739/01, Cândido Narciso Soares, 1870/1, No. 03/753/1219/02, Christiano Manoel Sá Bittencourt Câmara, 1879.
[38] APEB, SJ, Inv. No. 02/759/1225/4, Egídio Luís de Sá Bittencourt Camara, 1883.
[39] APEB, SJ, Ilhéus, Livro de notas No. 20.

and that attempted to assure Antonia's survival and the girls' freedom after his death. Clearly, *roças* meant freedom, and indeed a certain kind of freedom.

Enslaved men and women who obtained their freedom were not at liberty to leave the region. Rather, it was their responsibility to remain and work to free the rest of the family one by one. Couto and Antonia freed him first, then her, and then left property to his children in hopes of enabling them to become free. Maria and José Pedro Calasans purchased his freedom first and then hers. Freedman Verissimo Batista Lappa put the final payment on freedom for his wife, Luiza Francisca de Gusmão just before he died,[40]

Enslaved families were prioritizing the freeing of adult men. That is hardly surprising. For all the dangers that enslaved women and children faced, they were not at great risk of being permanently separated from their families, but healthy young adults or even middle aged men like José do Amparo were. There was no way for slaves sold to Rio de Janeiro or São Paulo to see their friends and family in Bahia. Sale south meant permanent separation.

There may also have been other reasons for prioritizing the freedom of men within enslaved families. As we have seen, many enslaved families involved children, some of whom were enslaved and others who had been born free under the 1871 Law of the Free Womb. Enslaved men and women as well as slaveowners considered women to have the primary responsibility for rearing young children. Women in their 20s and 30s, those with the best ability to care for a *roça* by themselves, were also frequently the mothers of minor children.[41] They were, therefore, less mobile than their male counterparts while the children were very young. The parents of *ingenuo* children were those most seriously on the horns of a dilemma: their children were not enslaved, so they could not be freed. Owners were not required to let their children go until they turned 21. Under these circumstances, keeping mothers and children together, while freeing men made more sense.

Yet a final consideration may have played into these decisions about whom to free first, and that is slaves' gendered notions that men were more suited than women to negotiating the commercial and legal networks with which farmers were required to interact. Nineteenth-century Brazilian society operated on hierarchies of race, class and gender, in which one's position depended upon a combination of factors. Enslaved or freed black women occupied a rung on that social hierarchy quite close to the bottom, as members of an inferior race and an inferior gender. Free or freed farmers who grew cacao needed to be able to negotiate with merchants or government officials like the land agent or the district judge, all of whom were male, educated and either white

---

[40] APEB, SH, Classificação dos escravos; SJ, Invs., No. 02/751/1217/03, Crispim Domingos Couto, 1878; No. 02/1270/1739/07, Verissimo Batista Lappa, 1868.
[41] APEB, SH, Classificação dos escravos.

or very light-skinned *mestiços*. Prioritizing the freedom of men within a family, therefore, may have been a determined strategy to level the playing field for illiterate black ex-slaves forced to deal with the white, male and educated representatives of commercial or political institutions.

By the 1880s, these efforts to use *roças* to obtain freedom were beginning to concern the local authorities. According to one 1888 government report, for years slaves have been spending long periods of time away from their owners' plantations and farms.[42] In some cases they were spending nights or days away, or at least devoting as many hours and days as they could to working their *roças*. Some had established their own *roças* on national lands beyond the boundaries of the properties where they had been enslaved. Some of these *roças* were approaching independent farms, in that they were not only groves in the forest, but properties with small huts on them as well. To obtain the resources to develop these farms, the enslaved were gathering *piassava* palm fronds, the principal roofing material among the rural poor, and much in demand among shipbuilders for the excellent rope that it made. These men and women were pushing the boundaries of the "*internal economy of slavery.*"

Taurino and Diogo do Nascimento, brothers enslaved to João Theodoro Farias, were among the men pushing the boundaries of slavery and freedom. In 1887, both had cacao *roças*, and Taurino had built a hut on his. Both traded with Aristides Gusmão, whose shop was several hours travel downriver from Embira, but neither man appears to have had any difficulty getting there. They both carried their machetes with them wherever they went, testimony to both the density of the semi-tropical undergrowth in southern Bahia and the ubiquity of poisonous snakes in the region, but raising questions about the boundaries between slavery and freedom. Diogo's was an expensive Martindale Aligator or "*Jacaré*" machete imported from England. Whenever possible, they identified themselves as freedmen and claimed to be living in town. Although they were not yet formally free, they would not admit it unless pressed.[43] The two men were, to the degree possible, anticipating freedom.

These cacao *roças* – or the possibility of developing them – allowed the enslaved men and women of Ilhéus to look forward to freedom as a time of potential prosperity and family unity. The crop that they grew on their owner's properties was the same one that they grew on their own, and that crop was in growing demand. Rather than labor on sugar plantations whose owners were struggling to compete with sugar producers in other parts of the world, slaves on cacao farms found themselves at the leading edge of an expanding agricultural region and a growing market for milk chocolate – a

---

[42] APEB, SH, 2 December 1888 Civil Engineer Miguel de Freire e Argollo to the presidente da província, maço 4850.
[43] APEB, SJ, Processo Crime: No 06/182/15, Homicídio, Diogo, escravo, 1887.

product that had only recently been invented. They were among the few people who knew how to grow the new crop, many already had groves of cacao trees in production – or coming into production – and owners seemed content to allow them to grow cacao on their properties. There was even land in the public domain available in Ilhéus, which the government was willing to sell in small parcels to farmers who would agree to settle it and bring it into production. Enslaved men and women had every right to believe that their lives would improve after emancipation.

On May 13, 1888, they began to try to create those new lives in earnest. They did not do so, however, by abandoning the region where they had been enslaved. There was no mass exodus from the cacao region for major cities to the north or south. While some people left, the 1890 census shows no precipitous drop in the number of black men and women in the county over the statistics reported in 1872.

Ex-slaves' tendency to remain close to the plantations and farms where they had been enslaved was, in large part because they were members of families which included both elderly people and young children who could not easily tolerate the long trek to the back woods or life in an area so isolated. Efraim SantAnna was probably living and farming on or near the SantAnna Plantation in 1891, because his mother was living there in 1891 when she died, and he took charge of reporting the death to the authorities after she was buried in the plantation cemetery. Maria da Hora, ex-slave of Ritta Constança Sá whose plantation lay on the Cachoeira River, was living and farming in the Cachoeira district when her daughter Maria died in 1891. Ligia de Farias, born a slave on the Farias family's Embira farm in 1864, had moved slightly downriver to the Fazenda Itariry when she died in childbirth, according to the report that her mother, Sinhorinha de Farias, made to the authorities. Fabrício Steiger, born and raised on Fernando Steiger's Victoria Plantation, was living in a house on the plantation when he died there in 1890 at age 40.[44]

Ex-slaves did not stay on or near the plantations where they had been enslaved only because of family. They also stayed because their *roças* kept them tied to the locales where they had been enslaved. Cacao groves in production represented a great deal of hard work. The trees that composed them would produce for upwards of 50 years once planted, and abandoning them for new territory farther west where they would have to start all over again represented a significant loss of investment. Ex-slaves with cacao *roças* did not move far away from their groves, if they could not convince their ex-masters to buy the trees. That is why, after emancipation Efrain SantAnna and others might live on or near the former slave quarters of the SantAnna Plantation and yet call themselves farmers.

---

[44] APEB, SJ, Livro de Registro dos Óbitos.

From Captivity to Freedom

They were not, however, prepared to continue to work those *roças* under the conditions they had experienced in enslavement. Rather, they began to try to formalize and legalize their relationships to their *roças*. On May 24, 1888 the Ilhéus land agent sent an urgent telegram to his superiors at the Ministry of Agriculture advising them that the freedmen were refusing to work for wages and instead were trying to buy public lands from the government in order to grow cacao. "*Given the great number of the petitioners and their impatience*," he felt it necessary to write to Rio to request further instructions.[45] These were not men and women unable to plan for the future, or who refused to work in agriculture after abolition, rather, these were ambitious men and women with visions of freedom linked to hard work and prosperity.

Ex-slaves began referring to themselves as *lavradores*, or farmers. Men who had once been slaves or *ingenuos* now gave themselves titles equivalent to those of free men. That was how José Pedro Calasans, Jorge Alves da Silva and Efraim de SantAnna identified themselves to authorities just after abolition. All three had been born slaves, yet, each claimed to have a farm. So did two women who had been born enslaved – Maria da Hora and Paulina Maria – while Jorge Alves da Silva reported that his brother Fidellis Rodriguez Cezar was also a farmer when he died.[46]

These men and women were not agricultural workers. Men and women who worked for others were registered as either, day laborers – *jornaleiros* in Portuguese – or farm service – *serviço da lavoura*. People who worked in farm service, especially just after abolition, were normally permanent workers who lived on the plantations, while day laborers on the other hand, lived in town and hired themselves out to do tasks of various sorts in the countryside. *Lavrador*, on the other hand, always referred to an individual who owned property, although not necessarily land. This indeterminate term, which did not reflect the size of the property in any way, indicated that the individual in question worked for himself or herself. He or she might be a squatter on national lands or on private property, or a person with a formal agreement with a landlord, but they were not permanent plantation or farm workers. In other parts of Bahia, the term *lavrador* was commonly modified by the type of crop that the farmer grew, but in Ilhéus it was not. Rather, it always referred to someone who grew crops for the market, and by the 1890s that crop was usually cacao.

---

[45] APEB, 24 May 1888, Ilhéus, Engineer Theodolo Augusto Cardoso, Juiz Commissário de Ilhéos, to the Minister of Agriculture, included in June 15, 1888, Rio de Janeiro, Rodrigo A. da Silva to the presidente da província, maço 783. I wish to thank Walter Fraga Filho for locating this document and passing it to me.

[46] APEB, SJ, Ilhéus, Livro de Registro dos Óbitos, 1889–1895.

From Slaves to Sergipanos

After abolition Southern Bahia was transformed. Former slaveowners there did not face the kind of devastating crisis experienced on the sugar plantations of the Recôncavo.[47] Rather, they faced an almost completely different situation. The southern Bahian countryside began to fill up with people in the years after abolition and so any labor shortage that planters and farmers had experienced prior to abolition or in its immediate aftermath soon disappeared. Despite the authorities' predictions of doom in the cacao sector in the spring of 1888, exports for that year were only slightly lower than those of 1887 or 1889. That was in part because farmers with no slaves had always made up about half of southern Bahia's annual cacao production, but it is also because slaveowners found new workers to take the place of ex-slaves who refused to work for free or for low wages. The new workers were single men originating in two distinct parts of the northeast: the dry northwestern Bahian backlands known as the *sertão* and a humid stretch of coastal Bahia and Sergipe stretching from Alagoinhas to Estancia – a center of slave-based sugar production in the nineteenth century.[48]

These men formed part of a larger migrant stream that brought people from a cross section of northeastern Brazilian society to Ilhéus. These migrants included the younger sons of planters, farmers, and rural shopkeepers as well as black and mixed race country people. The process had begun slowly around 1860, grown more rapidly in the 1880s and 1890s, and then exploded as the twentieth century opened. By 1900 it was bringing hundreds of impoverished migrants to the Ilhéus countryside every month. In 1926 and 1927, more than 13,000 people entered the region. As Chart 1 indicates, by 1920, the population had increased more than tenfold, from just over 7,000 in 1890 to just under 105,000 in 1920.[49]

Table 1: Population of Ilhéus, 1818–1920

	1818	1872	1880	1890	1920*
Free		4,631	9,023	7097	104,279
Enslaved		1,051	977		
Total	2,400	5,682	10,000	7,097	104,279

* Includes population figures for both Ilhéus and Itabuna, the latter having been created out of Ilhéus in 1915.
Sources: *Recenseamento*, 1872; *Recenseamento*, 1890; *Recenseamento*, 1920, IV(2), 453, 457.

---

[47] On the crisis in the sugar industry in the wake of abolition see Walter Fraga Filho's essay in this volume and Barickman 1996, pp. 581–633.
[48] dos Passos Sobrinho, 2000.
[49] *Recenseamento*, 1890; *Recenseamento* 1920; Município de Ilhéus, 1928.

Table 2: Percentage of Male/Female Population Ilhéus, 1872–1920

	1872	1890	1920
Male	47	52	56
Female	53	48	44
Total	**100**	**100**	**100**

Sources: *Recenseamento*, 1872, 3:278–9; *Recenseamento*, 1890; *Recenseamento* 1920, IV(2), 453, 457.

Most of these migrants were men. So many men migrated to Ilhéus that instead of being a place with more women and girls than men and boys, as it was in 1872, by 1890 it was a place where men and boys were predominant. By 1920, the trend was even more pronounced: 56 percent of the population was male, while only 44 percent was female. After abolition, the population's breakdown by sex looked more like that of the old plantation slave labor districts of the Recôncavo than it did before. Male migrants especially filled the agricultural districts. Male to female sex ratios were particularly skewed there: in Banco do Pedro men single men outnumbered women 1.38 to one; in Castello Novo, 1.4 to one, and in Cachoeira de Itabuna, 1.1 to one. The differences were even stronger when we look at the number of single men and women in the region. In fact, the only district in Ilhéus that continued to boast a larger number of women than men was the old second district, location of the Saint Anthony of the Rocks Plantation, the Embira Farm and several other properties dating from the nineteenth century where enslaved women and children had once provided much of the labor.[50]

At least in the early years, large numbers of these migrants appear to have been black or *pardo* (mixed).[51] Indeed, the 1890 census suggests that the proportion of black men in the community was increasing, something that could only happen if many of the newly arriving migrants were black. The death registers, on the other hand, suggest that nearly all of the migrants of African descent in Ilhéus between 1889 and 1915 were of mixed ancestry rather than black. That may be because the deaths of the darkest – and presumably the poorest – migrants were never registered with the authorities. That seems unlikely, however, because the death registers include entries for ex-slaves, indigents, rural workers, sharecroppers and the babies of poor people as well as for the elite.

Brazilians' fluid notions about race and color, and the efforts of the migrants to distance themselves from any past in slavery, may offer a more plausible

---

[50] *Recenseamento*, 1920.
[51] APEB, SH, 19 August 1889, José Pedro Calasans, Freedman, to the presidente da província of Bahia, maço 5025.

Table 3: Percentage of Male/Female Black Population, Ilhéus, 1872–1890

	1872	*1890*
Male	47	55
Female	53	45
Total	**100**	**100**

Sources: *Recenseamento*, 1872, 3:278–9; *Recenseamento*, 1890; *Recenseamento*,1920, IV(2), 453, 457.

Table 4: Percentage of Male/Female Mixed Race Population, Ilhéus, 1872–1920

	1872	*1890*
Male	47	51
Female	53	49
Total	**100**	**100**

Sources: *Recenseamento*, 1872, 3:278–9; *Recenseamento*, 1890; *Recenseamento*, 1920, IV(2), 453, 457.

explanation of the differences between the census and the death register. Census takers recorded the color that they observed when they prepared their spreadsheets of the population. The city clerks, however, did not necessarily observe the skin color of the deceased whose death they were registering. Rather, they relied on the reports of the friends, family, employers and neighbors of the deceased for information. The migrants rarely identified themselves as either ex-slaves or as freedmen when they registered deaths or imparted any other information about themselves. Rather they called themselves *Sergipanos* (natives of Sergipe) or *sertanejos* (natives of the Sertão), and reported that they were *pardos* or *mestiços*, in other words, mixed race people, rather than blacks.

Brazil is well known for having complex ideas about race and color, which go well beyond the binary opposition between black and white so common in the United States. Prior to abolition, Brazilians used at least four or five different terms for African descended people: *preto, negro crioulo, pardo, pardo claro* (light *pardo*) and *cabra*. In Ilhéus, both *preto* and *crioulo* referred to very dark skinned individuals who either were slaves themselves or their recent descendants. *Negro*, on the other hand, referred to black people who were free and had been for some time, while *pardo* and *cabra* referred to people who were mixed. With abolition, *mestiço* – another term for mixed – began to dominate. The terms also reflected class distinctions. *Preto* and *crioulo* were pejorative terms never used to refer to "respectable" people, whatever their color. The *sertanejos* and *Sergipanos* may have been sidestepping the issue of race or color altogether, developing a new label for themselves in this new place, that would deny the salience of color and highlight their roots in freedom and

Brazil rather than in slavery and Africa. Certainly they made no effort to ally themselves along racial lines with people emerging from slavery in Ilhéus itself, who could hardly obscure their roots given the size of the community.

Although they chose to highlight a Brazilian rather than an African identity, the Sergipanos did not avoid agricultural labor. Rather they attached themselves to whomever was able to pay their wages. They had no experience with growing cacao but planters and farmers did not seem to care. To a certain degree, that made sense: No part of cacao growing or processing demanded the precision or the technical skill of making sugar. Moreover, landowners were more interested in clearing the land – either of trees or of *lavradores* who refused to acknowledge that their farms lay on private property – and the migrants were perfectly capable of doing that.

The migrants were, for the most part, young single men, unencumbered by children, wives, parents, or other relatives to whom they owed allegiance. Nor did they form part of the complex community of ex-slaves and freed people or the patron-client ties that dated back to the period prior to abolition. They could be asked to harass, beat, rape or even murder individuals and families that owners found problematic for whatever reason and no conflicting loyalties inhibited their behavior.

By 1894, the owners of the large plantations and farms were particularly eager to clear their properties of *lavradores*, because the laws governing landholding in Bahia were changing. At the national level, abolition had been followed by the fall of the Brazilian empire and the formation of the first Brazilian Republic. In the process of decentralizing power, the new republican government had passed control over public lands to the states and a bill lay before the state of Bahia's legislature that would distribute uncultivated lands in southern Bahia in fifty hectare (about 100 acre) plots to farmers who would bring them into production.[52] The proposed law even took aim at the large estates, explicitly allowing any farmer who could prove that he or she had been peacefully cultivating their plot of land for at least ten years to purchase those lands from the state and receive legal title to them. The new law struck terror into long term southern Bahian planters and farmers who had allowed slaves and others to plant groves of cacao on their properties. The law was about to give the land under those groves to the tillers.

The planters, whose claims to land lay in land grants from the Portuguese Crown immediately called on the land agent, ordered their properties to be surveyed and began to clarify their relationship to the *lavradores* on their land. In 1894 Dona Maria Cerqueira Lima sent a *"crioulo"* by the name of Bomfim

---

[52] All public lands did not revert to the state, but a full discussion of exactly which public lands did and did not do so is beyond the scope of this article. For further discussion of the issue see Mahony, 1996, pp. 441–443.

to "*request*" that the *lavradores* at Conquista on her property sign rental agreements.⁵³ The Steiger family sent a notice to the newspaper in 1903 telling everyone occupying a land at Banco da Victória that they could not sell or otherwise transfer any of their property, something that tradition had allowed *lavradores* on other people's lands do to for at least a century if not more.⁵⁴ When the *lavradores* did not comply, Mrs. Cerqueira Lima and the Steigers took stronger measures. Other planters did not bother with the niceties of formal requests, but simply began the process of turning people who considered themselves property owners into sharecroppers or getting rid of them.

Hardly surprisingly, the districts that had been the center of nineteenth-century slave-based cacao growing exploded in violence at the end of the nineteenth century. Iguape, Itariry, Almada, and Banco da Victória all became sites of brutality, as landowners sent their hired hands, known locally as *capangas* or *jagunços* to get farmers to leave the plantations and farms that they had peacefully farmed for decades. The *Ilhéos Gazette* reported that the *jagunço* Avelino had become the terror of Almada, raping, burning, pillaging and otherwise disrespecting families in the second district.⁵⁵ He was, they reported, the local sheriff, but he feared no one because Domingos Adami de Sá, plantation owner and political power in the Almada district, protected him.

The men and women of Almada or Cachoeira de Itabuna who offended powerful local interests could find themselves on the receiving end of a visit from someone like Avelino. Punishments could involve torture or death or both. Farmer Henrique Alves dos Reis, one of Domingos Adami's political allies, was said to have a set of stocks on his farm and periodically left people in this remnant of slavery for days at a time. Adami himself was said to use particularly ruthless measures against people who may have been former slaves. According to a story that appeared in the *Ilhéos Gazette*,

> *Nero had a worker named José Grande, who they took on February 29 turning him over to a guy named Villa Nova who takes care of the fazenda that the big guy has in Alegrias, ordering Villa Nova, his guard and two more thugs to make José Grande disappear, and [as they took him along the road, they] never stopped beating the prisoner and whacking him with the machete and the people they passed on the road saw him leaving pools of blood behind him, and walking so strangely that it seemed as though he had been castrated. When they got to the plantation, they tied the guy up and then they killed him. After they buried him, they said that he fled.*⁵⁶

---

[53] FEBC, POVC, Manoel Bernardo dos Santos et al. v. Dona Maria Victoria Mendes de Cerqueira Lima, 1897.
[54] *Gazeta de Ilhéos*, 3 October 1902.
[55] *Gazeta de Ilhéos*, 1 January 1901.
[56] *Gazeta de Ilhéos*, 13 March 1904.

José Grande may have been an ex-slave. Although he does not appear on any of the extant slave lists, most enslaved men who were born between 1855 and 1871 do not. The baptismal register for the period of their birth is missing; they were too young to be listed by name in the slave register prepared for the Emancipation Fund and they do not appear in the *ingenuo* registry, because they were not married to the mothers of their children. On the other hand, enslaved men nicknamed Grande (Big) or Pequeno (Small), in other words, whose names included an indication of size, were common on Ilhéus plantations and farms, especially the large ones like those owned by Domingos Adami de Sá's family. Moreover, the reference to fleeing after death may reflect the concept of "*flying back to Africa*," described among Afro-descended populations in the Caribbean and the United States. Such an allusion in the newspaper story describing his death, suggests that José Grande was African, or had been raised by Africans.

José Grande had offended his former employer horribly to merit his torture and death. The offense may have been sexual, as witnesses reported signs of castration. He may not necessarily, however, have committed a sexual offense against a woman. Rather, he may have attempted to assert his masculinity – something that the ex-slaves of Ilhéus associated with farming cacao, and protecting family members. Slaveowners had frequently used exemplary punishment to demonstrate the consequences of violating the boundaries of slavery to the enslaved: perhaps Adami had used the same tactics on a free or freed man. Perhaps José Grande had refused to acknowledge Adami as the owner of the land under his *roça*.

José Grande may also have objected to something else: the treatment of women and girls in his circle of friends and family. By 1900, the presence of all the unattached men in the district was leading to the establishment of brothels and taverns in the countryside. In 1903, as an anonymous complaint to the *Ilhéus Gazette* informed readers, the three largest planters in the Cachoeira district – Manuel Misael da Silva Tavares, Domingos Pereira and Virgilio Amorim – had "*allowed*" a house of prostitution to develop "*at the back of their farms*" where a certain Manoel Panhoala had "*gathered a large number of women of the lowest classes*," which were attracting "*the workers of the neighboring fazendas on the holy days and every night in a complete orgy, getting drunk and carrying on.*"[57] Who could these women "*of the lowest classes*" have been, but those emerging from slavery. Women and girls who had provided farm labor for their owners and child care for their families were now required to support themselves in new ways.

---

[57] *Gazeta de Ilhéos*, 1 September 1902.

Conclusion

This paper began by arguing that notions of gender within enslaved families were central to the behavior of the enslaved prior to emancipation and to the newly freed thereafter. We have seen that enslaved men and women struggled to maintain connections to loved ones and to physically and emotionally protect each other and their children. These efforts were particularly clear in the way that the enslaved sought to negotiate their lives within slavery. Enslaved families assigned responsibility for the care of children and the elderly to women, and recognized that men were more capable than women of negotiating the patriarchal society outside the plantations and farms. They also recognized that men were more likely to be sold far away to southern parts than were women and children and, therefore, when they worked to free each other they tended to prioritize men. Thus, men were more likely to obtain their freedom than women, children and the elderly. After all, freeing a mother while a young child remained bound to a plantation was no solution to the problem of slavery. Gendered notions of family responsibility kept men from leaving the site of their enslavement while partners and children remained captive. Masters understood this and did not oppose enslaved men's efforts – after all, enslavement was above all a method of controlling labor. Masters had no reason to object to a process through which the enslaved paid for their freedom but remained available for agricultural work.

After emancipation, however, masters were much less interested in keeping the families of former slaves nearby. The late nineteenth century saw the beginning of an enormous wave of migration to the cacao region that originated in the nearby state of Sergipe. Most of these migrants, called Sergipanos, were mixed race men looking for agricultural work and they rapidly eradicated southern Bahia's nineteenth-century male labor shortage. Now benefiting from a male labor surplus, ex-masters preferred to clear their property of former slaves. No longer able to threaten to sell them in order to control them, planters and farmers now turned to violence to expel newly freed ex-slaves who would no go quietly.

Bibliography

Aguiar, D. V. de (1979), *Descrições práticas da província da Bahia: Com declaração de todas as distâncias intermediárias das cidades, vilas e povoações*, Preface by Fernando Sales, 2nd. ed, Rio de Janeiro.

Barickman, B. J. (1996), 'Persistance and Decline: Slave Labour and Sugar Production in the Bahian Recôncavo, 1850–1888', *Journal of Latin American Studies*, 28:3, pp. 581–633.

Barickman, B. J. (1999), *A Bahian Counterpoint*, Stanford.

Barickman, B. J. (1994), '"A Bit of Land, Which They Call Roça": Slave Provision Grounds in the Bahian Recôncavo, 1780–1860,' *Hispanic American Historical Review*, 74, pp. 649–687.

Brazil (1898), Ministério da Indústria, Viaçuoe Obras Públicas Diretoria Geral de Estatística, *Synopse do Recenseamento de 31 dezembro de 1890*, Rio de Janeiro: Officina da Estatística.

Calmon du Pin e Almeida, M. (1904), 'Memoria Sobre a Cultura do Cacau', *Gazeta de Ilhéos*, October 16–30, 1904.

Diretoria Geral de Estatística (1873–1876), *Recenseamento da população do Brazil a que se procedeu no dia 1 de agosto de 1872*, "Parochia de São Jorge dos Ilhéos, População considerado em relação a edades", 21 vols., Rio de Janeiro [*Recenseamento*, 1872].

Diretoria Geral de Estatística (1922–1930), *Recenseamento do Brasil realizado em 1 setembro 1920*, 16 vols, Rio de Janeiro.

Ferreira da Câmara, M. (1789), 'Ensaio de descripção fizica, e econômica da Comarca de São Jorge dos Ilhéos', *Memórias Economicas da Academia das Sciencias da Lisboa* 1, pp. 304–350.

Mahony, M. A. (1996), *The World Cacao Made: Society, Politics and History in Brazil's Cacao Area, 1822–1919*, Ph.D. Thesis, Yale University.

Mahony, M. A., (2006), 'The Local and the Global' in S. Topik, C. Marichal, and Z. Frank (eds.), *From Silver to Cocaine: Latin American Commodity Chains and the Building of the World Economy 1500–2000*, Durham, pp. 174–206.

Maximilian I, Emperor of Mexico (1868), *Recollections of my Life*. 3 vols., new edition with a preface by R. Bentley.

Miller, S. (2000), *Fruitless Trees*, Stanford.

Município de Ilhéus (1928), *Relatório Exercicio de 1927, apresentado ao Conselho Municipal pelo Intendente Dr. Mario Pessoa da Costa e Silva*, Bahia.

dos Passos Sobrinho, J. M. (2000), *Reordenamento do Trabalho: Trabalho Escravo e Trabalho Livre no Nordeste Açucareiro. Sergipe 1850–1930*, Aracaju.

Rodrigues de Souza, J. (1852), *Memôria sobre a lavoura de cacao e suas vantagens principalmente na Bahia*, Bahia.

Schwartz, S. (1985), *Sugar Plantations in the Formation of Brazilian Society: Bahia, 1550–1835*, New York.

Scully, E. and Paton, D. (eds.) (2005), *Gender and Slave Emancipation in the Atlantic World*, Durham.

Slenes, R. (1999), *Na Senzala uma Flor: Esperanças e Recordações na Formação da Família escrava, Brasil Sudeste, século XIX*, Rio de Janeiro.

Viotti da Costa, E. (2000), *The Brazilian Empire*, 2nd. ed., Chapel Hill.

Part 4

SLAVE REBELLIONS

REWRITING SLAVE REBELLIONS[1]

Theresa Urbainczyk

Spartacus is a name familiar to many, but this is due more to the efforts of Kirk Douglas than of any ancient historian. Spartacus was not the only leader of a slave revolt in antiquity, or even the most successful although he is today the most famous. In fact, whenever a slave revolt is reported by the ancient sources, there has been a growing tendency recently in modern scholarship to argue either that it is not a revolt or that those involved are not slaves. Both approaches logically result in a reduction in the number of events which can be termed slave wars or revolts. In a recent article, for instance, Pierre Piccinin suggests that, although there were slaves in Spartacus' army and although Spartacus and his generals were gladiators, the uprising in 73BC should not be called a slave war.[2] It was, rather, a war against Rome, a nationalist conflict of Italians against Roman rule. Piccinin's thesis is not new, as he admits; he is building on the work of Rubinsohn among others, who asked whether this was a servile war and concluded that it was not.[3] A consequence of accepting this radical hypothesis would be that we must disregard most of what our ancient sources wrote about this episode.[4]

Before the revolt of Spartacus there had been two major slave uprisings in Sicily in the 130s BC and in the 100s BC. Both these Sicilian wars have been interpreted in a way similar to that of Spartacus, that is, it has been argued that they were not slave rebellions but in fact nationalist uprisings involving the Sicilians, this time against their Roman and Italian overlords.[5] The sources for all three wars tell us that poor free people did join the slave

---

[1] In rewriting this article I am indebted to the participants of the conference in Galway, especially Stephen Hodkinson, and also to the observations of Christian Mileta and an anonymous reader for the publisher. All views and mistakes are my own.
[2] Piccinin, 2004, p. 198.
[3] Rubinsohn, 1971, pp. 290–299; see also Guarino, 1979.
[4] See Egerton's article in this volume for an account of the scholarly treatment of later episodes of slave resistance. Being unfamiliar with the modern material when I started researching slave revolts I was staggered when I read his paper for the first time since the problems he encountered echoed so strongly the ones I faced. His comments about Denmark Vesey that introduce his article, for instance, with a few minor changes, could have been written about Spartacus.
[5] See Verbrugghe in a series of articles from 1973, 1974, and 1975.

armies, so there is some evidence for their involvement, but there would have to be a drastic rewriting of the historical accounts to make them the instigators of the conflict.

As an indication of the accompanying decline in the twentieth century of scholarly attention to the mere topic of slave revolts, it is interesting to note the differences of treatment of slave wars of the Roman Republic in the first and second editions of volume IX of *The Cambridge Ancient History*.[6] The first edition, from 1932, dealt with the first Sicilian slave war in Chapter 1, on Tiberius Gracchus, and with the second war in Chapter 3, 'The wars of the age of Marius'; the slave wars were discussed, in other words, in their historical setting, since these events were thirty years apart.[7] The reader of the second edition, however, has to search in the subsection 'Sicily' of Chapter 2, 'The Roman empire and its problems in the late second century' to find two pages dealing with both slave wars together.[8] The second edition also puts Spartacus into a subsection of the chapter, 'The rise of Pompey', a subsection of some nine pages, entitled 'The wars against Sertorius and Spartacus 79–71', but only two of those pages are about Spartacus.[9] Sixty years earlier, the rebels under Spartacus had had a subsection to themselves entitled 'The war of the Gladiators'.[10]

Another still more violently reinterpreted episode is the revolt of Aristonicus. Although Joseph Vogt in *Slavery and the Ideal of Man* and Zvi Yavetz in *Slaves and Slavery in Ancient Rome* had both discussed the rebellion of Aristonicus, as if it were a slave uprising,[11] Aristonicus' name was not even in the index of Keith Bradley's 1989 book, entitled *Slavery and Rebellion in the Roman World*. Similarly the uprising in Pergamum is not included in Thomas Wiedemann's chapter on resistance in his source book *Greek and Roman Slavery*. The latter had explained in his introduction that because Aristonicus was not a slave himself

---

[6] 1st edition, Cambridge, 1932, edited by S. A. Cook, F. E. Adcock and M. P. Charlesworth; 2nd edition 1994 edited by J. A. Crook, A. Lintott and E. Rawson.

[7] Pp. 11–16 and 151–157. Both chapters were written by Hugh Last.

[8] Pp. 25–27, written by Andrew Lintott, who refers only obliquely to slave revolts when discussing 'The agrarian problem', see e.g. p.54: "*Hence Gracchus deplored not only the injustice which was being done to those who fought for Rome but the danger of replacing potential warriors with slaves, who could not be used for military service but might on the contrary rebel.*"

[9] Pp. 215–223. This chapter is by Robin Seager.

[10] Pp. 329–332, again by Hugh Last. In another textbook from recent years, Spartacus, the only slave leader to be mentioned by name, has only reference in the index of the 2004 The Cambridge Companion to the Roman Republic edited by Harriet Flower (which incidentally has no chapter – out of a possible 15 – with the word 'slave' or 'slavery' in the title.) The reference is to a section entitled 'Pompeius' in a chapter on the crisis in the Republic. In another survey, only Spartacus is mentioned and only once, in the 2002 *A History of the Roman Republic* by Klaus Bringmann, translated into English in 2007, although there are five references to slave revolts in this volume. However each of these refers only to a sentence or so, except for one which refers the reader to a paragraph on the Spartacan revolt. I mention these books only because they represent current attitudes in scholarship to the topic.

[11] Yavetz, 1988, pp. 45–66 and Vogt, 1974, pp. 93–102.

and did not want to abolish slavery this should not be classed as a slave revolt.[12] Brent Shaw did not feel the need to justify his exclusion of the event from his collection of sources in translation, called *Spartacus and the Slave Wars*, which contains extracts relating to the Sicilian wars as well as of the Spartacan uprising.[13]

It is certainly true that Aristonicus was no slave but the pretender to the throne of Pergamum at the same time as the first Sicilian slave war. Diodorus described the outbreak of the war in Sicily and linked it to events in Pergamum in this way:

> "*The result [of the maltreatment of slaves in Sicily] was that, without any communication between themselves, tens of thousands of slaves joined forces to kill their masters. Almost the identical thing happened in Asia at the same time, when Aristonicus claimed the kingship that was not rightly his. Because their masters had treated them so terribly, the slaves in Asia joined Aristonicus and were the cause of great disasters to many unfortunate cities.*" (my emphasis, Diodorus, 34/35.2.26)

Diodorus did not say that Aristonicus recruited slaves in order to fight his cause, but rather that the reason the slaves joined him was that they were badly treated. In other words, whatever was in Aristonicus' mind, the slaves made decisions of their own, and therefore had their own aims. If one were tempted to focus only on Aristonicus' intentions the result would be a disregard of our main source, which happens, quite remarkably, to be supported in this case by epigraphic evidence. There is an inscription from Claros which refers to a '*city of slaves*' (who were being a nuisance) in the chora of Colophon, lending some support not only to Diodorus' account but also perhaps to Strabo's remark that Aristonicus called his followers Heliopolitae, Citizens of the City of the Sun (14.1.38).[14]

Although it is easy to argue, and it has been, that Aristonicus merely wished to gain control of Pergamum and did not intend to abolish slavery, the role of the slaves here cannot be ignored, if our ancient evidence is taken seriously.

---

[12] Wiedemann states: "*this war should not be seen so much as slave rebellion than as an instance of slaves being promised their freedom in return for fighting on behalf of someone who saw himself as a legitimate ruler threatened by a foreign power. There is no evidence that Aristonikos envisaged the permanent abolition of slavery as an institution.*" 1981, p. 13.

[13] Shaw, 2001. By comparison, Aristonicus had had a subsection to himself in the first edition of the *Cambridge Ancient History*, pp.102–107, whereas in the second edition, he was given only a paragraph on p.34.

[14] Mileta, 1998, pp. 47–65; see also Robert and Robert, 1989, p. 13, col. 2, line 37, discussed pp. 36–8. The mention of the city of slaves appears among the problems facing the city for which the man honoured by the inscription, Ptolemaios, asked and received help from the Romans. Ferrary 1991 suggests that this decree dates to a slightly later period, but this does not affect the argument here. That these rebels survived in the area some time after the fall of Aristonicus is a perfectly reasonable suggestion.

From Captivity to Freedom

Quite apart from the consideration that the personal wishes of leaders may not have much influence on the historical course of events, there is also the possibility that ideas evolve over time with changing circumstances.[15] Toussaint Louverture in Saint Domingue did not even join the rebellion there immediately and it was only in the course of the war that the aim of the abolition of slavery developed.[16]

Keith Bradley argued that the two Sicilian slave wars and that of Spartacus were not in any sense political rebellions but merely slaves wanting to be free.[17] They were in fact trying to set up maroon communities in which they could lead an independent existence.[18] At the end of his book we read:

> *"The Roman slave wars were not revolutionary mass movements in any sense but to a large extent historical accidents precipitated by a combination of circumstances that never again reappeared in the long history of slavery in the Roman world."* (p.126)

---

[15] Orlando Patterson's comments in any case are apposite here, *"Certainly we know next to nothing about the individual personalities of slaves, or of the way they felt about one another. The data are just not there, and it is the height of arrogance, not to mention intellectual irresponsibility, to generalise about the inner psychology of any group, be they medieval Jewish merchants, New England Puritan farmers, or Scythian slave policemen in Athens."* 1982, p. 11.

[16] On which revolt, see still James, 1938 (here p. 73) and Dubois, 2004. As Dubois, 2004, p. 3 puts it *"the revolution began as a challenge to French imperial authority by colonial whites, but it soon became a battle over racial inequality, and then over the existence of slavery itself."* See also Davis, 1975, pp. 137–148 on the shifting alliances of this period.

[17] Bradley makes the point that we have no evidence of any aims on the part of the slaves of antiquity apart from their own personal freedom and that we can, thus, distinguish between their efforts and revolts in the modern world, for instance, on the Engeno Santana of Ilhéus, a large sugar plantation in Brazil in 1789 where slaves wanted an amelioration in their conditions. After rebelling for two years these had offered terms and said they would return as slaves if these were accepted. Unsurprisingly these terms were not conceded to them but Bradley adds: *"But they [the Brazilian slaves] represented all the same a revolutionary threat to the institution of slavery of a kind that is without parallel in the Roman world."* [my emphasis] 1989, p. 103. In other words, the slaves in Brazil were a completely different threat from the slaves in ancient Sicily because they asked for certain conditions, not because they achieved them. The aims of the slaves in Brazil were indeed revolutionary but one can see how they arose from their particular situation since we have a transcript of their demands. The slaves did not demand freedom and an end to their slavery in those words, couched in the vocabulary of the French Revolution for instance, but what they demanded was in reality an end to their slavery. Schwartz, 2003 reproduces the document in his appendix 2 (pp. 631–2). They wanted Fridays and Saturdays to work for themselves; that their masters provide them with canoes and nets, proper boats for working and clothes. They did not want to do certain tasks and asked to fix the amount of work for themselves; they asked for proper working conditions, and they wanted to choose their overseers. They wanted to be able to grow their rice wherever they wanted and be able to cut whatever wood they needed, and, as Schwartz points out, very importantly, they wanted the equipment for their work to remain in their control, *"reducing the concept of slavery to a farce."* Schwartz, 2003, p. 629. The last clause is haunting: *"We shall be able to play, relax and sing any time we wish without your hinderance nor will permission be needed."* Schwartz, 2003, p. 632. We have no evidence of what the slaves of antiquity asked for.

[18] Bradley introduced his book with the following remark: *"In the seventy years between 140 BC and 70 BC Rome was confronted by three major insurrections of slaves.... This series of events was unique in Rome's history, for slave uprisings on such a dramatic scale had never been known beforehand and similar episodes were never to recur despite the*

The expression '*in any sense*' is a little puzzling because it is undeniable that the slave wars were revolutionary mass movements in some sense, in that there were tens of thousands of slaves fighting their masters for years on end.[19]

However the argument here is that in all three episodes signs of these maroon communities can be observed. In other words this was not a war as much as a mass escape:

> "*Thus it cannot be assumed that slaves set out to make war, in any formal manner, against established powers; it can only be said that slaves were prepared to use military tactics to protect and sustain themselves in flight, to make continuous flight and the freedom it represented feasible. Almost paradoxically, however flight could not bring permanent freedom when so many fugitives were involved. The numerical dimensions of the slave uprisings were therefore the rebellions' fatal flaw.*"[20]

If one accepts this scenario, none of the slaves involved in any of the three wars wanted war; rather all of them wished merely to be free. Their mistake was to attract too many followers; if they had remained very few they could individually have escaped.

There are certain problems with this interpretation: if the slaves had only had as their aim to run off into the countryside, why did they collect an army

---

long endurance of slavery in the Roman world." 1989, p. xi. Peter Green commented in a similar fashion: "*The Roman slave revolts of the second and first centuries BC were unique. Nothing like them had ever happened before, and after the final suppression of Spartacus in 70 BC no comparable uprising ever took place again.*" 1961, p. 10. See also Joseph Vogt who began his chapter on slave rebellions: "*Everyone who considers the great slave revolts of the ancient world will be struck by the fact that they all occurred in the relatively short period of time between 140 BC and 70 BC.*" 1974, p. 39. Paul Cartledge had made a very similar point when discussing helot revolt, "*Not withstanding the fact that in servile revolts the participants typically aim at purely individual liberation rather than social transformation.*" 1985, pp. 16–46. Certainly in the case of slave revolts we have no evidence at all for what they may have intended. In any case, personal aims and historical conditions are more intimately involved than such a view would indicate. The intentions of individuals emerge from historical conditions as well as helping to determine them.

[19] Eugene Genovese in his study of slave revolts in the southern states of the US used terms in his very title, which are key in the debate about revolution. His volume is called *From Rebellion to Revolution* and his argument is that the particular historical circumstances of, for instance, the rebellion in St Domingue, meant that, unlike their ancient counterparts, these slaves were revolutionary and had revolutionary aims. (1979, p. xix). Until this age of revolution, when ideas about freedom and equality were formulated, slaves merely wished to withdraw from society, not change it. (pp. xiv, xxi.) Genovese says in his introduction: "*The history of slavery and of slave revolts in the Americas corresponds roughly to the transition from seigneurialism to capitalism.*" (p. xviii). Jacky Dahomay goes even further and says that the slaves on Saint-Domingue did not even understand the principles of the French Revolution and one cannot call this an anti-slavery revolution, but rather it was an anti-colonial revolution that incorporated anti-slavery uprisings. 2003, p. 4. The author goes on to ask "*is revolution thinkable before the advent of modernity?*" p. 12. It seems not and, thus, my use of the term 'revolutionary' is not in this technical sense. A consequence of looking for a precise 'revolutionary' content to the revolts, is that modern observers tend to emphasise the inevitable failure. What comes across quite strikingly however is that many times for the participants the prospect of escaping slavery overrode fears of a violent death.

[20] 1989, p. 125.

together, something which could hardly occur spontaneously, given the amount of planning and organization this entailed? As Piccinin points out, when discussing Spartacus, the slaves did not simply flee into the countryside; they recruited more and one must conclude, he argues, that the wish was for war not simply freedom.[21]

One must also attribute a lack of perception on the part of the slaves for this suggestion to work. The slaves involved in these three revolts, which in hindsight seem rather similar, would have all to have made the same mistake. Those participating in the first war might be forgiven but those in the following two should have learnt better, one would have thought. In addition, although there was only thirty years between them, then there must have been no memory lingering of these wars, since every time they made the same error of having too many in their army to escape the notice of the Romans.

An added difficulty for such a view is that Diodorus himself interpreted the events in Sicily as wars, and Appian and Plutarch described Spartacus as leading a slave rebellion. Why then is there this tendency, usually uncommon in ancient history, to discount the few explicit ancient sources which we have? It has to be granted that often Diodorus and Plutarch are not considered the most reliable historical writers, but one meets such a disregard with more esteemed authors such as Thucydides and Aristotle.

Take the example of Sparta, which has been called the place where one sees clearly the open hostility between free and slaves in the ancient world. The general view is that in most cities such antagonism is hidden because the slaves were inert and helpless and lacked unity, whereas the masters were always ready to unite against them. In Sparta however the helots spoke the same language, were from the same culture, were a people enslaved by invaders and therefore were unified in revolt. Moreover there was a great many of them. Thucydides in a passage not about Sparta but one merely trying to stress the number of slaves in Chios says *'There were many slaves in Chios – more, in fact, than in any other city except Sparta.....'* (8.40)

About this city, we are informed that every year the main magistrates, the ephors, declared war on the helots so that they could be killed without incurring any religious pollution (Plutarch, *Life of Lycurgus*, 28.7). Aristotle wrote that the helots were always on the look-out for any mischance that might befall their masters (*Politics*, 2.9.1269a38–9).[22] They were readier than other slaves to use violence against their masters, not as Finley points out because

---

[21] Piccinin, 2004, p. 194.
[22] See Thucydides, 4.80. As Luraghi points out, this kind of treatment probably contributed to a sense of helot identity and was a source of social cohesion which in turn rendered them more able to organize resistance, in Luraghi, 2002, p. 68.

they were more badly treated but because they were better organised.[23] The Messenian helots took advantage of the Theban army under Epaminondas entering the Peloponnese in 369–370 BC to win their freedom and to establish the city of Messene. Yet this is seldom called a successful slave revolt.

So the sources tell of continual hostility between the Spartans and their workforce which often resulted in violence. This seems to have caused more unease among ancient observers than the usual slave-master relationship in that they recorded it as being especially harsh and brutal. Plutarch, for instance, is keen to distance his hero Lycurgus from the famous aspects of helot treatment, in his biography. And we read the comment in Athenaeus,

> *"In book seven of his Greek history, Theopompos says of the Helots that they are also called Heleatai. He writes as follows: The conditions of the Helot race are in every respect inhumane and horrible. These people were enslaved by the Spartans a long time ago; some of them originate from Messenia, while the Heleatai formerly inhabited the territory called Helos in Lakonia." (Deipnosophistae 6.272.)*[24]

The view of the Spartans almost permanently at war with their own workforce has not however gone unchallenged.[25] One response has been to say that what we see are not slaves rebelling since helots are not slaves,[26] and the other more recent strand is to say that they were slaves but in fact did not rebel very often in spite of what the ancient evidence says.

Richard Talbert has put forward the argument that the helots did not revolt very often because they had no leadership potential.[27] Although our

---

[23] Finley, 1959, pp. 145–164 observes that it is not maltreatment that leads to revolt but opportunity. Revolt requires organisation, courage and persistence, p. 159.

[24] One can see a similar sympathy in the remarks of Dio Chrysostom: *"Look at the example of the Messenians; after an interval of how many years was it that they got back both their freedom and their country? After the Thebans had defeated the Spartans at Leuctra, they marched into the Peloponnese together with their allies and forced the Spartans to give up Messenia; they resettled all the people who were descended from the Messenians who had previously been the Spartans' slaves and were called Helots. No one says that the Thebans did this unjustly, but rather with great honour and great justice."* On Slavery and Freedom, 2.28.

[25] Paul Cartledge comments in his article (1985, p. 42) that the helots revolts should be seen as slave uprisings adding the caveat that we should interpret the term slave loosely. Thomas Figueira, 1999, pp. 211–244 argues that the helots' uprising is not a slave rebellion but nationalist revolt. The two are not mutually exclusive although this is not how he argues the case. Figueira points out the special nature of the helots, which helps to account for their favourable treatment in ancient sources.

[26] This is too large a debate to enter into here. Those who see a sharp distinction rely on Pollux, *Onomasticon* 3.83 where he describes helots as being between slave and free. For the moment it should be noted that there are plenty of references in the ancient sources to the helots as slaves. See for instance Thucydides 5.23.2 which appears to be a verbatim treaty between the Spartans and Athenians.

[27] *"In brief we should expect helots to have been relatively ignorant, simple people, almost without education or awareness of the outside world. Few, if any, can even have gained the chance to develop the skills, let alone the sophistication, to make them natural leaders or agents for change."* Talbert, 1989, p. 30.

From Captivity to Freedom

sources record the helots as continually dissatisfied and rebelling whenever possible, this is not acceptable for Talbert who simply rejects the stories as wrong. Helots may have smarted under their haughty rulers but they suffered them passively, whatever Aristotle or Thucydides might say.[28] Talbert observes:

> *"Like the lower orders in many societies throughout human history, helots knew their place within severely limited horizons, clung to it and seldom thought coherently about how to alter it, regardless of how humiliating or undesirable it might seem to others."*[29]

Michael Whitby also challenges the conventional view of the Spartans as constantly afraid of their own workforce, who rebel on every conceivable opportunity.[30] His argument is that, although the Spartans may have cruelly exploited their helots, they were not afraid of them. For him, those who suggested otherwise are simply wrong:

> *"Thus the two most intelligent ancient sources, Thucydides and Aristotle, support the negative interpretation. But intelligent judgments need not be right or universally valid and this may be true of Sparta."*[31]

With an approach similar to the argument that gives more prominence to the free participants in the Roman Republican slave wars, Nino Luraghi has put forward the idea that the *perioikoi* were more important in the helot revolts than our sources have led us to believe because they had more leadership potential, echoing Talbert's disbelief that the such lowly people as the helots could produce leaders.[32]

The argument that the helots are not properly slaves is perhaps a more convincing one. The helots clearly are a special case and this can be seen in the sympathy with which ancient sources describe them. Nevertheless it is

---

[28] As he observes at the end of his article 1989, p. 39.

[29] He further remarks that although the Spartans had very little to fear from their slaves: *"Nonetheless it did still make sound sense for the remarkable tradition of an annual declaration of war upon the helots by the ephors to be maintained."* 1989, pp. 33–34. He goes on to say that the *krypteia* where young Spartans went out murdering helots was also useful as the main purpose was not so much to cull the helots as to blood the Spartans. And, he adds, it probably did not happen that often because the Spartans would not want to provoke the helots.

[30] *"I prefer the alternative of a Sparta whose citizens were sufficiently arrogant to believe the myths of their own superiority."* Whitby, 1994, p. 111.

[31] 1994, p. 108. He doubts the reality of the slaughter of 2,000 helots related by Thucydides, p. 98 and refers to Talbert's article as if the latter had some arguments in favour of his view apart from the fact that he did not believe it. In fact all Talbert says is *"Assuming that the story is to be credited at all..."* 1989, p. 24.

[32] Luraghi, 2002, p. 68, although there was even a word for the leaders of the helots, the mnoionnomoi, discussed by Ducat, 1990, p. 63.

very difficult not to see a connection between helots and slaves.[33] They were not free, although they could be set free, they performed the work that slaves performed in other societies and therefore when they fought back, it might seem quite logical to include this among slave revolts, while admitting that there were special circumstances which enabled them to be more successful than the average slave.

However the tendency has been *not* to include these rebellions as uprisings of slaves, continuing the trend of denying the ability or the inclination to rebel to those in bondage. This is most puzzling when one considers what the sources say. It is nevertheless true that one cannot, and should not, simply adopt the attitudes of the ancients. On the other hand, to discount all the evidence, which points to the involvement of slaves, is an unusually rigorous procedure, and not only unprecedented but ultimately sterile.

Plutarch and Appian both give accounts of an enormous and damaging slave rebellion in Italy under the leadership of Spartacus. Diodorus clearly describes two slave wars in Sicily, which according to him were provoked by the cruel treatment by their masters. Indeed he goes on to generalize to say that, if masters treat underlings badly, they will want to kill them. He does not say they will want to run away.[34]

And he also describes how the slaves felt – which one would think was not the emotion of those avoiding warfare:

> *"All of them [the slaves] were equipped with the best of weapons: a rage that was directed at the destruction of their arrogant and overbearing masters".* (Diodorus Siculus, 34/35.2.24b).

All the more puzzling is the fact that these episodes are unique in bringing these usually invisible persons, that is slaves, to the forefront of the historical narrative. One might think they would receive special attention rather than being dismissed either as the product of a peculiar set of circumstances, which were nevertheless condemned to fail from the start, or simply nationalist uprisings in disguise. In fact, what seems more to be the case is that there are peculiar circumstances surrounding the sources which inform us of these episodes and that, in fact, slave revolts were probably more common than the state of our ancient texts would indicate.

The issues facing the ancient historian may be highlighted by a comparison with revolts in the modern world. A glance at Aptheker's study of American slave revolts reveals a heavy reliance on personal letters and contemporary newspapers, exactly the sort of primary source not extant from the ancient

---

[33] Xenophon in his *Constitution of Sparta* does not even mention helots but refers only to slaves. I am grateful to Noreen Humble for this observation.
[34] See his comments at 34/35.2.33.

world. Even with this type of evidence, the modern historian faces, as Aptheker illustrated most effectively, exaggeration, distortion and censorship, which we can see more clearly in the modern world because of the nature of the evidence we have.[35] Aptheker's conclusions are as fitting for the ancient as for the modern world:

> *"Yet, it is highly probable that all plots, and quite possibly even all actual outbreaks, that did occur, and that are, somewhere, on record, have not been uncovered. And the subject is of such a nature that it appears almost certain that some, perhaps many, occurred and were never recorded."*[36]

Yet this book itself, *American Negro Slave Revolts*, provides an example of the fate of publications on the wrong side of the debate. Orlando Patterson noted in his survey of slavery for the *Annual Review of Sociology* in 1977 that whatever the faults of Aptheker's work:

> *"the total rejection of Aptheker has gone too far. The man and his works have literally been purged from the company of polite scholars."*[37]

Aptheker's thesis was that there were more slave revolts in the US than had previously been thought and his book is a careful documentation of the all the different episodes. He concludes

> *"The evidence, on the contrary, points to the conclusion that discontent and rebelliousness were not only exceedingly common, but, indeed, characteristic of American Negro slaves."*[38]

Such a conclusion, and such a survey of revolt, has, as Patterson observes, been treated with surprising hostility. And as Egerton points out so vividly in the companion essay to this one, the tendency to present slaves as passive grows.

In the twentieth century there had been a largely unsuccessful attempt for scholars from the old 'eastern bloc' countries to build up slave revolts into events of tremendous significance, and to interpret them as early struggles for socialism.[39] The atmosphere of the Cold War led to a general suspicion of enquiry into slavery, and especially slave revolts. The very study of slave revolts betrayed one's political sympathies and both Aptheker and Genovese

---

[35] 1993, pp. 150–161. See Egerton's comment on the difference between recent accounts of Vesey's revolt with the extensive documentary record (article in this volume). See also Jordan's acknowledgement of the role of an assistant archivist who brought to his attention the crucial document for his book, 1993, p. xiv. This type of document or non-literary record is much scarcer for antiquity.
[36] 1993, p. 161.
[37] 1977, p. 426.
[38] 1993, p. 374.
[39] Documented precisely and briefly for Soviet historiography by Rubinsohn, 1987. See McKeown, 2007, especially pp. 30–41 for an overview of the political attitudes affecting scholarship on slavery.

have been labelled Marxists.[40] It would seem that a frequent response to the exaggeration of the importance of the slave revolt has been to minimize their significance. Unfortunately this has meant in some cases an almost total disregard for the evidence given to us by our ancient sources. With the Cold War long gone, it is to be hoped that a more nuanced approach is possible. We need not lose some of the most exciting episodes of ancient history by refusing to believe our eyes when we read about slave revolts.

Bibliography

Aptheker, H. (1993), *American Negro Slave Revolts*, New York (6th edition, first publ. 1943).
Bradley, K. (1989), *Slavery and Rebellion in the Roman World, 140BC–70BC*, London.
Cartledge, P. (1985), 'Rebels and Sambos in Classical Greece', in P.A. Cartledge and F.D. Harvey (eds.), *Crux:Essays in Greek History presented to G E M de Ste Croix*, London, pp. 16–46.
Dahomey, J. (2003), 'Slavery and Law: Legitimations of an Insurrection', in Dorigny (ed.) 2003, pp. 3–16.
Davis, D. B. (1975), *The Problem of Slavery in the Age of Revolution*, Ithaca.
Dubois, L. (2004), *Avengers of the New World: The story of the Haitian revolution*, Cambridge, Mass.
Ducat, J. (1990), *Les Hilotes*, Paris.
Dorigny, M. (2003), *The Abolitions of Slavery*, New York, originally published as *Les abolitions de l'esclavage* (1995) Paris.
Ferrary, J.-L. (1991), 'Le status des cités dans l'empire romain a la lumière des inscriptions de Claros.' *Comptes rendus de l'Academie des Inscriptions et Belles- letters*, Paris, pp. 557–577.
Figueira, T. (1999), 'The evolution of the Messenian Identity', in S. Hodkinson and A. Powell (eds.), *Sparta: New Perspectives* ed., London, pp. 211–244.
Finley, M. I. (1959), 'Was Greek civilisation based on slave labour?', *Historia*, 8, pp. 145–164.
Genovese, E. D. (1979), *From Rebellion to Revolution: Afro-American Slave Revolts in the Making of the Modern World*, Baton Rouge.
Green, P. (1961), 'The first Sicilian Slave War', *Past and Present*, 20, pp. 10–29.
Guarino, A. (1979), *Spartakus: Analyse eines Mythos*, Naples (transl. into German by B. Gullath, Munich 1980).
Heuman, G. and Walvin, J. (2003), *The Slavery Reader*, London.
James, C. L. R. (2001), *The Black Jacobins*, Harmondsworth (first published 1938).
Jordan, W. D. (1993), *Tumult and Silence at Second Creek: An Inquiry Into a Civil War Slave Conspiracy*, Baton Rouge.
Luraghi, N. (2002), 'Becoming Messenian', *Journal of Hellenic Studies*, 122, pp. 45–69.
McKeown, N. (2007), *The Invention of Ancient Slavery?*, London.

---

[40] One of the very few English ancient historians who would describe themselves as Marxist, Geoffrey de Ste Croix, 1981, p. 61 quoted a passage from the preface to the second German edition of 1869 of The Eighteenth Brumaire by Karl Marx: "*In ancient Rome the class struggle took place only within a privileged minority, between the free rich and the free poor, while the great productive mass of the population, the slaves, formed the purely passive pedestal for these conflicts.*" Many modern scholars would seem to subscribe to this view. Ste Croix himself professes not to agree with Marx on this point but he himself in his book gives surprisingly little attention to the fight between slave and free.

Mileta, C. (1998), 'Eumenes III und die Sklaven', *Klio*, 80, pp. 47–65.
Patterson, O. (1977), 'Slavery' *Annual Review of Sociology*, 3, pp. 407–449.
Patterson, O. (1982), *Slavery and Social Death*, Cambridge, Mass.
Piccinin, P. (2004), 'Les Italiens dans le Bellum Spartacium', *Historia*, 53, pp. 173–199.
Robert, L. and Robert, J. (1989), *Claros I. Decrets hellenistiques*, vol. 1, Paris.
Rubinsohn, W. Z. (1971), 'Was the Bellum Spartacium a servile insurrection?', *Rivista di filologia e d'instruzione classica*, 99, pp. 290–299.
Rubinsohn, W. Z. (1987), *Spartacus' Uprising and Soviet Historical Writing*, Oxford.
de Ste Croix, G. E. M. (1981), *The Class Struggle in the Ancient Greek World*, London.
Schwartz, S. B. (2003), 'Resistance and accommodation in eighteenth-century Brazil', in Heuman and Walvin (eds.), pp. 626–634, reprinted from *Hispanic American Historical Review*, 57 (1977), pp. 69–81.
Shaw, B. (2001), *Spartacus and the Slave Wars*, Boston, Mass.
Talbert, R. J. A. (1989), 'The role of helots in the class struggle at Sparta', *Historia*, 38, pp. 22–40.
Verbrugghe, G. P. (1973), 'The "*Elogium*" from Polla and the First Slave War', *Classical Philology*, 68, pp. 25–35.
Verbrugghe, G. P. (1974), 'Slave rebellion or Sicily in revolt?', *Kokalos*, 20, pp. 46–60.
Verbrugghe, G. P. (1975), 'Narrative Pattern in Posidonius', History' *Historia*, 24, pp. 198–204.
Vogt, J. (1974), *Slavery and the Ideal of Man*, Oxford (transl. T. Wiedemann, first published 1965).
Whitby, M. (1994), 'Two Shadows: Images of Spartans and Helots', in A. Powell and S. Hodkinson (eds.), *The Shadow of Sparta*, London, pp. 87–126.
Wiedemann, T. (1981), *Greek and Roman Slavery*, London.
Yavetz, A. (1988), *Slaves and Slavery in Ancient Rome*, New Brunswick.

DENYING THE EVIDENCE: SLAVE REBELLIOUSNESS AND THE DENMARK VESEY DEBATE

Douglas R. Egerton

Former slave Israel Nesbitt was a very old man when WPA interviewer Stiles Scruggs knocked on his door. Nesbitt spoke of his own hard life, and how he advised his children *"to get all de schoolin' they can"* and to *"trust in God."* But then he began to tell a story that caught Scruggs's attention. His great-grandfather, he said, was Robert Nesbitt, a man who knew all *"'bout de Vesey uprisin'."* According to Israel's grandfather, who heard the tale from Robert himself, Nesbitt and Denmark Vesey were *"friends,"* and as such, Robert found himself invited to a nocturnal gathering at the black carpenter's house. *"My great-granddaddy attended a meetin' one night,"* Israel insisted. Vesey spoke of his planned exodus from Charleston, but Nesbitt wanted no part of it. *"[H]e tried all de time to show Vesey he was ridin' to a fall and was playin' wid dynamite. . . . He tell Vesey he was takin' too big a dare."*[1]

Poor, deluded fool. Had Israel Nesbitt been lucky enough to live in our enlightened time, or had wit enough to discern the truth for himself, he would have understood that the stories told to him by his grandfather were a colossal fraud. His great-grandfather could not possibly have attended a secret meeting at Vesey's Bull Street house, since no such meetings existed. Were he a bit less credulous, Israel would have realized that one of two things were true. Either his great-grandfather was a liar of the first order, who bragged to his family of acquaintances he in fact did not have. Or, and this is more likely, since it would be irrational to boast of a friendship with a man who in fact was quite unimportant, Israel simply failed to grasp the sad fact that his ancestor was part of a far-flung conspiracy of Charleston magistrates, white clergymen, black ministers, and lowcountry planters designed to shut down the city's African Methodist Episcopal (AME) Church and identify the innocent Vesey as a convenient *"fall guy."*

---

[1] Interview with Israel Nesbitt, in Rawick, 1972, pp. 261–263. Robert Nesbitt, *"A Free Man,"* was arrested on July 3 but discharged, *"the testimony against [him] not being sufficient to bring [him] to trial."* See Kennedy and Thomas, 1822, p. 187.

From Captivity to Freedom

For well over a century following the events of 1822, Denmark Vesey was regarded as the mastermind of the largest slave conspiracy in North American history. Born a slave in the Danish colony of St. Thomas around 1767, Denmark was purchased and brought to live in Charleston by Captain Joseph Vesey. Winning a city lottery in 1799, Denmark purchased his freedom, and for the next twenty-two years earned his living as a carpenter. Unable to purchase his children, and furious with city authorities for routinely closing the AME Church, Vesey resolved to orchestrate a rebellion followed by a mass exodus from Charleston to Haiti. His plan called for Vesey's many recruits to rise at midnight on Sunday, July 14 – Bastille Day – slay their masters, and sail for Haiti and freedom.

But starting in the early 1960s, this commonly accepted story came under fire from a number of historians who have, as one scholar has put it, "*attempt[ed] to make Denmark Vesey disappear.*" This chapter surveys the historiography of the past four decades and compares the recent revisionists' accounts of the Vesey affair with the extant documentary record. In the process, it discusses the profound differences between the two, as well as the extraordinary leaps of logic that one must engage in to wish Denmark Vesey away. Finally, the chapter explores *why* it is that some modern writers appear to have a hard time accepting the reality that a man like Vesey could exist, and why he was able to recruit so many followers during the spring of 1822.

The idea that men like Robert and Israel Nesbitt remembered stories that never existed is an old one and dates back to 1964. In that year, Richard C. Wade, the author of a pioneering and still sound study of *Slavery in the Cities*, suggested in a now-famous essay that the Vesey conspiracy was little more than angry, "*loose talk*" on the part of black Charlestonians. Despite its publication in the prestigious *Journal of Southern History*, Wade's essay never found many adherents, and for a variety of sound reasons. First, the entire theory was fundamentally at odds with the data presented in his own monograph, which demonstrated that the slave controls necessary to uphold the peculiar institution tended to break down in urban areas. Moreover, Wade's thesis was informed by the flawed notion that urban slaves, enjoying the relative freedom of southern towns, would not risk their precious quasi-liberty by banding together with men like Denmark Vesey. For some men, like Robert Nesbitt, that was obviously true, although one suspects that had Nesbitt been a country slave, his caution would have been just as strong. But as to Wade's larger theory, the late John Lofton, who wrote an early account of Vesey's plot, had an obvious response: "*Revolutionary movements have usually been led and widely supported, not by the most deprived class but by those who were better off*" and so "*wanted to remove remaining vestiges of tyranny precisely because they could visualize and appreciate the advantages of freedom.*"[2]

---

[2] Wade, 1964, pp. 143, 148; Lofton, 1983, p. xi.

Far more seriously, Wade not only constructed his theory on a faulty premise, he supported his argument with faulty data. He misidentified key actors in the saga, such as Peter Prioleau, whom he rechristened "Devany Prioleau," and even fused mulatto turncoats William Penceel and George Wilson into a single individual named "George Pencil." Worse still, as William W. Freehling observed in an influential rebuttal essay, Wade carefully crafted his prose in way that implied that important white contemporaries shared his *"loose talk"* thesis. "*Governor [Thomas] Bennett probably believed in a plot of some kind*," Wade suggested at one point. Bennett's niece, "*if she believed that a conspiracy existed at all*," he wrote in another, "*thought it surely had not extended far enough to justify the massive retaliation of the courts*." These artfully phrased sentences, to be blunt, were disingenuous at best, since, as Freehling noted, Bennett absolutely *did* believe that there was a deadly conspiracy afoot. Even a cursory glance at the Bennett family correspondence – and Wade's research indicated that he gave it far more than that – clearly revealed that their only doubts pertained to the Charleston court's methods, not their conclusions. As Bennett's niece, Anna Hayne Johnson, put it: "*I have never heard in my life, more deep laid plots or plots more likely to succeed.*" It gives me no pleasure to say this, but if one of our students read that letter and then concluded that Anna in fact doubted the existence of a conspiracy, we would probably accuse them of consciously twisting data to fit a preconceived theory. In fact, it is hard to read Freehling's devastating deconstruction of Wade's essay without concluding that this was far more than simply an example of sloppy scholarship.[3]

Perhaps because of this, Wade's theory was generally relegated to dismissive footnotes, when it was mentioned at all. Scholars who touched upon Vesey in the years since 1964 – Norrece T. Jones, Bernard Powers, Margaret Washington, Stanley Harrold, Marcus Rediker, and of course William Freehling – rarely even bothered to cite Wade's article.[4] Then came 2001, and the publication of Michael P. Johnson's essay in the *William and Mary Quarterly*, not so much an updating as an extension of Wade's thesis. No longer was this a misunderstanding of "*angry talk*" on the part of the enslaved, but rather a Machiavellian plot in which Vesey was merely a passive "*fall guy*" and his friends "*victims of an insurrection conspiracy conjured into being*" by Mayor James Hamilton and five or six other white politicians bent on closing Charleston's African Methodist Episcopal Church.[5]

---

[3] Wade, 1964, pp. 152–153 (emphasis added); Freehling, 1994, p. 279 note 20; Anna Hayne Johnson to Elizabeth Haywood, July 18, 1822, Haywood Papers, Southern Historical Collection (SHC), University of North Carolina.

[4] Jones, 1990, p. 287; Washington, 1988, p. 380; Harrold, 2000; Rediker and Linebaugh, 2000, p. 299; Freehling, 1990, p. 579.

[5] Johnson, 2001, pp. 915–917.

Johnson devised this argument after noticing the differences between the handwritten trial documents housed in the South Carolina Department of Archives and History, and the pamphlet version that magistrates Lionel Kennedy and Thomas Parker published in late 1822 under the title of *An Official Report of the Trials of Sundry Negroes*. There indeed are differences, apart from small editorial changes, such as cleaning up grammar or adding the first names of the men who occasionally represented the accused. The pamphlet version includes a long narrative of events, as well as references to later trials, such as that of coachman John Horry, for which the handwritten documents are silent. Johnson even suggests that there is no evidence that Vesey himself ever stood trial, since that event, as well as *"the presence in court of . . . G.W. Cross as his counsel"* is mentioned only in the *Official Report* and not clearly indicated in the far messier trial documents.[6]

The explanation for this, however, is quite simple, and requires no elaborate hoax on the part of Charleston magistrates. The court documents that remain from the Virginia trials of 1800, when the enslaved rebel Gabriel and his followers organized for their freedom, ranged anywhere from lengthy, carefully drafted depositions to hastily scribbled notes on small scraps of paper. By comparison, the handwritten trial documents from 1822, which were prepared at the governor's direction to be turned over to the state assembly, are uniformly neat and precise. No hurried scrawl mars the roughly eighty-six pages of documents, each drawn by the same patient hand. Clearly, the extant handwritten materials, like the later *Official Report*, were based upon fragmentary court scraps that were tossed away after being transcribed by a Charleston clerk. Lacking modern stenographic capabilities, and uninterested in modern archival or preservation techniques, the court obviously saw no reason to retain random bits of data that now existed in two more readable forms.

Curiously, Johnson admits as much by conceding that neither version of the trials included any of *"the questions the court posed to witnesses,"* although he has no doubt that such questions indeed *"preceded certain testimony."* But if Johnson acknowledges that neither the extant manuscripts nor the *Official Report* contain a record of every single word spoken in the workhouse courtroom, it is unclear why he then insists that neither Vesey nor Horry ever actually stood trial. There is, of course, another explanation. George Cross, Vesey's attorney and sometimes landlord, was, like Robert Nesbitt, either a colossal liar or part of Mayor Hamilton's elaborate hoax. Johnson observes that the handwritten manuscripts never mention *"the presence in court of . . . G.W. Cross as [Vesey] counsel,"* while the pamphlet version did. Johnson's longtime friend, former colleague, and Beatle biographer Jon Wiener agrees that *"[t]here is*

---

[6] Johnson, 2001, p. 933.

nothing suggesting" that Vesey ever stood trial. But, would not George Cross know whether he had been present at a trial? And if not, would he be willing to allow Kennedy and Parker to insist that he had been in their *Official Report*, which Johnson alleges "*routinely falsified the June court proceedings?*" Clearly then, the nefarious Cross was part of Hamilton's conspiracy. So too, evidently, was the white witness who told Martha Proctor Richardson that he had sat in on Horry's trial and heard the coachmen tell his master that he intended to "*kill him, rip open [his] belly & throw [his] guts in [his] face.*"[7]

Not surprisingly, Horry swung from the gallows after that confession. Johnson, however, has his own explanation for who died, and who lived. Allowing "*for exceptions,*" he writes, "*black men [like Vesey] who did not admit guilt were executed,*" whereas those who played along with the magistrates Machiavellian hoax and confessed were spared.[8] Even leaving aside the fact that one of those exceptions was Denmark's son Sandy Vesey, who like Nat Turner and John Brown, pled guilty but was transported rather than executed, it might appear that Johnson could actually use numbers to prove his theory. There are, however, other ways to analyze this data. Typical for most failed slave conspiracies in North America was the hard fact that the first rebels to be captured were virtually doomed to swing. Once white fury dissipated, however, those rebels who were captured late had a better chance of survival. This was certainly the case with Gabriel's men in 1800. Those fortunate enough to be tried after Thomas Jefferson warned Governor James Monroe that "*there is a strong sentiment that there has been hanging enough*" were virtually guaranteed a sentence of transportation rather than execution.[9]

The same holds true in Charleston in 1822. Of the forty-seven men tried between July 2 and July 26, thirty were hanged, ten were acquitted, two were whipped, four were transported, and one died in the jail. Or, 63% were hanged, and 8.5% were transported. But on July 26, twenty-two men were hanged in one ghastly morning along the low wall called The Lines. Some were shot while slowly strangling, and white Charleston's collective wrath finally began to dissipate. "*The day before I felt strangely firm about*" the executions, confessed Mary Beach, but "*by evening my distress about the business returned.*"[10] At this point the numbers reversed. For the fifty-seven men tried *after* that date, five were hanged, fourteen were acquitted, one was whipped, one died in jail, two emigrated, and thirty-four were transported. Or, now 8.7% were hanged, but fully 59.6% were transported. As Thomas Carlyle

---

[7] Wiener, 2002; Johnson, 2001, p. 933; Johnson, 2002, p. 196; Martha Proctor Richardson to James Screven, August 7, 1822, Arnold and Screven Papers, SHC.
[8] Johnson, 2001, p. 947.
[9] Thomas Jefferson to James Monroe, September 20, 1800, Jefferson Papers, Library of Congress.
[10] Beach to Gilchrist, July 25, 1822, Beach Letters, SCHS. This letter is misdated, since Beach writes in the past tense of the "*22 [who] were executed*" on July 26.

aptly observed, "*you might prove anything by figures*," and there is quite a danger is supposing that Johnson's numbers sustain a theory supported by *no* contemporaneous voice, black or white.

The myth that some Carolina whites expressed uncertainty about the reality of a conspiracy in 1822 is an old one, but utterly without foundation. Writing in the *Quarterly* in 2001, book review editor Robert Gross erroneously insisted that "*[d]oubts were raised at the time.*" Michael Johnson continued to perpetuate this myth by writing that the "*doubts about the plot expressed by Governor Thomas Bennett and [his brother-in-law,] United States Supreme Court Justice William Johnson,*" were solid enough to convince Richard Wade that there was no conspiracy. Justice Johnson's extensive correspondence, however, makes it quite clear that the only caveats he expressed were about the courts' methods, not its findings. And what about Governor Bennett's alleged doubts? Writing to Charles Cotesworth Pinckney and the other board members of the Charleston Bible Society on October 1, the governor spoke of "*the late conspiracy*" and what he learned about it from "*one of the conspirators, whose veracity was unimpeached by the Court.*" The plot, Bennett insisted, in an attempt to remove its geographic focus away from Bull Street and his own house, originated in "*the mind of Gullah Jack and not of Vesey.*" Who was the conspirator of whom Bennett spoke, the man in whom he placed such confidence? According to both Mary Lamboll Beach and John Potter, Thomas Bennett accompanied Jacob Axson, the expensive Charleston attorney he had hired, to the trial of his domestic slave Rolla Bennett. Insisting that he would not believe in Rolla's guilt until "*he heard it from his own lips,*" the governor sat stunned when Rolla sadly replied that while he would not have killed his master himself, he had found another rebel to undertake the task for him.[11]

Poor naive Governor Bennett. Despite the best efforts of Wade, Gross, and Johnson to transform him into a nonbeliever, the governor not only clearly accepted the existence of a conspiracy, but he appears to have believed that he actually heard Rolla wish him dead on the afternoon of June 19. Perhaps he too was a member of the vast conspiracy designed to shut down the African Church and crush his own political career. Unhappily, however, from the perspective of those modern scholars who would like to make "*Denmark Vesey disappear,*" as Eugene Genovese once put it, Bennett's views were shared by a good many of his black neighbors. Writing in mid-century, Carolina-born Daniel Alexander Payne, the third great leader of the Philadelphia AME Church, wrote of the suppression of the Charleston congregation after the efforts of "*the heroic, but luckless Denmark Vesey, to overthrow the infernal system*" of

---

[11] Gross, 2001, p. 913; Thomas Bennett to Charles Cotesworth Pinckney, October 1, 1822, SCHS; Beach to Gilchrist, July 5, 1822, Beach Letters, SCHS; John Potter to Langdon Cheves, July 10, 1822, Cheves Papers, SCHS.

slavery. Payne also noted that when a white mob began to search for the Reverend Morris Brown, "*General James Hamilton interposed, and after secreting Elder Brown in his own house for a certain time, gave him a safe passage*" to the north.[12]

Payne told much the same story in his later *History of the African Methodist Episcopal Church*. From whom did he get this information? And why would Mayor Hamilton risk his political career by protecting Morris Brown if his goals were advance his own political career by shutting down Brown's church? According to his autobiography, *Recollections of Seventy Years*, Payne served as the "*illiterate*" Brown's "*private secretary*" in the years between his banishment and death in 1850. Who else could have told him of these events besides Brown and Charles Corr, who was also banished to Philadelphia in late 1822? Or are we to believe that for nearly two decades, Payne labored as Brown's secretary, yet the two men never spoke of Vesey? As for Mayor Hamilton's behavior, perhaps the simple answer is that he distinguished between "*guilty*" conspirators like Vesey and innocent men like Brown and Corr and so risked his career by hiding Brown within his own home, a fact that has yet to appear in any of the new, revisionist accounts of the episode.[13]

More to the point, as the cautious Morris Brown well knew, Charleston's African Church was routinely in violation of two state laws, which is why city authorities consistently closed it down. Under South Carolina statutes of 1800 and 1803, blacks were permitted to gather for religious worship, but only after the "*rising of the sun*" and before the "*going down of the same.*" Moreover, state laws demanded that a "*majority of [the congregation] shall be white persons.*" Hamilton and his city council had no need to concoct an elaborate hoax; if they wished the African Church closed, the mayor had both cause and the legal authority to do so.[14]

Faced with this troublesome fact, of late Johnson has said less about Morris Brown and the church, and more about how Mayor Hamilton concocted the story as a "*wedge issue*" to advance his own political career at the expense of big government nationalists like Thomas Bennett. According to this theory, Hamilton was an incipient nullifier as early as 1822, who seized upon states' rights and proslavery ideology as a convenient path to power. Unhappily, Robert S. Tinkler's recent biography of James Hamilton hardly supports such a theory. Tinkler not only demonstrates that young Hamilton was a neo-Federalist who believed in broad construction, but that his nationalism even survived the Missouri debates. As late as 1824, Hamilton even supported the colonization of emancipated slaves in Liberia. Indeed, Tinkler argues that

---

[12] Genovese, 1979, p. 14; Payne, 1866, pp. 23–24.
[13] Payne, 1891, p. 45; Payne, 1888, p. 94.
[14] 'An Act Respecting Slaves, Free Negroes, Mulattoes, and Mestizoes', December 20, 1800, in Cooper and McCord, 1840, 7, pp. 440–443; 'An Act Regarding Religious Worship', 1803, in Brevard, 1814, 2, p. 261.

Hamilton's *"postwar nationalism was more than a financial or political one . . . it was also emotional and psychological."* As Tinkler adds in his footnote to the debate, he found absolutely no documentation to support any view besides the one that *"James Hamilton believed there was indeed a Vesey plot, and [that] he ruthlessly sought to root it out."* In short, William Freehling clearly had it right nearly four decades ago, when he argued that it was only *after* Vesey's conspiracy that the *"tidewater gentry had grim second thoughts about congressional slavery debates."* To argue otherwise is to engage in teleology. Mayor Hamilton could not have concocted this hoax as a *"wedge issue"* against his enemies, since, as Freehling observes, before 1822 *"most South Carolina planters were inclined toward the optimism of Calhoun rather than the forebodings of [Charles Cotesworth] Pinckney."*[15]

So where does this leave us? Subtle differences between the extant trial documents and the 1822 *Official Report* pamphlet are easily explained by the fact that both are most likely based upon fragmentary court documents, the existence of which even Johnson seems to take for granted. Critics of the courts' legal procedures, most notably Governor Bennett, were critical only of their methods, and not their conclusions, despite persistent attempts by Wade, Gross, and Johnson to hint otherwise. Patterns of executions and hangings can be configured in any number of ways. Black voices in later years – from Israel Nesbitt to Denmark's son Robert Vesey to likely Vesey acquaintance David Walker – spoke of the conspiracy with authority. And Mayor Hamilton, who is now depicted as an ambitious sectionalist, in fact risked his political career by hiding the Reverend Morris Brown in his home and by endorsing the American Colonization Society two years after the events of 1822.[16] Given the complete lack of data to support the view that Vesey was an innocent *"fall guy,"* given the fact that absolutely no document written by a white or black correspondent in 1822 supports this theory – in fact, just the reverse – how does one explain the fact that it keeps returning in various incarnations?

Perhaps a clue may be found in the single word that appears most often in the writings of Johnson and those historians who have found his theory attractive: *heroic*. Johnson suggests that to believe, as did the Reverend Morris Brown, that Vesey planned an extensive slave conspiracy is to adhere to a *"heroic interpretation."* Jon Wiener picks up the chorus in his brief essay on this debate in *The Nation*, as does Winthrop Jordan, who now insists that *"we need to stop requiring slaves to have behaved in ways that we now think would have been heroic."*

---

[15] Tinkler, forthcoming, chapter 2; Freehling, 1965, p. 109.

[16] Hinks, 1997, p. 38, builds a convincing case that one of Vesey's young disciples was David Walker, who moved from his birthplace in North Carolina to Charleston around 1817. At the time that he rebuilt the Charleston AME Church in 1865, Robert Vesey evidently bragged to the Philadelphia Christian Recorder, October 14, that he was the *"son of Denmark Vesey,"* a proud statement that obviously implied he believed his father to be something more than an innocent *"fall guy."*

Drew Faust agrees. "*I have problems with finding heroism as the purpose of history*," she told Wiener.[17]

This is truly curious. Would any modern scholar actually suppose that the "*purpose of history*" is to identify heroes and villains? Black minister Daniel Payne used the term, but one may search the vast historiography of recent slave studies in vain hopes of finding the word "*hero*" or even hints of such hagiographic interpretations in recent studies of Nat Turner, Caesar Varrick, or the Stono rebels. Indeed, recent studies of Vesey emphasize his less attractive traits, such as his domineering manner and his cold willingness to accept the death of non-combatants. Certainly Robert Paquette employed no such gloss to the Cuban insurgents he wrote about in his 1988 study of the conspiracy of La Escalera. And why is this charge leveled only at scholars who write about black abolitionists? Was Henry Mayer accused of embracing a "*heroic interpretation*" of white activist William Lloyd Garrison in his *All On Fire*? Or Stanley Harrold in his balanced and nuanced biography of Gamaliel Bailey?[18] As we enter the 21st Century, is it truly necessary to craft titles like *Denmark Vesey: A Biography of an Exceedingly Complicated and Problematical Personality*?

This raises another question. Does writing a study of Vesey or the New York City revolt of 1712 imply that one believes that slaves were perpetually at the barricades? Michael Johnson has argued that it does, and that books on Vesey or Turner explicitly support Herbert Aptheker's theories of relentless slave rebelliousness. Since a number of writers, and most notably Eugene Genovese in his influential *From Rebellion to Revolution*,[19] have laid out a demographic case for why large slave revolts were less common in North America than in Brazil or the Caribbean, it appears obvious that any biographer of Vesey has merely accepted the task of explaining why the context of Charleston in 1822 allowed for such a vast conspiracy to take place. Would Johnson care to argue that a biographer of Thomas Jefferson is implicitly suggesting that all white Virginians during the age of revolution were hypocritical geniuses with a personality disorder? Would Drew Faust wish to suggest that Andrew Burstein's new character study of Andrew Jackson reveals a hidden penchant for "*finding heroism as the purpose of history*?" If not, why this strange double standard when it comes to biographies of notable black activists?

Moreover, if scholars working in slave studies have declined to paint the men and women they write about in simplistic, glowing terms, why do Johnson, Wiener, and Jordan go to such lengths in demolishing such an obvious straw man? "*I've always written about people so far from being heroes*," Drew Faust

---

[17] Johnson, 2001, p. 915; quotations from Wiener, Jordan, and Faust all appear in Wiener, 2002.
[18] Paquette, 1988; Mayer, 1998; Harrold, 1986.
[19] Genovese, 1979, especially chapter one.

noted, as if she were the only biographer to ever take on a dislikable subject.[20] Since these historians appear eager to embrace the idea that Vesey was no violent abolitionist, but instead a passive victim, perhaps the word *"hero"* might better be replaced with the term *"activist."* After all, that, at bottom, is what Johnson is disputing. But given the paucity of data to support Johnson's theory, what informs this reading of the documents, this attempt to make black agency disappear?

The late Winthrop D. Jordan's contribution to the debate is especially illuminating. Having once given Edward Pearson's collection of Vesey documents a positive review, Jordan then criticized not Pearson's scholarship, but his introduction. In particular, Jordan seized upon Pearson's rather sensible explication of how women resisted their enslavement in ways different from their husbands. Female slaves, Pearson observes, rarely banded together with rebels like Vesey and instead found other ways to resist their bondage, such as feigning illness, stealing, and on rare occasions, administering poison. None of this is a revelation, of course, and one can find references to all of these practices in the writings of Philip Schwarz, Mary Beth Norton, and Marie Schwartz. Yet Jordan disparaged this reasonable observation by writing: *"Clearly we are not yet free from ideological posturing about slave revolts."* Jordan then turned to Richard Wade, who we are to understand was guilty of no such thing. Despite the fact that Pearson was never accused of any transgression worse than sloppiness, and despite the fact that Wade managed to mangle more sources in a single article than Pearson did in a large book, what did Jordan have to say about his scholarship? *"[K]udos for Richard C. Wade."*[21]

"Kudos for Richard C. Wade?" Here is another curious double standard. Why has only William Freehling subjected Wade's scholarship to the sort of grueling test now reserved for Edward Pearson? To ask this is not to excuse Pearson's work, and he himself has conceded that his *"transcription of the trial record is deeply flawed."* But why, decades after Freehling demonstrated just how flawed Wade's *research* was, was Jordan so willing to sign hosannas to Wade's *conclusions*? Perhaps the answer lies not so much in a determination to make Denmark Vesey go away, but rather to make any evidence of black rebelliousness disappear. Admittedly, just as writing a biography about a single black rebel does not necessarily imply that *all* slaves were constantly in a state of overt rebellion, suggesting that Vesey was an innocent victim does not necessarily imply that no slave conspiracies existed in North America. But witness Philip Morgan's impressive list of other slave plots that most likely never existed: New York City in 1741, Antigua in 1736, the Chesapeake in the 1790s, and southern Virginia in 1802. What Marcus Rediker and Peter

---

[20] Faust quoted in Wiener, 2002.
[21] Schwarz, 1988, pp. 92–113; Norton, 1980, pp. 32–33; Schwartz, 2000, pp. 24–25; Jordan, 2002, p. 178.

Linebaugh regard as "*cycle[s] of rebellion[s],*" Morgan depicts as more "*witchcraft scares than slave revolts.*"[22]

The study of history, of course, is never static, and as new data comes to light, old interpretations are inevitably overturned. Leaving aside for a moment the fact that no new data has come to light regarding 1822, it is theoretically possible that Rediker, Linebaugh, Graham Hodges, Peter Hoffer, Barry Gaspar, and Sylvia Frey all have it wrong. All, perhaps, have failed to grasp the essential truth of slave passivity throughout the western hemisphere. Yet Morgan is so anxious to transform Vesey from a black abolitionist into a passive victim that he actually lightens Vesey's skin and turns him into a Charleston brown. Morgan cites page six of Archibald Grimké's pamphlet as evidence that he was a mulatto, but in fact that page says absolutely nothing about Vesey's color. Instead, on the first page of his 1901 study, Grimké employed the single word "*black*" to describe Vesey, as did the 1822 court, which called him "*a free black man.*" Michael Johnson once scoffed that "*[n]o source documents Vesey's physical size,*" and that historians had conveniently substituted the myth of Vesey as a "*big man*" to support the legend of a big conspiracy. Grimké, of course, wrote of Vesey's "*royal body,*" which was "*noted for its great strength.*" It is interesting how the same pamphlet that Johnson ignored when it came to Vesey's size is now being miscited by Morgan when it comes to Vesey's color.[23]

Clearly, the spirit of Stanley Elkins is alive and well, although in a new permutation, much in the same way that Wade's old thesis is alive again in a new formulation. Whereas Elkins refused to recognize the existence of men like Denmark Vesey because they gave the lie to his theory of dehumanized, docile Sambos, "*the perpetual child incapable of maturity,*" this new denial of black rebelliousness in 1822 – or 1736, or 1741, or the 1790s, or 1802 – appears to be based on something quite different, a sense of black cultural independence that militated against overt resistance. As Morgan explains in his *Slave Counterpoint*, the "*major triumph [of the enslaved] was the creation of a coherent culture, [which was] the most significant act of resistance in its own right.*" In short, by "*carving out some independence for themselves*" through their work culture, and especially through the task system of labor, slaves were able to oppose "*the dehumanization inherent in their status. In this way,*" Morgan argues, "*slaves constantly achieved small victories.*" Perhaps, therefore, the implication goes, they did wish to risk their lives by organizing for large victories. Just as Richard Wade once suggested that urban slaves had too much to lose by gambling on a plot like Vesey's, Morgan now argues that by "*creating an autonomous culture, slaves also eased the torments of slavery.*"[24]

---

[22] Pearson, 2002, p. 139; Morgan, 2002, p. 166.
[23] Morgan, 2002, p. 161; Grimke, 1901, p. 1; Johnson, 2001, p. 918.
[24] Elkins, 1959; Morgan, 1998, p. xxii.

Perhaps Morgan's most illuminating remark is his explanation for why there is no separate chapter on resistance in his very large work. "*In a sense,*" he writes, "*the whole book is a study of resistance.*" But do enslaved rebels truly fit into Morgan's model? Peter Coclanis once criticized such studies of the informal slave economy as failing to properly account for the enormous power of the master class and its tendency to use every form of barbarity to control the black working class. Slave life, Coclanis wrote, was "*about labor, black labor, hard, black labor, mostly for the benefit of whites.*" For more specialized studies, such as those written by Betty Wood or Larry Hudson, which stake no claims at being comprehensive studies of slave life, that may be an unfair criticism. But for *Slave Counterpoint*, a book that weighs in at 703 pages, the absence of enslaved rebels is curious indeed. The Stono insurgents receive but two paragraphs, and Gabriel, but three short paragraphs more. In such an interpretation, men who resisted their enslavement by sharpening a sword or picking up a gun simply do not exist. On the other hand, if "*the struggles between masters and slaves were [as] profoundly unsure*" as Morgan theorizes, it also remains unclear why Charleston magistrates would be forced to concoct such an elaborate hoax to shut down an institution as therefore unimportant as the city's AME Church.[25]

Our job is not to create heroes, and perhaps not even to define which of our subjects were heroic or villainous. But neither is it to erase black agency so that the conduct of the enslaved better fits our latest models of labor culture. Nor should we ignore a wealth of documentation that fails to suit our preconceived notions of how the enslaved should behave. Most of all, no scholar should ever forget the cruel reality of the South Carolina planter class, or the fact that the builders of the Charleston workhouse used thick, sand-filled walls to better muffle the screams of those being tortured inside. When Smart Anderson warned Vesey that it was a sin to "*kill the women and children,*" Vesey retorted that Smart "*had not a man's heart [and] that he was a friend to [the] Buckra.*" Our job is not to judge the magnanimity of that reply, but rather to understand the world that produced it.[26]

Bibliography

Aptheker, H. (1943), *American Negro Slave Revolts*, New York.
Brevard, J. (ed.) (1814), *An Alphabetical Digest of the Public Statute Laws of South Carolina*, Charleston.
Coclanis P. (1995), 'Review Essay: Slavery, African-American Agency, and the World We Have Lost', *Georgia Historical Quarterly*, 79, pp. 873–884.

---

[25] Morgan, 1998, p. xxii; Coclanis, 1995, pp. 880–881.
[26] Confession of Smart Anderson, July 12, 1822, Records of the General Assembly, Governor's Messages, South Carolina Department of Archives and History.

Cooper, T. and McCord, D. J. (eds.) (1840), *The Statutes at Large of South Carolina*, Columbia.
Creel, M. W. (1988), *"A Peculiar People": Slave Religion and Community-Culture among the Gullahs*, New York.
Egerton, D. (1993), *Gabriel's Rebellion: The Virginia Slave Conspiracies of 1800 and 1802*, Chapel Hill.
Elkins, S. M. (1959), *Slavery: A Problem in American Institutional and Intellectual Life*, Chicago.
Freehling, W. W. (1966), *Prelude to Civil War: The Nullification Controversy in South Carolina, 1816–1836*, New York.
Freehling, W. W. (1990), *The Road to Disunion: Secessionists at Bay, 1776–1854*, New York.
Freehling, W. W. (1994), *The Reintegration of American History: Slavery and the Civil War*, New York.
Frey, Sylvia R. (1991), *Water from the Rock: Black Resistance in a Revolutionary Age*, Princeton.
Genovese, E. D. (1979), *From Rebellion to Revolution: Afro-American Slave Revolts in the Making of the Modern World*, New York.
Genovese, E. D. (1974), *Roll, Jordan, Roll: The World the Slaves Made*, New York.
Grimké, A. (1901), *Right on the Scaffold, or The Martyrs of 1822*, Washington.
Gross, R. (2001), 'Introduction', *William and Mary Quarterly*, 58.4, pp. 913–915.
Harrold, S. (2000), *The American Abolitionists*, New York.
Hoffer, C. P. (2003), *The Great New York Conspiracy of 1741: Slavery, Crime, and Colonial Law*, Lawrence.
Johnson, M. P. (2001), 'Denmark Vesey and His Co-Conspirators', *William and Mary Quarterly*, 58.4, pp. 915–976.
Johnson, M. P. (2002), 'Reading Evidence', *William and Mary Quarterly*, 59.1, pp. 193–202.
Johnson, M. P. (2003), 'A Conversation with Michael Johnson', unpublished lecture delivered at Yale University, Centre for the Study of the United States.
Johnson, M. P. (2005), 'Captive Minds: What Can Historians Learn From False Confessions?' *Huntington Frontiers* [http://www.huntington.org/Information/frontiers/captiveminds.htm]
Johnson, M. P. and Roark, J. L. (1984), *Black Masters: A Free Family of Color in the Old South*, New York.
Jones, N. T. (1990), *Born a Child of Freedom, Yet a Slave: Mechanisms of Control and Strategies of Resistance in Antebellum South Carolina*, Hanover.
Jordan, W. D. (1993), *Tumult and Silence at Second Creek: An Inquiry into a Civil War Slave Conspiracy*, Baton Rouge.
Jordan, W. D. (2002), 'The Charleston Hurricane of 1822; Or, the Law's Rampage', *William and Mary Quarterly*, 59.1, pp. 175–178.
Kennedy, L. and Parker, T. (eds.) (1822), *An Official Report of the Trials of Sundry Negroes*, Charleston.
Lofton, J. (1964), *Insurrection in South Carolina: The Turbulent World of Denmark Vesey*, Yellow Springs.
Lofton, J. (1983), *Denmark Vesey's Revolt: The Slave Plot. That Lit the Fuse to Fort Sumter*, Kent.
Morgan, P. D. (1998), *Slave Counterpoint: Black Culture in the Eighteenth-Century Chesapeake & Lowcountry*, Chapel Hill.
Morgan, P. D. (2002), 'Conspiracy Scares', *William and Mary Quarterly*, 59.1, pp. 159–166.
Paquette R. L. (2004), 'From Rebellion to Revisionism: The Continuing Debate about the Denmark Vesey Affair', *Journal of the Historical Society*, 4.3, pp. 291–334.
Paquette, R. L. and Egerton, D. R. (2004), 'Of Acts and Fables: New Light on the Denmark Vesey Affair', *South Carolina Historical Magazine*, 105, pp. 7–47.
Payne, D. A. (1866), *Semi-Centenary of the African Methodist Episcopal Church in the United States of America*, Baltimore.
Payne, D. A. (1888), *Recollections of Seventy Years*, Nashville.
Payne, D. A. (1891), *History of the African Methodist Episcopal Church*, New York.

Rawick, G. P. (ed.) (1972), *The American Slave: A Composite Autobiography*, Supplement, Series 1: 2, Westport.
Rediker, M. and Linebaugh, P. (2000), *The Many-Headed Hydra: Sailors, Slaves, Commoners, and the Hidden History of the Revolutionary Atlantic*, Boston.
Tinkler, R.S. (forthcoming), *Ashes of Greatness: Politics and Reputation in the Antebellum World of James Hamilton*, Baton Rouge.
Wade, R. C. (1964), 'The Vesey Plot: A Reconsideration', *Journal of Southern History*, 30, pp. 143–161.
Wiener, J. (2002), 'Denmark Vesey: A New Verdict', *The Nation*, March 11.

Part 5

FREEDOM AFTER SLAVERY

'INDEPENDENT' SLAVES IN CLASSICAL ATHENS AND THE IDEOLOGY OF SLAVERY

Nick Fisher

In the mid fourth century BC, Hermias was (allegedly) a eunuch slave from Bithynia working as a manager for the banker Euboulos of Bithynia; the banker established himself as tyrant over the small Asia Minor cities of Atarneus and Assos, and Hermias, set free, succeeded not only to the bank but also to the tyranny.[1] This Hermias had attended Plato's and Aristotle's lectures in Athens and while he was in power (a sort of philosopher-King) he established his own philosophical school, entertained Aristotle and others at Assos and married Aristotle's niece. After he was brutally killed by the Persians, he was rewarded by Aristotle with a fine burial and a poem celebrating his lifelong and trouble-strewn pursuit of Virtue (*Arete*) and the life of the mind. Our sources do not inform us how long he was a slave and how he came to be castrated; nor is it quite certain that he was originally non-Greek.[2] *Prima facie* there might seem to be a contradiction between Aristotle's close friendship and marriage ties with this eunuch ex-slave, and his forthright defence of the theory of 'natural' slavery, resting on the belief that some peoples were inherently inferior in intelligence and decision-making capacities to Greeks, especially those who came (by a happy coincidence) from the same countries which supplied most of their slaves, countries which by their climatic conditions and/or political regimes inhibited the formation of the capacities

---

[1] Strabo 13.1.57 and Didymus, *On Demosthenes* cols 4–6, and other sources. Didymus' lengthy excursus on him (on which see Harding, 2006, pp. 124–62) emphasises the various different accounts of his career and moral character, quoting among other earlier sources Theopompos, *FHG*, 115 frr.250 and 291, who presents him more as a brutal and murderous tyrant, and also Aristotle's praise poem (which is quoted also by Athenaeus 696a–697b).

[2] It is possible that the sources' assertion that he was a non-Greek, eunuch, slave, may all reflect contemporary rhetorical vituperation (Wormell, 1935; Harding, 2006, p. 128); apparently he was accepted as a competitor at the Panhellenic games. He may have been a Greek living in Bithynia, who suffered enslavement and mutilation.

for free existence.[3] This problem finds its analogues in other aspects of his theory, such as the apparently contradictory opinions regarding the terms under which friendship between master and slave may exist,[4] and between the theory of natural slavery and the recommendation found both in his and a pupil's works that manumission should be offered to slaves as a major incentive.[5]

However that may be, Hermias' career can stand as a striking example of the remarkable possibility of social advancement open to at least a few slaves of unusual talent in the Greek world, and the ways in which such changes of fortune make patent the contradictions of an exploitative system that attempts to justify itself rationally. This paper identifies some slaves in Athens who, like Hermias, seem to have progressed from operating as slaves in the banking, commercial and public spheres to free status, some wealth and in a few cases to citizenship and some political power. It also observes how systematically indeterminate and ambiguous many descriptions of such people in many of our sources are; and finally presents a few, also contradictory, examples of Athenian official responses in the period 355–330 BC with regard to the presence of such independent slaves, more of whom were being manumitted, and thus be thought to have constituted a threat to the ideology of exclusive citizenship.

From at least as early as the 420s BC, conservative sources grumbled at the numbers of independent slaves in the streets of Athens, earning their own money, indistinguishable in appearance and clothes from the free and unable to be punished as slaves should be.[6] It is clear in general that in many economic sectors in Athens and in many other urbanised Greek communities many slaves operated as the trusted agents or managers for bankers, shipowners, overseas traders, and the like. Many operated as craftsmen working in their own small houses or workshops, paying a proportion of their earnings as a fixed fee (*apophora*) to their masters (or to those to whom he had hired them out).[7] Something like a thousand slaves were owned by the state, a good few

---

[3] Cf. e.g. Garnsey, 1996, pp. 107–27. Aristotle would doubtless have avoided the contradiction by believing Hermias to have been one of those relatively few slaves who had been enslaved unjustly and contrary to nature, especially if he had claims to being Greek.

[4] See Aristotle, *Politics*, 1255b 4–15 and *Nicomachean Ethics*, 1161 a30–b10.

[5] Aristotle, *Politics*, 1330a 25–33, Ps. Aristotle, *Oikonomika*, 1344b, 15–17. Some recent studies argue that Aristotle's notion of 'nature' was not immutable for an individual, and hence his idea of 'natural' and beneficial slavery does not exclude the possibility that careful training by good masters might fit certain slaves for freedom, undo the effects of their original 'natures', and so justify manumission: see e.g. Dobbs, 1994 and Frank, 2004. If so, the contradictions may be removed or at least diminished, though it may be allowed that if this was his view, Aristotle has not exactly made his heterodox position clear. I am grateful to Kelly Joss for alerting me to these interpretations.

[6] Pseudo-Xenophon, *Constitution of Athens*, 1.10–12; Plato, *Republic*, 563b.

[7] e.g. Aeschin., *Against Timarchos*, 1.97

of whom had literacy skills and responsibility to deal with citizens and other free persons, e.g. as under-clerks to the governmental bodies such as the Council, as regulators of money-changing operations in the *agora* and the Piraeus, or in service to the military.[8] Finally, a few of the many slaves who worked as professional sex-partners might have operated with some level of day-to-day independence and choice of whom to accept as punters. These are the categories of slaves above all who would be likely to be offered the possibilities of earning or purchasing their liberty and to respond to this incentive.

There is no agreement on the likely rates of manumission in classical Athens; the limited evidence available does not lend itself to quantification, and scholars disagree on which models or comparisons to apply. For example, the most systematic overall comparative assessment of manumission rates across a very large number of slaveholding societies, in Orlando Patterson's *Slavery and Social Death*,[9] concludes, with all proper caution, that in urbanised and commercial areas of Athens and other cities in classical Greece rates were "*very high*" (though not as high as in Roman Italy in the late Republic and early empire). Paul Cartledge's cross-cultural comparison of likely rebelliousness among slaves and other un-free groups such as the Spartan helots gives a rather different impression, stating that manumission in classical Greece "*seems to have been infrequent, at least in comparison to Roman practice*".[10] I shall argue that there are indications that some Athenians at least had a perception of an increase in manumission through the fourth century: at this stage I shall mention only Xenophon's statement that "*the state itself too would gain if the citizens served in the ranks [of the land army] together, and no longer found themselves in the same company with Lydians, Phrygians, Syrians, and barbarians of all sorts; for there are many such people among the metics*".[11] 'Metics' (*metoikoi*) were foreigners who, if they stayed in Athens longer (probably) than a month, were required to register as resident in an Athenian *deme* with an Athenian as their designated representative; manumitted slaves joined this metic class. This sentence is best explained on the assumption that the majority of those among the metics serving in the army so disparagingly described as 'barbarians' – i.e. non-Greeks – were manumitted slaves. Patterson assigns urban Greek communities to his fourth group of societies, which include most of the slave-societies of nineteenth-century Latin America, whose distinctive patterns included relatively high levels of manumission and the formation of a distinct category of freedmen excluded from citizenship while fully participating in economic life. Characteristic of this group is a relatively high number of slaves operating

---

[8] See Stroud, 1974 = *SEG* 26. 72; *IG* II2 502; *SEG* 25.81.
[9] Patterson, 1982, ch. 10
[10] Cartledge, 2003, p. 145.
[11] Xenophon, *Revenues* 2.3; c. 355 BC.

fairly independently, especially in urban environments. Some of them might have acquired considerable wealth for themselves as well as for their masters and other free operators. Such slaves were more likely to be motivated effectively by the inducement of buying their freedom (or having others buy it for them), or winning it by loyalty and efficiency, rather than by the forceful persuasion of strict discipline. Conversely, a major reason for widespread use of slaves in these sorts of jobs in these societies (including the Greek cities) was the considerable reluctance of free men and especially citizens to be seen to work directly for another; mainly because this type of work diminished their inter-related senses of identity, masculinity, and freedom.[12] Consequently, in these societies, unlike at Rome, manumission did not bring citizenship (in Athens freed slaves joined the metic class). Instead, manumitted slaves joined a separate social space, where they did not compete politically with the citizenry, which guarded its privileges so jealously.[13]

The terminology of 'independent slaves' in Greek is in fact tenuous and problematic and modern scholarship gives a misleadingly consistent picture; this in itself makes a helpful start to the argument. Most accounts employ the Greek phrase οἱ χωρίς οἰκοῦντες those living separately – for these independent slaves operating their own business operations from houses/workshops where they live separately from their owners.[14] Some scholars seek to draw further (misleading) conclusions from the supposed meaning of this phrase in Greek; for example Cohen suggests – but disputably – that linguistically it should mean running their own household (*oikos*), not just living on their own.[15] The implication of these modern accounts is often that this was a commonly used, semi-official, designation. In fact, occurrences of the term in Greek are remarkably few and they do not suggest either that it is a fixed or official category or that it indicated a clearly defined group. It may be applied ambiguously to slaves, ex-slaves, or both, who live on their own.[16] In the single case where the phrase is applied to a class or group of people in our fifth- and fourth-century sources, Demosthenes hypothesises that during a crisis the Athenians in an assembly might waste time unnecessarily debating

---

[12] Patterson 1982, pp. 253–6, 281–4; for a brief, nuanced comparison between manumission in Brazil and the United States, see also Degler, 1970, pp. 1010–1013; detailed studies of manumission in Brazil and Argentina include Schwartz, 1974, Johnson, 1979 and Nishida, 1993.

[13] See also, on how such conceptions of freedom may themselves have been sharpened the more the slaves occupied such roles, see Patterson, 1991 with the qualifications in Raaflaub, 2005.

[14] E.g. Beauchet, 1897, pp. 445–50; Harrison, 1968–72, I, p. 167; de Ste Croix, 1981, p. 142 (though both note carefully the few references specifically using this term and that a number certainly or probably refer to freed persons); Garlan, 1988, pp. 70–1; Fisher, 1993, pp. 52–3; Trevett, 1992, p. 155; Whitehead, 1977, p. 17; and Zelnick-Abramovitz, 2005, pp. 215–6 are properly cautious.

[15] Cohen, 2000, p. 148.

[16] Fullest account in Perotti, 1974; but see also Bieżuńska-Malowist, 1974, esp. pp. 35–37, and her comments on Perotti's paper in Perotti, 1976, pp. 192–3.

whom to mobilise as rowers on the fleet: the metics or 'those living separately' (*choris oikountes*).[17] Later, lexicographers citing this passage were divided on whether *choris oikountes* here designated just freedmen (the majority view) or perhaps both freedmen and slaves.[18] Some say none the less that it must mean slaves, not ex-slave metics;[19] others are doubtful.[20] As Hunt has shown,[21] the Athenians seem to have made extensive use of slaves as rowers in their triremes, but a prudent orator might perhaps not wish to draw attention to this fact unambiguously in the assembly. It is most plausible, I suspect, that Demosthenes deliberately combines with 'metics' an ambiguous phrase which might cover both ex-slaves with their own establishments (who were of course also metics) and also the 'better class' of slaves who operated on their own (some of whom, as we shall see, might have been traders and used to sea-travel). Elsewhere the phrase is explicitly used of a freedwoman, an individual domestic slave who had moved out after being manumitted and lived with her husband ('she was living separately', χωρίς οἰκεῖ).[22] Two conclusions seem to follow: first, that the *choris oikountes* was not an Athenian status-term for a specific category of slaves, however convenient this label may be for us; and second, importantly for this paper, systematic or deliberate ambiguity is likely to characterise orators' discussions of those of non-citizen status.

On the other hand, more specific phrases, 'fee-earning slaves' (*andropoda misthophorounta* or variants) do indicate categories of relatively independent slaves and may be applied both to those slaves who were hired out to another for a daily *misthos* paid to the master and those who lived and worked independently in their living quarters, operating on their own, and paid fixed amounts as a return to their masters (*apophora*).[23]

We do in fact find a systematic indeterminacy of status in reference to individuals in many law court speeches. At times, this may reflect a genuine

---

[17] Demosthenes, *First Philippic*, 4. 36–7.
[18] Harpokration, Suda, Photios and the Lexica Segueriana s.v. *khoris oikountes*, all state in similar terms that the phrase should mean freedmen because only they would 'live apart' from their masters (which of course begs the question); only the entry in the Lexica Segueriana allows the possibility that it might also mean slaves who lived apart.
[19] e.g. Cohen, 2001, p. 150 n.101
[20] e.g. de Ste. Croix, 1981, p. 142, n.9; Zelnick-Abramovitz, 2005, pp. 215–6
[21] Hunt, 1998.
[22] Demosthenes, *Against Euergos and Mnesiboulos*, 47. 67. In the same speech, Demosthenes uses the phrase of a citizen who now maintained his estate separately from his brother (47.35); in other fourth-century authors, Plato so describes the nurses who will look after the children in his new ideal state in a distinct part of the city (*Rep.* 460c), and Aristotle refers to the hypothetical case of citizens of different states who lived apart from one another, but had mutual laws of protection, but even so would not be a single polis (*Pol.* 1280b 17). These cases make it even less likely that it was used as a specific status-designation for slaves.
[23] See especially Perotti, 1976. Examples occur at Aeschines, *Against Timarchos*, 1.97 (slave craftsmen), and Menander, *Arbitrants* 379–80, 408, where the herdsman slave Syros has his own dwelling (though the term *choris oikon* is not used) and is said to pay apophora to his master.

uncertainty in real-life situations, or cases where an individual's status was one of the issues under dispute. Alternatively, explanations in terms of different rhetorical strategies may be offered in different legal contexts, as the importance of identifying status may seem crucial (if difficult) in some cases, and carefully avoided in others. Many individuals mentioned in our law court speeches who seem to be exercising independent agency in banking, overseas trade, or state service, are designated in ways which leave it unclear whether they are slaves or freedmen; and in some cases, narratives reveal that their status was disputed in the courts. More than once Edward Cohen asserts that in such disputed cases the characters are certainly slaves. As part of his general position, which has much to recommend it, that many scholars have been reluctant to face up to the considerable fluidity and mobility in Athenian economic and social life, and to the numbers of extremely wealthy and independent slaves, he berates scholars for refusing to accept the slave status of some of these characters when the sources "*state*" it unambiguously (in his view). He attributes this reluctance to the influence on scholars of their awareness of slavery in North America.[24] A detailed look at the texts suggests rather that there remain genuinely irresolvable, and deeply revealing, ambiguities in many of these texts.

The most successful slaves we hear of fall in the banking sector, in terms of the scale and extent of their managerial roles, and their greater opportunities for attaining manumission, and in a few cases, citizen status. The best-known case is that of the bank originally owned by the citizens Archestratos and Antisthenes. They left the business to their slave-manager Pasion, who was given his freedom either before or after he took over the bank; subsequently, in return for very substantial gifts to the state of warships and shields, he was rewarded with citizenship. His own slave-manager Phormion followed the same career path, first leasing the bank under the terms of Pasion's will (which also established him as guardian to Pasion's sons and second husband to his wife) and then accumulating further wealth through ship-owning[25] and in all probability through his own bank as well.[26] Like Pasion he rose all the way from slavery to freedom and citizenship, and is mentioned casually in a speech of c. 348–6 as one of the richest of the citizens.[27]

It is likely that slaves working in a bank owned by another as chief cashiers could exercise considerable financial power and arrange substantial loans and other deals; and possible that they could manage banks outright. But all our

---

[24] Cohen, 1992; 2000. As we shall see, however, at times he acknowledges ambiguities of status in the sources.
[25] Demosthenes, *Against Stephanos*, I, 45.64.
[26] Demosthenes, *Against Stephanos*, I, 45.66.
[27] Demosthenes, *Against Meidias*, 21.157. See e.g. Davies, 1971, p. 435; Trevett, 1992, pp. 14–17. It is likely that most or all of the metic bankers we hear of who were granted citizenship during the fourth century had similarly started their careers as slaves: Aristolochos: (Demosthenes, *Against Stephanos*,

instances are strikingly marked by disputes and uncertainty. An early example from Pasion's bank concerns his chief cashier, Kittos, who appears in a speech of the 390s arranging substantial loans and deals, while evidently still being treated as a slave, since the proposition that he should give evidence under torture was actively canvassed; as was usual with such challenges to apply evidentiary torture to slaves, it was not actually put into practice. It is remarkable that according to this hostile account Pasion kept switching his ground, between accepting that Kittos was a slave, and claiming that he had been freed and could not be subjected to torture.[28] Whether slaves could manage banks completely in their own right, taking all current financial decisions on loans, investments and so on, remains doubtful, and two instances again from Pasion's bank have produced irresolvable debate. The date of Phormion's manumission by Pasion is not stated and hence it is uncertain whether he had already been manumitted when he acted as *'friend and business partner'* in a maritime loan of the citizen Timosthenes.[29] An even more interesting case is that of the leasing of the bank to four men in 362 by Pasion's sons Apollodoros and Pasikles. Xenon, Euphraios, Euphron and Kallistratos leased it for ten years.[30] At the end of the lease it is stated that Apollodoros and Pasikles "*released them to be free (ἐλευθέρους ἀφεισαν) as they had had very good experience of their activities*". The slightly easier interpretation of this phrase is perhaps "*set them free*", i.e. "*manumitted*";[31] but the alternative meaning "*released them*", i.e. "*set them from all claims*"[32] cannot be excluded. Which way a jury would take it would depend on their expectations of the possible status such lessees might have, which is precisely the point we cannot easily determine. But there is no doubt that slaves performed a variety of important, independent and trusted roles in banking, and the practices of choosing your slave manager to inherit the business and often to marry the bank-owner's widow or into his family seem to be frequent and systemic.[33]

I, 45.63, see Davies, 1971, pp. 60–1); perhaps Blepaios: (Demosthenes, *Against Boiotos*, II, 40.52, IG II2 1675. 29–33); Epigenes and Konon (*Dein.* 1.43). See Davies, 1981, pp. 64–6, Trevett, 1992, pp. 160–2. On the economic roles of Athenian banks, see e.g. Millett, 1991, Cohen, 1992, and the balanced survey of Shipton, 1997.

[28] Isokrates, *Trapezitikos*, 17.11–23, 49–55. Bogaert, 1968, pp. 64–67; Cohen, 1992. The Kittos who appears as a banker in Demosthenes 34.6 is most unlikely, on chronological grounds, to be the same man, but may conceivably be a descendant (see Bogaert, 1968, p. 83).

[29] Pseudo Demosthenes, 49.31; cf. also Phormion's actions reported by Apollodoros in Pseudo Demosthenes, *Against Kallippos*, 52. 5–7. Davies, 1971, pp. 431–2 (also Trevett, 1992, pp. 6–7) argues Phormion must have been freed, to be so acting; Cohen, 1992, pp. 75–6, and Cohen, 2000, pp. 134–5 and 146–7 believes he was still a slave.

[30] Demosthenes, *For Phormion*, 36.10–14.

[31] So Cohen, 2000, p. 134.

[32] So Davies, 1971, pp. 432–3; see also Trevett, 1992, p.38.

[33] Stated explicitly by Demosthenes at Demosthenes, *For Phormion*, 36.28ff. See Cohen, 1992, pp. 61–85; Zelnick-Abramovitz, 2005, pp. 325–6.

Similar issues are raised in the world of overseas trade, the increasingly compartmentalised and separate 'world of the *emporion*'. The most problematic case has long been recognised to be that of Lampis, a shady character in Demosthenes' speech 34 (327/6). Two passages seem to suggest that Demosthenes and his client Chrysippos wished the jury to think of Lampis as a slave. Lampis is described as the 'domestic' (*oiketes*) of Dion,[34] and in the shipwreck he had helped to engineer "*he was saved with the other 'boys' (paides = slaves) belonging to Dion*". The term *oiketes* most commonly (but not invariably) refers to a slave; in this context, *paides* must surely mean 'slaves' rather than 'sons', though it must also be pointed out that the grammatical use of *allos* 'other' in Greek does not necessarily imply that Lampis too is a *pais*. The two passages taken together give a very strong impression that the intention was to suggest Lampis was a slave, while leaving an element of uncertainty.[35] It is surely appropriate to question whether this implied status was correct, or even whether Chrysippos, his brother and his associates know for certain (or cared) what his precise status was, presumably in relation to the laws of a city other than Athens. What seems to me to be particularly interesting is that, though the speaker implies Lampis is a slave and treats him throughout as a crook who is up to a host of deceitful scams with Dion and others, he nowhere makes rhetorical capital out of his slave status or barbarian origins in order to increase the jury's hostility to him. The hint that Lampis was Dion's slave rather than his freedman helped, but was not crucial to his argument; labouring the point might be unhelpful. Lampis is presented as a substantial operator in his own right, he is described as a *naukleros* (ship-owner or one in charge of doing the trading deals for a ship)[36] and is shown working in close association with Dion. He arranged deals and loans both in Piraeus and Bosporus; gave evidence freely before the arbitrator and allegedly 'cheats' the Athenian people by exporting corn from the Bosporus. Taking advantage of the rule allowing exporters to Athens not to pay duty, he then unloads it at Akanthos;[37] it seems likely that he was registered as a metic in Athens, as he is said to be "*living at Athens, with his wife and children here with him*".[38] One might have expected a speaker in an Athenian court not merely to clarify his status but to insist on the insult inflicted both on himself and on the whole city by this no-good slave or at least argue that he was registered as a metic under false pretences. But he chooses not to go down this route. Part of the explanation

---

[34] Demosthenes, *Against Phormion*, 34.5.
[35] Apparently there were three hundred (or, according to a possible emendation of the text, thirty) other 'free persons' lost on the ship.
[36] See Reed, 2003, pp. 102–4.
[37] Demosthenes, *Against Phormion*, 34.37.
[38] Demosthenes, *Against Phormion*, 34.37. Cohen (2000, p. 149) asserts he is "*specifically designated as one of the choris oikountes residing at Athens*" but the word choris is not used.

is probably that the speaker Chrysippos and his brother and partner are themselves non-Athenians, long-term *emporoi* and bottomry lenders (also probably registered as metics, as they spent some time in Athens);[39] Chrysippos appeals, as a benevolent outsider, to the interests of the Athenian people in encouraging traders to bring grain to Athens and in upholding fair trading and punishing cheats to make the market work well.[40] It might well then be dangerous for him to appeal too vigorously to the prejudices of Athenians and to elaborate on an allegation of servile status, especially if it were likely to be disputed, or if indeed Chrysippos was not in fact certain of Lampis' exact status and relation to Dion.[41]

What is clearly also relevant to this reticence is the particular nature of the courts at which these trials take place; the special 'commercial courts' (*dikai emporikai*) instituted c. 350,[42] whose creation reflects both the importance to Athens (highlighted by Chrysippos) of keeping good relations with merchants, ship-owners and bottomry lenders and the cosmopolitanism and indifference to status of the denizens of the *emporia* themselves. These courts ensured swift dealing with cases (probably during the summer trading system)[43] essentially decided on the criterion of whether those who made a deal had complied with the written contract. The procedures in these courts ignored status-distinctions meticulously observed elsewhere, as slaves, freedmen, foreigners and citizens gave evidence in the same way (there was here no torture of slaves).[44] Those from this world, especially if not citizens themselves, were used to dealing with those who might well have been slaves, while acting as agents with authority to strike deals and owning substantial property (including slaves). Such people might often have been in genuine doubt if those they were dealing with were slaves, freed, or free. So, when non-Athenian litigants came to these courts, it might well not seem appropriate to seek to make rhetorical capital out of the hostility and contempt for slaves, standard in other Athenian formal settings. At most they might have thrown out a suggestion, which might have had a more subtle effect, while simultaneously claiming that their opponents were acting as fully responsible agents.

A comparable case occurs in Demosthenes' speech against another shady trader, Zenothemis, delivered around 340. Zenothemis is introduced as an '*underling*' or '*servant*' of Hegestratos the *naukleros* but later is called his partner

---

[39] Reed, 2003, p. 104.
[40] Demosthenes, *Against Phormion*, 34.38–40.
[41] On the deliberate ambiguities in the treatment of Lampis, and a subtle treatment of the rhetorical strategies of Athenians and metics in such legal cases, see Seager, 1966, esp. pp. 180–4.
[42] See Gernet, 1955; Cohen, 1973; Wilson, 1997; Reed, 2003, App. 3; Lanni, 2006, pp. 149–74.
[43] See Hansen, 1983, against Cohen, 1973.
[44] Note especially Demosthenes, *Against Phormion*, 34.28 and 31, where the rhetorical point is made that his opponent called no witness, slave or free. Cf. Lanni, 2006, p. 153.

(*koinonos*).⁴⁵ The term translated as 'servant' (*hyperetes*) can be used to indicate types of slaves, such as a public slave,⁴⁶ but it can also refer to a free man acting as a supporter or collaborator of a more powerful man.⁴⁷ This speech too seeks to excite the hostility of the jury not against merchants and lenders in general, but against a particular "*gang*" of crooks who "*deceived*" the poor victim, Demon; even less attempt is made here to clarify his status or to make anything of a possible slave status. Even though in this case the speaker is Demon, an Athenian and a cousin of his speechwriter Demosthenes the politician, here too the hint of slave status is not developed in the denunciation of these alleged fraudsters.

In other courts it could be very different. Perhaps the most extreme cases of unpleasant and offensive exploitation of prejudice are found in the forensic invectives uttered, strikingly enough, by the son of a slave and a man well experienced in the world of banking and trade deals we have just considered. The many speeches delivered by Pasion's son, Apollodoros, which have survived under the name of Demosthenes but which may well have been largely or wholly composed by Apollodoros himself,⁴⁸ exhibit to a very high degree and in classic form the obsessive sensitivity to personal honour and new status of the ex-slave and new citizen. We can identify in him a touching desire to win honour and approval from the community, through a successful political career and substantial expenditure on liturgies and trierarchies, despite facing much prejudice, insults and hostility from other rich men who frustrated him and treated him with contempt.⁴⁹ Allegedly, he was also prone to display his wealth lavishly on *symposia, hetairai,* and to show off in the streets with a brash manner, loud voice, and a train of three slave-attendants.⁵⁰ More relevantly, among his many appearances in court was a fierce attempt to defend the citizenship laws against alleged abuses in the form of his prosecution of a political enemy, Stephanos, and his alleged long-term lover Neaira, a retired *hetaira*.⁵¹ Finally

---

⁴⁵ Demosthenes, *Against Zenothemis*, 32; cf. Reed, 2003, pp. 100–1.

⁴⁶ e.g. in Pseudo-Demosthenes, *Against Euergos and Mnesiboulos*, 47.35.

⁴⁷ For example, merchants in league with Cleomenes when he ruled Egypt, Pseudo-Demosthenes, *Against Dionysodoros*, 56.7.

⁴⁸ See in general, Trevett, 1992; Zelnick-Abramaovitz, 2005, pp. 328–9.

⁴⁹ He reports one insult – "*the mouse has tasted pitch – he did want to be Athenian*" – Demosthenes, *Against Polykles*, 50.28, and no doubt there was much worse that he did not care to report to a jury. On his liturgies and extravagance, Davies, 1971, pp. 440–2.

⁵⁰ Demosthenes, *For Phormion*, 36.45–56; 45.77–8.

⁵¹ Pseudo-Demosthenes, *Against Neaira*, 59. Apollodoros' preparedness to be deceitful when prosecuting is now further illustrated by the intriguing lead letter, written by Pasion at some point in his career and recently published by Jordan, 2003. In this Pasion instructs a friend or underling Satyrion to "*take revenge on and pursue*" (i.e. prosecute in the courts? or dispose of more violently?) the same Nikostratos and Arethousios whom Apollodoros prosecuted in the courts some time later, with what can now be seen to be deeply misleading statements about their earlier close friendship: see Pseudo-Demosthenes, 53 passim.

and most offensively, his staggeringly hypocritical assault on Phormion, his father's trusted manager and future citizen, includes the absurd allegations that he forged Pasion's will to gain the management of the bank and a 'marriage' with Archippe, Apollodoros' mother, which is even presented as a serious affront to his own honour (*hybris*).[52] At the same time he does not hide the fact that his own citizenship came as a result of the grant from the Athenian people to his father, but he none the less adopts the pose of the orthodox and passionate citizen and slave-owner, and attacks Phormion as a ungrateful barbarian who cannot speak good Greek,[53] a debauched adulterer,[54] and as his ex-slave, who should not insult him, but treat him with respect, as the ordinary jurymen would expect of their own '*Manes*' or '*Syros*'.[55]

Somewhere between these cases there is a comparable, but interestingly different, case of deliberate ambiguity and contradictory rhetorical elaboration in a narrative featuring one Pittalakos, whom a forensic speech asserts, possibly incorrectly, was a public slave. It forms a crucial and dramatic part of Aeschines' prosecution of Timarchos. There were certainly several hundred, perhaps over a thousand public slaves, owned, and maintained by the Athenian state.[56] Many of them probably lived independently and a few seem to have been quite well-off and been themselves owners of slaves. The clearest evidence for this is one, and probably two, instances of owners on the 'lists of freedmen's bowls', *phialai exeleutherikai* (on which more below).[57] In the early Hellenistic period one such slave received public honours for his service to the Athenian army: Antiphates, identified as a *demosios*, who had apparently been assisting a general on a campaign, had in 302/1 BC his grants recorded on a stone adorned with a sculptural relief.[58] Unfortunately the fragmentary inscription gives out before revealing what honours he received (freedom or extra privileges as a metic).

Pittalakos, then, the putative public slave in Aeschines' speech appears as an operator on quasi-equal terms in leisure contexts, in somewhat raffish areas of Athenian life – and here too there are serious ambiguities. In his speech against Timarchos (delivered late in 346/5 BC), Aeschines says more than

---

[52] Demosthenes, *Against Stephanos*, I, 45.4, 6, 35, 39.
[53] Demosthenes, *Against Stephanos*, I, 45.30.
[54] Demosthenes, *Against Stephanos*, I, 45.73.
[55] Demosthenes, *Against Stephanos*, I, 45.86–7.
[56] Jacob, 1928; Lewis, 1990, pp. 254–8; Hunter, 2000, pp. 11–13.
[57] The certain one is ....*kleides demosios*, recorded as manumitting or releasing a slave at *IG* II2 1570.78–9; the possible one occurs at *IG* II2 1566: 33–5 – x son of –achos demo. On 'independent' slaves who owned slaves in the town of Salvador in Brazil, and in some cases supplied them as the price of their own freedom, see. Schwartz, 1974, pp. 625–7, Nishida 1993; on free Negroes who owned slaves in the southern states (often freedmen buying out their loved ones, and hoping to manumit them later), see e.g.. Koger, 1985.
[58] *IG* II2 502; *SEG* 25.81; Lawton, 1995, no. 57 on the relief. On public slaves in military service, Jacob, 1928, pp. 121–2, 171–2.

once that Pittalakos was a state slave (*demosios*) but he does not specify what his job was. Later the narrative reveals that two other characters each had different views on his status. Timarchos' friend and Aeschines' other main target, Hegesandros, brother of a significant politician Hegesippos who was associated with Demosthenes, claimed at one point at least that Pittalakos was his own slave, whereas Pittalakos' defender Glaukon claimed in public he was now free and sought to defend his free status by the legal process of *aphairesis eis eleutherian*: this procedure was designed to rescue an individual wrongly subjected to treatment as a slave, so that the disputed issue of status would be determined in a court. Many scholars have argued that Pittalakos' status is unclear but that he may well have been a state slave who has been manumitted by the time of these events.[59] Cohen[60] states at one point that Aeschines' statement that he was a state slave should be accepted, but earlier[61] added this to a long list of cases where individuals' status was unclear and disputed. In fact, the situation is even more confusing; Aeschines himself (like Demosthenes with Lampis) presents an inconsistent picture for identifiable rhetorical reasons. In the first half of the story he presents him as a state slave with a house and some wealth, involved in gambling alongside wealthy and prominent Athenians, perhaps running some games and cockfights, and engaged in an affair with Timarchos, an attractive free Athenian youth. Here, the story is slanted to emphasise the shame and degradation involved in Timarchos' submitting to the unspeakable sexual desires of a state slave;[62] labelling Pittalakos a slave suits this argument. But it is very remarkable that he does not make the further point that this renders Pittalakos liable to the very laws Aeschines cites later in the speech[63] forbidding a male slave from acting as the 'lover' of a free youth or boy, though it would help his case, and despite the fact that in many other places he falsely asserts that other lovers of Timarchos, even though Athenian, were breaking laws.[64] In the second stage, however, Pittalakos becomes more of a victim, for whom the jury seems to be invited to feel some sympathy, as he is savagely whipped – i.e. is treated with extreme humiliation as a disobedient slave – by Timarchos' new lover, Hegesandros, and ruthlessly frustrated in his legitimate attempts to get legal revenge for the grievous insult (*hybris*).[65] At this point in his narrative Aeschines ascribes to Pittalakos legal rights in assault cases which would be surprising in an

---

[59] Jacob, 1928, pp. 147–89; Todd, 1993, pp. 192–3; Hunter, 1994, p. 231.
[60] Cohen, 2000, p. 131.
[61] Cohen, 2000, p. 111, n. 45.
[62] Aeschin., *Against Timarchos*, 1.54.
[63] Aeschin., *Against Timarchos*, 1.139.
[64] e.g. at Aeschin., *Against Timarchos*, 1.72, 87, 90.
[65] Aeschin., *Against Timarchos*, 1.59–63.

ordinary slave in Athens, though perhaps conceivable for a state slave. Specifically, he began an action against his assailants and the destroyers of his property, though he felt forced to give it up because of the political influence of his opponents. If he were still a state slave, we could conclude that as independent trading slaves had for a decade or so before this speech exercised similar rights in strictly defined commercial cases, some public slaves had acquired exemption from important legal restrictions imposed on others. But it is remarkable that Pittalakos' defender, Glaukon chose, it seems, to oppose Hegesandros' abuse of Pittalakos by invoking the legal procedure known as 'taking away to freedom' (*aphairesis eis eleutherian*), rather than asserting that he belonged to the city, not to a citizen;[66] this strongly suggests the possibility that Pittalakos was an ex-slave, and had been able to accumulate enough wealth to purchase his freedom, whether he had previously been a public or private slave.[67] It might even be, as I have speculated elsewhere, that he had been owned by a collective association, the *genos* of the Salaminioi (a group to which Hegesandros and his brother the more famous politician Hegesippos belonged), who had cultic functions in relation to the sanctuary of Athena Skiras at Phaleron, which may have been a centre of gambling.[68] But the more important point is that Aeschines treats Pittalakos' status in the same contradictory way that he does his role in the story. It helps Aeschines' case to treat him, *qua* lover of Timarchos, as a slave, because he can then claim that Timarchos further degraded himself by this sexual relationship; but Aeschines would not wish to concede Hegesandros' case that he used to belong to him. He prefers to label him a public slave but gives no details of his specific duties. On the other hand, *qua* victim of Hegesandros' violence and contempt, the impression is given (though not made explicit) that Pittalakos is (now) a freedman. We cannot be sure what his actual status was at this time, nor what it may have been in the past; nor can we securely deduce from this text what legal powers a state slave might have, nor be sure of the allegations of a sexual relationship. But we can suggest that slaves who were state-owned (or were owned by a smaller collective group such as the Salaminioi) might be supposed to be able to acquire wealth, associate with the rich in social activities and have a good chance of being freed. But, perhaps most important of all, we see another striking case where an indeterminacy of status is

---

[66] Though at 1.62 Aeschines none the less repeats the claim that he was the property of the city.
[67] See also Zelnick-Abramovitz, 2005, p. 298, who suspects, following Todd, 1993, pp. 192–4, that Pittalakos has been freed, and does not doubt that Pittalakos was, or had been, a public slave. Beauchet's suggestion (1897, pp. 465–6) that this was the appropriate procedure to claim that some one was a public slave seems implausible.
[68] Fisher, 2001, pp. 357–62; 2004. On the Salaminioi and their cultic and social position in Athens, see Taylor, 1997; Lambert, 1997a; 1999.

persistently exploited in a law court speech and a ex-slave (if Pittalakos was such) can be represented as still a slave and carrying the stigma of slavery, where it suited the orator's case.

Given these structural uncertainties and ambiguities over status, it should not then be surprising that we can find in this same period (c.350–320BC) several indications that the Athenian people and politicians took an interest in the barriers between citizenship and other statuses and in changing patterns of the manumission of slaves and its registration. Their responses, however, took the form of clarifications of individual statuses or modifications to manumission procedures, not attempts to reduce the numbers of manumission, as may have occurred in some slave societies facing crises of confidence.[69] One crucial event was the decision to operate a complete review, *diapsephisis*, of citizenship lists in all the *demes* in 346–5BC, which was no doubt stimulated by many internal hatreds and disputes in the *demes*, and certainly produced many further bitter court cases.[70] Those who voted for this proposal must have believed a good many abuses had taken place across the 139 *deme*s, resulting in the enrolment of many who might prove on examination not to be the children of a citizen and a wife of Athenian citizen family. Such a result might be thought to occur where a rich metic or freedman paid a poor family to present his son(s) as their own;[71] where a foreigner claimed to be a citizen (perhaps a citizen captured by pirates, and returned);[72] or where a citizen presented as legitimate the son(s) produced by intercourse with his slave, or with a metic or a foreign mistress, or married a daughter so produced to an Athenian: these are the central allegations in Apollodoros' speech against Neaira and Stephanos, delivered at very much the same time, perhaps in fact shortly before the decision to carry out the general review.[73] Such abuses might well have been relatively easier to perpetrate (or to allege), because of the inadequate documentation of registration of males and the non-registration of

---

[69] Contrast e.g. the frequent attempts (but often ineffective) in many southern states between 1830 and 1860 to limit or prevent manumission of slaves and/or to expel free Negroes from their state, Matison 1948, pp. 149–53; Genovese, 1972, pp. 405–9; Patterson, 1982, p. 259; Schafer, 2003 on Louisiana.

[70] Demosthenes, *Against Euboulides*, 57.49 alludes to it as a time *"when the whole polis, angered at those who had shamelessly jumped into the demes, were all in an agitated state"* (*paroxunesthai* – cf. the same word at Demosthenes, *Against Euboulides*, 57.2); Aeschin., *Against Timarchos*, 1.77–8. See especially Davies, 1977/78.

[71] See perhaps the case in Aeschin., *Against Timarchos*, 1.114–5.

[72] Demosthenes, *Against Euboulides*, 57.

[73] Pseudo-Demosthenes, *Against Neaira*, 59. This trial is usually dated two or three years later than the review, c. 343 BC (e.g. Trevett, 1992, pp. 48–9; Carey, 1992, p. 3; Kapparis, 1999, pp. 28–31). For a strong case that it may predate the diapsephisis see Wallace, 2000; a further argument for this view is that Apollodoros' failure to mention the diapsephisis in his speech would be surprising if the trial took place soon after it (contrary to the statement in Fisher 2001, p. 63); if Stephanos and his sons, and also perhaps the husband of his daughter Phano, had survived the scrutiny process in their demes, Apollodoros would have had to offer an explanation of this fact and rebut Stephanos' attempt to exploit it in his favour.

women in the *demes*. Furthermore, they would become gradually the easier, because many citizen families had moved away from their own *demes* (that where their Kleisthenic ancestor was living in 508/7) and each *deme* therefore contained many citizens of other *demes* and foreign metics (described as '*resident in...*') who were not full members. It should be pointed out that all the arguments in speeches such as Demosthenes' 57 and 59, deployed in cases of disputed citizenship, focus on the need to demonstrate the Athenian parentage on both sides of those whose citizenship is in dispute; this, among much else, renders impossible Cohen's recent argument that well-embedded metics might be included in those called *astoi*, as distinct from *politai* (citizens by birth), and be legitimately accepted as citizens on the *deme* lists.[74] But such well-established metics, many of whom were ex-slaves, as well as some slaves living independently, and as we have seen, acquiring some wealth,[75] no doubt existed in many *demes*, especially those in the city of Athens, the Piraeus and neighbouring *demes*; some are likely to have developed close business, financial or sexual ties with citizens and may have been aided by their friends and an incautious or trusting *deme* assembly in order to get themselves or a relative enrolled into a citizen family. As the state increasingly recognised that it faced a major external political threat from Philip II of Macedon, enough voters, perhaps aroused by some famous scandals (such as, conceivably, the Neaira case), were persuaded that a dangerous situation needed the radical solution of a complete review. It seems only too likely, however, that the review itself exacerbated rather than ameliorated personal hatreds and uncertainties.[76]

In the period after the defeat at Chaeroneia, the first desperate response by the people was to accept Hypereides' proposal to restore rights to the disenfranchised and enfranchise any metics and free slaves who would agree to sign up to fight, if Philip invaded Attica.[77] Immediately subjected to a legal

---

[74] Cohen, 2000, ch. 2. There are many other arguments against this view, and the texts he cites do not support him: see e.g. Osborne, 2002.

[75] E.g. the case a little later of one Agasikles, prosecuted by Dinarchos for illegal acquisition of citizenship (*a graphe xenias*): see Hypereides, *For Euxenippos*, 3, Dinarchos, Fr. 16, Dion Hallicarnasseus, *Din.*, 10. Allegedly, he, like his father, a 'Scythian', before him, had been operating as a controller of weights in the agora (*prometretes*), which may well have been the occupation of a public slave, as an attendant to the *metronomoi* (whether or not Sauppe's emendation in Harpokration s.v. *prometretes of en demotiais* to *en demosiois* is correct). He is said later to have bought his way into the *deme* of Halimous, and to have been denounced while participating as a citizen in the *euandria* (manhood-contests) in the Panathenaia; apparently he was prosecuted for *xenia*, false acquisition of citizenship, in a heavy-handed procedure using the serious public process of *eisangelia*. See Jacob, 1928, pp. 119–21; Whitehead, 1985, pp. 292–3, and on Hypereides, *Euxenippos*, 3.

[76] Demosthenes, *Against Euboulides*, 57; Isaeus, *For Euphiletos*, 12; Aeschines, *Against Timarchos*, 1.77, 114–5; *On the Embassy*, 2.182.

[77] Athens had reacted similarly to a desperate crisis in the last years of the Peloponnesian war, when they set free and gave citizenship to slaves who had fought at Arginusai in 406 (see Hunt, 2001); and see for many other parallel cases, Patterson, 1982, pp. 287–93, Hunt 1998, and the essays in Brown and Morgan, 2006.

From Captivity to Freedom

challenge by Aristogeiton, under the procedure of the *graphe paranomon*,[78] it was apparently just dropped, as the danger from Philip receded. Hypereides later defended the proposal as purely the product of the defeat and Lykourgos strikingly presented it as the most pitiable feature of those dark days.[79] Overall, the event displays the commitment to defend the existing restrictive rules, if at all possible. In the next fourteen years, conventionally and with good reason characterised as the 'Lykourgan age', three complex snippets of evidence seem to reveal continuing concerns about procedures and rates of manumission and the maintenance of the boundary between slaves and free.

First, Aeschines in his speech against Ctesiphon of 330 BC cites and discusses recent laws regarding Ctesiphon's proposal (originally made in 336 BC, though the case took six years to reach the court) to award Demosthenes a crown in the theatre of Dionysos, in recognition of his overall political achievements.

> '*When the tragedies were taking place in the city, some people used to make proclamations, without seeking the approval of the people, some that they were being crowned by their tribes, others by their demes; some others used to set their slaves free by proclamation, making the Greeks their witnesses*'

This rash of proclamations had been checked by a new law that prevented the theatre proceedings from being disrupted.[80] This seems likely to have been a recent law (though certainty is impossible). Other evidence suggests that the Lykourgan period saw sustained efforts to increase the dignity and classic impressiveness of the performances at the City Dionysia, when many foreigners were present, as part of the presentation of Athens as a centre of Greece's cultural heritage: the theatre was given its new stone setting with special seats for cultic and civic dignitaries; a new stoa was added; the texts of the three great fifth-century tragedians were stabilised and re-performed frequently;[81] and increasing care was taken at this time to ensure that relevant business (such as honorific decrees for those with theatrical connections) was conducted at the assembly held in the theatre itself, which followed immediately after the festival (in the period 17th–19th Elaphebolion), and was published on stone subsequently. This may again suggest an emphasis on giving wide publicity on an occasion where many foreigners may still have been present to appropriate

---

[78] This procedure introduced in the later fifth century enabled an orator to challenge a decree of the assembly by prosecuting its proposer in a law court. See e.g. Hansen, 1991, pp. 205–12
[79] Lykourgos, *Against Leokrates*, 1.36–42, Hypereides, frr. 32–6.
[80] Aeschin., *Against Ctesiphon*, 3.41–44.
[81] Pseudo-Plutarch, *Moralia*, 841e. See Faraguna, 1992, p. 259; Humphreys, 2005, p. 87,; see also *IG* II2 354 = Schwenk, 1985, no 54, honours for Androkles the priest of Asklepios for maintaining *eukosmia* in relation to the theatre as well as in his shrine.

state acts which furthered the reputation of the theatre and its activities, and the support of the community for them; and less publicity to individuals proclaiming achievements unrelated to the theatre.[82] In our passage Aeschines is of course primarily concerned with honorific decrees and crowns, given that his case is against the crowning of Demosthenes; that he mentions manumission proclamations as well suggests that an increase in such proclamations, delaying the performances, had been observed, caused some irritation, and contributed to the passing of the restrictive legislation.[83] This increase in itself might suggest that both ex-owners and ex-slaves welcomed publicity for the act of manumission, slave-owners seeking public recognition of their generosity and freed slaves with good grounds wanting to secure public record and recognition of their manumission, above all because, as we have seen, proving one's free status and resisting attempts by a former master or others to get one back into slavery could be very difficult.[84]

These concerns about the appropriate locus for registering manumission may then be related to what seems to have been a new procedure relating to manumitted slaves introduced at about the time of the Crown speech. A substantial series of inscriptions, the so-called 'freedmen's silver bowls' (*phialai exeleutherikai*) documents, apparently dating from the period c. 330–320, presents a cryptic and abbreviated record of a large number of acts concerned with manumission; these often fragmentary documents unfortunately present almost as large a number of unresolved problems.[85] What seems to be going on is the recording of the results of prosecutions brought by masters against ex-slaves for not performing some residual obligations, using the procedure known as a *dike apostasiou*, a lawsuit for the 'abandonment' by the ex-slave of his legal obligations. But in all cases the slave is in fact acquitted and, thus, finally released from all obligations. Further, in all but a couple of early cases, a silver bowl (*phiale*) of a fixed weight of 100 drachmae is recorded as dedicated to Athena. The inscriptions usually designate the previous occupation of the slave. Of those for whom occupational terms survive the majority

---

[82] See Lambert, 2003 for a plausible argument that *IG* II2 410, honouring the priest of Dionysos and others, was originally intended to be published in the theatre at Piraeus, in the immediate security alarm after Chaironeia but publication was then moved to the theatre in the city. I am most grateful to Stephen Lambert for sharing his further thoughts on these matters.

[83] Fragments of an Isaios speech delivered after 358/7 (frr. 15–16 Thalheim:) suggest a manumission procedure in a law court was also a possibility.

[84] On the frequent involvement of other sanctuaries, and hence the sanction of the gods as witnesses, in a variety of manumission documents from Delphi and other places in Central & Northern Greece, see e.g. Westermann, 1944; Hopkins, 1978, pp. 133–171; Tucker, 1982; Darmazan, 1999; Zelnick-Abramovitz, 2005 passim, esp. pp. 184–208.

[85] There is one large inscription of which various fragments survive, and smaller fragments of some 20 documents. They can all be dated to the period 330–20 BC. See Lewis, 1959, 1968.

of women are called 'woolworkers' (*talasiourgoi*), and some of them have partners and children also being released; on one view this is a term used for general female domestic slaves (otherwise absent from the lists) and specifying the skill most readily transferable to life after slavery; alternatively it may be a sign that they worked in a more commercial clothes-manufacturing operation, or refer euphemistically to a side-line performed by those primarily offering sexual services (there are also a few musicians and entertainers on the lists).[86] The males are mostly divided across a wide range of crafts (c. 25), retail and transport of goods (c. 14) and overseas trade (c.6), with a not insignificant number engaged in agriculture – perhaps mostly as farm-managers (c.15), and a smattering of musicians. The majority are thus likely to have been slaves who enjoyed some independence and capacity to accumulate money to buy their freedom and perhaps contribute to a *phiale* (the texts do not reveal who paid for it); some were able to free their children as well.[87] The *deme* of residence of slaves is most commonly the city or Piraeus. Their citizen owners in almost all cases come from a different *deme*. However, it is impossible to estimate from this how many slaves had been 'living apart' from their masters, since we cannot say of any citizen whether he still lived in the ancestral *deme* in which he was registered for citizenship purposes or not. In some cases, though, metic slave owners appear as living in different *demes* from where their ex-slaves were now registered. Here it seems likely that the slaves had been operating independently, based in different *demes*, before they were set free.

What these documents represent is an unresolved problem. One view, strongly restated in two recent works, is that they are, as they appear, real cases of genuine disputes under the *dike apostasiou* procedure between former owners and their ex-slaves subsequent to an earlier manumission.[88] If that is the case, and given that there are over 300 cases in a period of less than 10 years on our very fragmentary documents, it would follow that the overall levels of manumissions were remarkably high, since presumably many more manumissions did not lead to such subsequent challenges, and some at least of those which did led to convictions (see also below). It has been noted, however, that on a couple of these texts it looks as if a good many cases were handled on the same day, or on very few days.[89] Hence the alternative view has won much support, that we have here forms of agreed 'fictitious' and collusive cases, whereby masters, slaves and the relevant magistrate and court used the mechanism of an

---

[86] Rosivatch, 1989, Todd, 1997.
[87] Jameson, 1977/78; Cohen, 2000, pp. 152–4. Some comparable evidence for occupations of manumitted slaves in Salvador in Brazil can be found in Nishida, 1993, p. 382.
[88] See Klees, 1998, pp. 334–54; Zelnick-Abramovitz, 2005, esp. pp. 282–92; she suggests a reason for so many cases of manumission and subsequent challenges may be the uncertainties of the corn shortages and political problems in the 320a.
[89] Lewis, 1959, p. 238; 1968, pp. 372–3; but see Klees, 1998, p. 345.

apparent *dike apostasiou* to achieve a consensual form of complete manumission accompanied by a formal registration, which included a lasting record on a stone stele and the dedication of a silver bowl as a form of payment to 'Athena'.[90] On this hypothesis, there is a further uncertainty, whether these are collusive initial manumissions, in the form which led straight away to a complete freedom, or collusive second stage releases from any further obligations (if so, again it would be even more indicative of widespread manumission in general).[91] Opponents of this hypothesis find it difficult to believe that politicians like Lycurgos and the voting assembly would agree to such a fictitious and cumbersome procedure, and that so many (ex-)masters would agree to forfeiting all rights over their ex-slaves.[92]

These complex issues cannot be further explored here, though the highly formulaic and truncated form of recording, the numbers involved, and the fixed dedication/payment to Athena seem to me more easily reconcilable with some form of consensual procedure of registration and state-payment for those gaining complete release from slavery, than with the idea of genuinely contested cases; we may have to allow that Lycurgan politicians persuaded the people to vote to establish this convenient legal mechanism. We may yet cautiously conclude first that manumissions, especially for those slaves with independent occupations, were at this period relatively frequent in Athens (thus, tentatively, supporting Patterson's judgement); whatever procedure is going on here, it seems likely that other less formal mechanisms of manumission coexisted with it. Secondly, it is likely that there was a sustained desire for a formal record of the slave's release, perhaps coming above all from those who were thus freed and/or completely released from obligations to their former masters; this procedure may be seen as a sort of replacement for earlier public announcements. Thirdly, there is a financial concern on the part of the state (perhaps with the involvement of Lykourgos): while to require (as in other cases) a dedication to Athena for this privilege would not immediately increase the state's revenues, there may have been the idea that such 'reserves' could be resorted to *in extremis*.[93]

On the other hand, there was reportedly another law passed at the same time by Lykourgos, which, as Klees[94] has plausibly argued, should probably be translated and interpreted as follows:

---

[90] Lewis, 1959; 1968; Todd, 1993, pp. 191–2.
[91] Westermann, 1946.
[92] Klees, 1998, pp. 348–52; Zelnick-Abramovitz, 2005, esp. pp. 284–6
[93] At least twice, in 321/0 (*IG* II2 1469. ll. 3–7), and again in 313/2 (*IG* II2 1480, ll. 8–11, Lewis, 1959, p. 236), some of these *phialai exeleutherikai* (so named on the documents) were melted down and reconstituted as large silver water-vessels (*hydriai*). On Lykourgan reserve-raising mechanisms involving dedications to the gods, see Lewis, 1968, pp. 374–7; Lambert, 1997b; Humphreys, 2004, pp. 121, 125–6.
[94] Klees, 1998, pp. 334–54

> *'His third measure was that it should not be possible for any Athenian or any one living in Athens to buy a free(d) person, of those who have been convicted, without the approval of the former master'.*[95]

If so translated, it indicates that Lykourgos was (also) interested in the results of genuinely disputed cases of *dikai apostasiou*. Here, where the master won his case, but decided, not unnaturally, that he no longer wished to keep on the 'ungrateful' slave, it was then felt appropriate that he retained a say in who did buy him, to avoid unwelcome possibilities such as that a friend of the slave, or an enemy of the previous master, might buy the slave and treat him better than he 'deserved'. The precise relation of this to what lies behind the *phialai* documents remains unclear. If those documents record genuinely contested legal court cases, as Klees believes, then this law fits in as an integral part of new procedures detailing with the consequences of both acquittals and convictions in such actions; if all or most of the documents reflect consensual manumissions or final releases, then the 'conviction' law confirms that Lycourgos, his colleagues and the people were concerned to regulate widely on manumission issues, including both new mechanisms for public recording of the transactions and payments to the city's goddess, and the consequences of a breakdown of ex-slaves' relations with their former owners.

In conclusion, both individual Athenians, and the collective *demos* when legislating, passing decrees, honouring benefactors and trying cases in court, could recognise how widespread and how economically important independent slaves and ex-slaves could be in the commercial, banking and other economic sectors; and hence they were to some degree aware of the many benefits such slaves brought to the economy and to their masters' prosperity. From the 350s they agreed, solely in strictly defined commercial cases, to treat such slaves legally as if they were free, along with all members of this separate world of overseas traders, agents and bankers. As in many other slave-holding societies, a good many other slaves in Athens were permitted to live relatively independent lives, subject to their providing money for and respecting their masters; they might of course at any time be downgraded to more miserable forms of servitude. Such slaves hoped to accumulate some wealth and to buy their freedom (sometimes with help from others, many of who might be ex-slaves); while other slaves might have enjoyed social or sexual relations with masters (or clients) which could seem affectionate and relaxed, and lead to their freedom, though they too were always subject to the threat of reversion to the servile experience of absolute power and cruelty, as exemplified by

---

[95] Pseudo-Plutarch, *Lives of the 10 Orators*, *Moralia* 842. Previously the term translated here as 'convicted' had been taken to mean 'captured', and concerned those enslaved as a result of war or piracy.

Hegesandros' beating of Pittalakos.[96] Overall, it seems likely that frequency of manumission in Athens, always substantial, increased steadily through the fourth century, and that this did not escape notice among the slave-owners.

These developments and perceptions did not, however, diminish the power of the standard ideology of Greek superiority over their slaves, and in many social and legal contexts strong prejudices about the inherent inferiority of slaves and their barbarian origins might at any time be dredged up and employed against independent slaves and ex-slaves. The existence of independent slaves and ex-slaves, the perceived increase in manumission, and the difficulty of maintaining the boundaries and identifying statuses in daily life all contributed to increased social tensions, especially at times of crisis, and induced a variety of contradictory official responses, in the form of citizenship grants, or restrictive scrutinies and lawsuits and a number of changes to the laws, both procedural and substantive.

Acknowledgments

My thanks to all present at the Galway colloquium on 'Slavery and Slave Systems' and above all to Constantina Katsari and Enrico dal Lago, its superbly enthusiastic and efficient organisers, and to Constantina for her excellent editing; to audiences at Sydney and Leeds who heard similar papers, and especially for their comments to Hans van Wees, Roger Brock, Malcolm Heath and Emma Stafford, and to Kelly Joss and Stephen Lambert for informing me of other work, sharing their work with me, and commenting in detail on a draft.

Bibliography

Beauchet, L. (1897), *L'Histoire du droit privé de la république athénienne*, 4 vols, Paris.
Bieżuńska-Malowist, I. (1974), 'Formen der Sklaverei in den Krisenperiode Athens', in E. Welskopf (ed.), *Hellenische Poleis: Krise – Wandlung – Wirkung*, Berlin, I, pp. 27–45.
Bogaert, R. (1968), *Banques et banquiers dans les cités grecques*, Leiden.
Brown, C.L. and Morgan P.D. (eds.) (2006), *Arming Slaves from Classical Times to the Modern Age*, New Haven.
Carey, C. (1992), *Apollodoros, Against Neaira [Demosthens 59], Translated with an Introduction and Commentary*, Warminster.
Carnsey, P. (1996), *Ideas of Slavery from Aristotle to Augustus*, Cambridge.
Cartledge, P. (1985, 2003), 'Rebels and Sambos in Classical Greece', in P. Cartledge and F.D. Harvey, *Crux: essays presented to G.E.M. de Ste Croix.*, Exeter, pp. 16–46, reprinted in 2003 (no editor) Cartledge, P., *Spartan Reflections*, London, pp. 127–152.

---

[96] Cf. again on similar opportunities for urban slaves in colonial Latin America, Schwartz 1974, 622–30, Nishida 1993, 386–91; and in the US, e.g. Genovese 1974, 388–401; Whitman 1995.

Cohen, E.E. (1973), *Ancient Athenian Maritime Courts*, Princeton.
Cohen, E.E. (1992), *Athenian economy and society: a banking perspective*, Princeton.
Cohen, E.E. (2000), *The Athenian Nation*, Princeton.
Darmazin, L. (1999), *Les affranchisements par consécration en Béotie et dans le monde grèc hellénistique*, Paris.
Davies, J.K. (1971), *Athenian propertied families*, Oxford.
Davies, J.K (1977/8), 'Athenian citizenship: the descent group and its alternatives', *Classical Journal* 73, 105–121.
Davies, J.K. (1981), *Wealth and the power of wealth*, New York.
Degler, C (1970), 'Slavery in Brazil and the United States', *Americal Historical Review*, 75, pp. 1004–1028.
Dobbs, D. (1994), 'Natural Rights and the Problem of Aristotle's Defense of Slavery', *The Journal of Politics*, 56, pp. 69–94
Faraguna, M. (1992), *Atene nell'eta di Alessandro*, Rome.
Fisher, N. (1993), *Slavery in Classical Greece*, London.
Fisher, N. (2001), *Aeschines Against Timarchus*: *translated, with introduction and commentary*, Oxford.
Fisher, N. (2004), 'The Perils of Pittalakos: Settings of Cock Fighting and Dicing in Classical Athens', in Bell, S. & Davies, G. (eds), *Games and Festivals in Classical Antiquity*, Oxford, pp. 65–78.
Frank, J. (2004), 'Citizens, Slaves and Foreigners: Aristotle on Human Nature', in *American Political Science Review*, 98, pp. 91–104.
Garlan, Y. (1988), *Slavery in ancient Greece*, Ithaca.
Genovese, E.D. (1972), *Roll, Jordan, Roll: The World The Slaves Made*, New York.
Gernet, L. (1938, 1964), 'Sur les actions commerciales en droit Athénien', *REG* 51, 1–44, reprinted in *Droit et société dans la Grèce ancienne*, Paris, pp. 173–200.
Hansen, M.H. (1983), 'Two Notes on the Athenian *Dikai Emporikai*', in Dimakis P. Biezuńska (ed.), *Symposion 1979*, Cologne, pp. 167–175.
Hansen, M.H. (1991), *The Athenian Democracy in theAge of Demosthenes*, Oxford.
Harding, P. (2006), *Didymus: On Demosthenes: translated, with introduction, text and commentary*, Oxford.
Hopkins, K. (1978), *Conquerors and Slaves*, London.
Humphreys, S.C. (2005), *The Strangeness of Gods*, Oxford.
Hunt, P. (1998), *Slaves, Warfare, and Ideology in the Greek Historians*, Cambridge.
Hunt, P. (2001), 'The Slaves and the Generals of Arginusae', *Americal Journal of Philology*, 122, pp. 359–380.
Hunter, V. (1994), *Policing Athens: Social Control in the Attic Lawsuits, 420–320 BC*, Princeton.
Hunter, V. (2000), 'Introduction: Status Distinctions in Athenian Law', in V. Hunter and J. Edmonson (eds.), *Law and Social Status in Classical Athens*, Oxford, pp. 1–29.
Jacob, O. (1928), *Les esclaves publics à Athènes*, Liège.
Jameson, M.H. (1977/8), 'Agriculture and slavery in Classical Athens', *Classical Journal*, 73, pp. 122–145.
Johnson, L.L. (1979), 'Manumission in Colonial Buenos Aires, 1776–1810', *Hispanic American Historical Review*, 59, pp. 258–279.
Jordan, D. (2003), 'A Letter from the Banker Pasion', in D. Jordan and J.Traill (eds.), *Lettered Attica: A Day of Attic Epigraphy*, Toronto, pp. 22–40.
Kapparis, K.A. (1999), *Apollodoros, Against Neaira, A Commentary*, Leiden.
Klees, H. (1998), *Sklavenleben im klassischen Griechenland*, (Forschungen zur antiken Sklaverei 30) Stuttgart.
Koger, L. (1985), *Black Slaveowners: Free Black Masters in South Carolina, 1970–1860*, North Carolina and London.

Lambert, S.D. (1997a), 'The Attic *Genos* Salaminioi and the Island of Salamis', *Zeitschrift für Papyrologie und Epigraphik*, 119, pp. 85–106.
Lambert, S.D. (1997b), *Rationes Centesimarum: Sales of Public Land in Lykourgan Athens*, Amsterdam.
Lambert, S.D. (1999), '*IG* II2 2345, Thiasoi of Herakles and the Salaminioi', *Zeitschrift für Papyrologie und Epigraphik*, 101, pp. 93–130.
Lanni, A. (2006), *Law and Justice in the Courts of Classical Athens*, Cambridge.
Lawton, C. (1995), *Attic Document Reliefs*, Oxford.
Lewis, D.M. (1959), 'Attic manumissions', *Hesperia*, 28, pp. 208–238.
Lewis, D.M. (1968), 'Dedications of *phialai* in Athens', *Hesperia*, 37, pp. 368–380.
Matison, S.E. (1948), 'Manumission by Purchase', *The Journal of Negro History*, 33, pp. 146–67.
Millett, P. (1991), *Lending and Borrowing in Ancient Athens.* Cambridge.
Nishida, M. (1993), 'Manumission and Ethnicity in Urban Slavery: Salvador, Brazil, 1808–1888', *Hispanic American Historical Review*, 73, pp. 361–391.
Osborne, M.J. (1981–3), *Naturalization in Athens*, 4 vols in 3, Brussels.
Osborne, R. (2002), review of E.E. Cohen, *The Athenian Nation*, 2000, in *Classical Philology*, 97, pp. 93–98.
Patterson, O. (1982), *Slavery and Social Death: a Comparatve Study*, Cambridge MA.
Patterson, O. (1991), *Freedom in the Making of Western Culture*, London.
Pečirka, J. (1966), *The Formula for the Grant of Enktesis in Attic Inscriptions*, Prague.
Perotti, E. (1974), 'Esclaves *Khoris Oikountes*', in *Actes du colloque d'histoire sociale 1972 sur l'esclavage*, Paris, pp. 47–56.
Perotti, E. (1976), 'Contribution a l'étude d'une autre categorie d'esclaves attiques: les misthophorounta andrapoda', in *Actes du colloque d'histoire sociale 1974 sur l'esclavage*, Paris, pp. 181–194.
Raaflaub, K. (2003), 'Freedom for the Messenians? A note on the impact of slavery and helotage on the Greek concept of freedom' in N. Luraghi and S.E. Alcock (eds.), *Helots and their masters in Laconia and Messenia : histories, ideologies, structures*, Cambridge Mass., pp. 169–190.
Reed, C.M. (2003), *Maritime Traders in the Ancient Greek World*, Oxford.
Rosivatch, V.J. (1989), '*Talasiourgoi* and *Paidia* in IG ii^2 1553–78: A Note on Athenian Social History', *Historia*, 38, pp. 365–370.
Schwartz, S.B. (1974), 'The Manumission of Slaves in Colonial Brazil', in *Hispanic American Historical Review*, 54, pp. 603–635.
Schafer, J.K. (2003), *Becoming Free, Remaining Free: Manumission and Enslavement in New Orleans, 1846–1862*, LSU Press.
Schwenk, C.J. (1985), *Athens in the Age of Alexander: the Dated Laws and Decrees of the Lycurgan Era, 338–322 BC*, Chicago.
Seager, R. (1966), 'Lysias against the Corndealers', *Historia*, 15, pp. 172–184.
Shipton, K. (1997), 'The Private Banks in Fourth-Century B.C. Athens: A Reappraisal', *Classical Quarterly*, 47, pp. 396–422.
Ste Croix de, G. E. M. (1981), *The class struggle in the ancient Greek world from the archaic age to the Arab conquests*, London.
Stroud, R. (1974), 'An Athenian Law on Silver Coinage', *Hesperia*, 43, pp. 157–188.
Taylor, M.C. (1997), *Salamis and the Salaminioi*, Amsterdam.
Todd, S.C. (1993), *The shape of Athenian law*, Oxford.
Todd, S.C. (1997), 'Status and Gender in Athenian Public Records', in G .Thur (ed.), *Symposion 1995*, pp. 113–124.
Trevett, J. (1992), *Apollodoros, son of Pasion*, Oxford.
Tucker, C.W. (1982), 'Women in the Manumission Inscriptions at Delphi', *Transactions of the American Philologial Association*, 112, pp. 225–236.

Wallace, R.W (2000), 'Investigations and Reports by the Areopagos Council and Demosthenes Areopagos decree', in *Polis and Politics, Studies in Ancient Greek History Presented to M. H. Hansen*, Copenhagen, pp. 591–595.

Westermann, W.D. (1946), 'Two Studies in Athenian Manumission', *Journal of Near Eastern Studies*, 5, pp. 92–104.

Whitehead, D. (1986), *The demes of Attica*, Princeton.

Whitman, S. (1995), 'Diverse Good Causes: Manumission and the Transformation of Urban Slavery, *Social Science History*, 19, pp. 333–370.

Whitman, S. (1997), *The Price of Freedom: Slavery and Manumission in Baltimore and Early National Maryland*. Lexington.

Wilson, J.-P. (1997), 'The Nature of Greek Overseas Settlements in the Archaic Period', in L.G. Mitchell & P.J. Rhodes (eds.), *The development of the polis in archaic Greece*, London/ New York, pp. 199–207.

Wormell, D.E. (1935), 'The Literary Tradition concerning Hermias of Atarneus', *Yale Classical Studies*, 5, pp. 57–92.

Zelnick-Abramovitz, R. (2005), *Not Wholly Free: The Concept of Manumission and the Status of Manumitted Slaves in the Ancient Greek World*, Leiden.

THE ABOLITION OF SLAVERY AND PLANS FOR FREEDOM IN LATE NINETEETH CENTURY BRAZIL

Walter Fraga Filho[1]

On May 13, 1888, when the newspapers announced the definitive abolition of slavery in Brazil, slaves and freedpersons took to the streets of the cities and towns of the sugar districts of the Bahian Recôncavo in celebration.[2] One person in authority from the town of São Francisco do Conde reported worriedly that the freedmen burst into "*noisy*" sambas during the nights following the announcement.[3] In Recôncavo cities just beyond the centers of sugar production, slaves recently liberated from the sugar plantations joined the urban poor in parades and general revelry sponsored by abolitionist associations. A newspaper from the city of Cachoeira reported that, on the night of May 13, "*the people spilled out into the streets*" accompanied by two bands. Speeches and cheers eulogizing the great day burst from the balconies of working class houses.[4] In Salvador, the capital of the province, abolitionists, students, the free poor and ex-slaves occupied the streets and paraded through the city center to the sound of marching bands. Fireworks illuminated the facades of private homes and public buildings night after night.

---

[1] The paper has been translated from the Portuguese by Mary Ann Mahony.
[2] The Recôncavo is a region that circles the Bay of All Saints and the city of Salvador in the northeastern Brazilian state of Bahia. It is quite warm and humid and, therefore, propitious to the cultivation of sugar cane and other crops. In the colonial and imperial periods, it was Brazil's most important center of sugar production, and the home of many Brazilian aristocratic families whose wealth and power dated back to the early days of colonization. The best discussion of the role of the Recôncavo and sugar plantations there in Brazilian history is in Schwartz, 1985. This study deals only with slaves who worked on sugar plantations, the "*grande lavoura*" in Portuguese, but this does not imply that the Recôncavo was exclusively a plantation region or that all slaves lived on large properties. B. J. Barickman, 1999, alerts us to the limits of this "*plantationist*" vision of Brazilian history and demonstrates that the region included a large variety of agricultural activities and methods of exploiting captive labor.
[3] Arquivo Público do Estado da Bahia (APEB), Delegados, 6227 (1885–1889), correspondence of the sheriff of the town of São Francisco, Luís de Oliveira Mendes, to the chief of police, 16 June 1888.
[4] Instituto Geográfico e Histórico da Bahia (IGHB), 'Ultimas palavras', O Tempo, 19 May, 1888, p. 1. On the festivals of May 13 see also, "Festejos abolicionistas", O Tempo, 23 May 1888, p. 1.

From Captivity to Freedom

The celebrations of the 13th of May turned into a huge popular demonstration, reflecting the extent of the anti-slavery social movement in Bahia and impressing observers their size. Two days after abolition, local newspapers referred to "*a hugely attended popular rally*," to the "*enormous multitude*" or to the "*great mass of the people*" that had taken over the streets of the city.[5]

Nevertheless, the local elite feared that "*mass of the people*" in the streets, a large part of which was composed of people recently released from slavery, and believed it would have dangerous consequences. On the 14th of May, one member of the Bahian Legislative Assembly protested at the reduction of the effective police force in the province, something which to him made no sense given the presence of around 80,000 people newly freed from slavery.[6] Elite residents of the cities of the Recôncavo and other Bahian regions sent requests for more police protection to the state chief of police. Three days after abolition, the planter and merchant Aristides Novis, confided his concerns about the events of May 13 in Salvador in a letter to the Baron of Cotegipe, one of the Brazilian Emperor's advisors. According to him, since that day "*we are living in complete delirium!*"

> "(...) *Hurray for the 13th of May, hurray for immediate abolition without indemnification, they are the saviors of the Homeland! Since the 13th of May we are living in complete delirium! Commerce was closed all day yesterday, marches in the streets, they went to find the Independence floats at Lapinha and they put them in the Palace Square; every night there is revelry; carnival, Independence day and the celebration of abolition! Imagine all three rolled into one, what an impact they've had, there are more than 3,000 blacks here who have come from the plantations. Just yesterday, speaking with the governor and the Chief of Police, I requested that as soon as these celebrations are over, that they make sure that these workers go back to the plantations, if not we will shortly be seeing an outbreak of thievery and murder.*"[7]

Novis' fear at thousands of freedmen mixing with the free poor in the streets of the city is obvious, as is his concern that the people's excitement had incorporated the dimensions and the meaning of Bahia's two most important popular celebrations. To his despair, the celebration of freedom had turned into a potentially explosive synthesis of Carnival and the Independence of Bahia.[8] The former slaveowner found it intolerable to watch, at one and the same

---

[5] Biblioteca Pública do Estado da Bahia (BPEBa), Diário da Bahia, 15 May 1888, p. 1. On the festivals of May 13 in Salvador see Brito, 1996, pp. 142–143.

[6] BPEBa, Anais da Assembléia Legislativa, vol. 1, sessão de 14 de maio de 1888, p. 68.

[7] Instituto Histórico e Geográfico do Brasil (IHGB), Collection of the Baron of Cotegipe, Box 918, file 23. Aristides Novis to the Baron of Cotegipe, 16 May 1888.

[8] Although Brazil declared its independence from Portugal on September 7, 1822, Bahia did not achieve liberation until July 2 of the following year, because of Portuguese resistance. Bahians therefore

time, the inversion of order that was Carnival and the commemoration of Independence. Behind this was his greater fear that the celebration would turn into a serious threat to order. For this reason, he did not hide his concern at the presence of more than 3,000 "*blacks*" in the streets of the city and pushed for repressive measures from the provincial authorities.

In the same letter, Novis revealed the reactions of his uncle, the Baron of Santiago, a major planter in the region, at the surprising changes in attitudes on the part of his ex-slaves since abolition and at the ways in which they had thrown themselves into the celebration of freedom. According to Novis "*(...) Santiago is well, but concerned, seeing the children he raised with such zeal take to the streets, etc. etc.*"[9] It seems that, for the old Baron of Santiago, the loss of his enslaved property was less of a shock than being unable, on that auspicious day, to interfere in the decisions of his esteemed "*wards.*" The Baron's concern grew out of the complete inefficacy of the traditional forms of control developed under slavery. The paternalism with which he had treated his domestic "*wards*" was worth nothing on that first day of freedom.

In those days, ex-slaves found the opportunity to openly question the basis and etiquette of seigniorial command, or to simply ignore the masters' orders. In this article, I attempt to demonstrate that abolition and the days that followed were important moments, in which ex-slaves tried to deepen the transformations in day-to-day power relations on and off the plantations. In the eyes of the ex-masters, the freedmen's behaviors were nothing but careless acts, the outgrowth of "*drunkenness*" and enthusiasm. The changes in attitudes of the men and women who emerged from slavery were also related to their expectations about the acquisition of free citizenship. Nevertheless, the days that followed abolition were actually loaded ones – in which were placed in dispute the possibilities and the limits of the condition of freedom and citizenship.

The Days Following Abolition

Many ex-masters were surprised at the perceptible changes in the behavior, language and attitudes of the men and women who until then had served them as captives. To confirm their freedom, the ex-slaves sought to distance themselves from an enslaved past, rejecting roles central to their former condition. On various plantations, the ex-slaves refused to accept the daily food ration, to go to work in the cane fields, or to work without pay. In

---

celebrate both holidays, but July 2 has historically been the more important one, commemorated by parades and street festivals in Salvador and many Bahian cities and towns. On July 2nd celebrations see Kraay, 1998. On Carnival as an inversion of the social order, see da Matta, 1988.

[9] IHGB, Collection of the Baron of Cotegipe, Box 918, file 23. Aristides Novis to the Baron of Cotegipe, 16 May 1888.

asserting their status as freedmen, many began to express themselves in a language that the ex-masters considered "*bold*" and "*insolent*." During that period, words and actions easily crossed the lines of what ex-masters understood as the appropriate etiquette of respect and deference. Few masters could later avoid bitter memories of the manner in which their former captives began to behave.[10]

In 1933, an ex-slave named Argeu recounted they way in which the captives of the plantation on which he lived celebrated the "*day of liberty*." He said:

> "*It was a terrible thing! Mr. Mata Pinto [the plantation owner] got everybody together, about 100 of us, for a samba, he ordered wine opened, cane liquor, molasses with tapioca, and at dawn he says that everybody's free. What the devil! We already know, and the bonfire cracked all night.*"[11]

Here we see the master's careful efforts to prepare a party to announce the good news of freedom to his ex-slaves becoming frustrated, because the slaves knew ahead of time that slavery had been abolished. On the following morning, the master was even more disgusted to discover that his slaves did not respond to the call to work, since, according to the elderly ex-slave, "*the following day nobody was left on the plantation.*" According to what he said, the domestic slaves also declared their liberty as well, since, the big house was almost completely silent; you could only hear "*the noise of the flies, in that house that the devil had taken over.*"[12]

Years after abolition, local chronicler Isaias Alves tried to use family memories to reconstruct what happened in the "*slaves' souls*" on the day that abolition took place. According to him, his grandfather's plantation filled with music and bonfires. In the town of Santo Antônio, one old family slave named Vitorino, spent the night "*insolent and provoking,*" and proudly marching through the streets shouting loudly "*Long live equality.*" The ex-masters were surprised at his behavior, since, until that point he had always been considered respectful and "*a good guy.*"[13] What most shocked the ex-masters was the perception that, in Victorino's head, and possibly those of other freedmen, the ideas of liberty and equality were mixing dangerously. It was a potentially explosive combination in a society fundamentally based on social and racial

---

[10] Foner, 1988, p. 12, affirms that in the U.S. south, ex-slaves attempted to liberate themselves from the "*marks of slavery*" in various ways, among which was destroying the authority that ex-masters could exercise over their lives.

[11] Interview with the ex-slave Argeu in 'O drama do cativeiro' (The drama of the captivity), O Escudo Social, São Felipe, 14 October 1933, p. 2.

[12] Interview with the ex-slave Argeu in 'O drama do cativeiro' (The drama of the captivity), O Escudo Social, São Felipe, 14 October 1933, p. 2.

[13] Alves, 1967, pp. 257–258.

inequality. Without realizing it, the author was revealing the way that the behaviors and attitudes of the ex-slaves frightened the "*souls*" of the former owners.

The ability to issue orders and to be obeyed, that was a basic condition of seigniorial authority, disappeared in the days following the 13th of May. According to Alves, on his grandfather's Outeiro Plantation, on the morning of May 14th "*after the news [about abolition], one [ex-slave] appeared with his head bandaged, another claimed that he was sick, and, asked why the others hadn't come to work, said that they were now free. The old man [the planter] at being informed of everything wasn't angry, just sad and worried.*"[14] For those freedmen, pretending to be sick and even openly refusing to come to work were ways of showing that their lives would no longer be dictated by the designs and wishes of the ex-masters. Doubtless, from the point of view of the former owners, the abolition of slavery was traumatic.

In alleging that they "*were now free,*" the freedmen on the Outeiro Plantation attempted to say that they no longer felt obliged to observe daily labor routines. Possibly they understood that working in the canefields was a "*continuation of slavery.*" For that reason, they refused to bend their backs in labor or to take part in any activity on the plantations. That is why, at dawn on the 14th of May, they refused to respond to the overseer's shouts or to the whistles that blew to announce the beginning of the daily grind in the cane.

The Baron of Vila Viçosa, the owner of large plantations in the city of Santo Amaro, registered his view of those days in various articles published in the Bahian press. On the 24th of January 1889, he wrote that, after the announcement of the law of May 13th, there was what he defined as "*general agitation in the [sugar industry],*" growing out of "*demoralization*" and flights. At the news that "*all Brazilian hearts should fill with recozijo*", the "*reflective spirits*" were overcome with apprehension about the economic future of the province. After their initial excitement about the law passed, they became depressed about the loss of workers and the lack of resources to pay salaries: "*since the 13th of May, labor has become completely disordered. The ex-slaves don't do anything except vagabond about, dancing and getting drunk.*" According to the Baron, most of them abandoned the plantations and went to the city of Santo Amaro, and the "*laziest*" of them stayed in their houses without working at all.[15] In the Baron's view the behavior of the freedmen was thoughtless, the result of unthinking desires and an enjoyment of sloth, vagrancy and drunkenness.

In the article the Baron of Vila Viçosa related his bitter experiences on the day after abolition. His words could not hide his chagrin at the loss of moral

---

[14] Alves, 1967, p. 54.
[15] BPEBa; 'A lavoura de cana de açucar, as causas de sua decadência nesta provincial e o seu estado depois da Lei de 13 de Maio', Diário da Bahia, 24 February 1889, p. 2. The article carries the suggestive title.

authority over people who, shortly before, had owed him obedience. He wrote that:

> "*I had left by train for Santo Amaro on the 12th of May, leaving the sugarmill functioning, and when I returned on the 14th I had no way to continue grinding the cane, but that didn't surprise me; because I'd come from the city without my servant who had been drinking since the 13th, and even the following day couldn't move, and only on the day after he shows up all embarrassed to tell me that he doesn't want to be my servant any more and that he was going to look for another way of making his living.*"[16]

In this passage, the Baron contradicted himself, since the decision of the servant to leave him wasn't motivated by sloth but by a desire for "*another way of making his living.*" Even then, for our Baron, the servant's decision grew out of the exhilaration and joy at the events of the previous day. Vila Viçosa tried to imagine the ex-slaves' logic: "*if when we were slaves we had to work every day, now that we are freedmen, we shouldn't have to work any more.*" In his view, with slavery extinct, sloth was all that remained to the ex-slaves, but he imagined that their minds obeyed "*only the habits of indolence and the temptations of vice and unruly passion.*"

To complete his portrait of the moral degeneration that abolition had unchained, Viçosa further observed that the cities had become "*overrun by black women throwing themselves into prostitution.*" The Baron tried to demonstrate that slavery had been a moral constraint on people he considered "*naturally*" inclined toward indolence, sloth, "*vice*" and "*unruly passion.*"[17] Vila Viçosa had supported the indemnification of planters for the loss of their enslaved laborers and he was a harsh critic of the way in which the government had decreed the law of the 13th of May. He hoped to show that, in addition to the loss of their human property, the ex-masters suffered disobedience and flight from the plantations, but it is evident that, behind his statements, was a great deal of dissatisfaction at his inability to control people who had belonged to him shortly before.

Inscribed in the words of Vila Viçosa's and the other observers is the notion that abolition represented much more than the loss of enslaved laborers; it had destroyed a way of life based on patterns and etiquettes of command and obedience. Beyond that, it had dangerously threatened to invert the "*places*" that individuals occupied in the social hierarchy. It was for no other reason that the Baron of Vila Viçosa deplored the day in which "*mothers of quality*" (read, white women and ladies of the big houses) were obliged to head for the kitchen and their children went without breast milk.[18] Truly, the Baron's

---

[16] BPEBa, Diário da Bahia, 24 February 1889, p. 2.
[17] BPEBa, Diário da Bahia, 24 February 1889, p. 2.
[18] Ibid, 2.

language expressed the laments of his social class at the destruction of the hierarchical rules and values that had benefited them for centuries.

The trauma that Bahian masters experienced at the end of the slavery even appeared in the pages of novels. In 1908, two decades after abolition, the writer Anna Ribeiro de Goes Bittencourt, herself the daughter of a large Recôncavo planter, explored the contrary feelings of the old slaveowners at the loss of their captive labor forces in her novel *Letícia*. The plot follows the matrimonial misadventures of Letícia, only child of old Travassos, a rich Recôncavo planter, set against the abolition of slavery, the fall of the Brazilian Empire and the proclamation of the Republic, crucial points with which the author punctuates the changes taking place in the private world of the mansions.[19] Letícia's personal drama becomes confused with the decline of the "*sugar aristocracy*," the social class to which the author belonged. Written by someone who lived through the tense period that followed abolition, the novel reveals the personal dramas of the planters whose wealth vanished as a result of the loss of their enslaved labor forces. And more than that, the novel serves as an important historical testimony of a person who experienced the end of slavery from the heights of the big plantation mansions.

In one piece of the novel, the author reproduces Travassos' speech at what he defined as the "*disordering of labor*" growing out of the end of slavery:

> "*– It is impossible to live like this! I never thought that our slaves, having been so well treated, would leave us without a thought. I always heard tell that slavery brought villainy, but many times I responded to this noxious maxim with the sentence by the author of Uncle Tom's Cabin: 'Treat them like dogs and they will behave like dogs; treat them like men and they will behave like men.' But what! (...) When I told them that they were free, I said to them: Those who don't want to remain with me can leave: I won't hold it against them; I only ask them that they let me know in advance so that I can organize the work to be done. They all insisted that they wouldn't leave me; some even added: 'Even if my master throws me out, I won't leave; I'm going to die here. We didn't have a master, but a father.*'"[20]

In the excerpt above, the master's surprise is evident at the change in the ex-slaves' behavior and the ineffectiveness of the traditional forms of seigniorial order. We see that the planter evaluated the freedmen's behavior through a paternalist lens, such that he interpreted the decision to leave the property as a sign of "*ingratitude*."

---

[19] Brazil became independent in 1822 as the the hemisphere's only monarchy. That monarchy fell in 1889, in part as a result of abolition, to be replaced by a republican government. On the transition from monarchy to republic, see Viotti da Costa, 2000.

[20] Bittencourt, 1908, pp. 68–69.

In another excerpt, the author revealed:

> *"So, I set a day to grind the cane, I let everybody know, the crates are full of cane, I get to the mill and some people are missing; where are they? They left without giving me the least satisfaction. Could anyone suffer this patiently? Madness, lies, it's like a plan to make me crazy."*[21]

Bittencourt perceptively recreated the masters' traumas at seeing themselves deprived of the services and comforts provided by the possession of enslaved men and women. In one scene, Travassos' family and guests – among them several planters – gathered around the antique table in the huge formal dining room of the plantation house. After serving the soup course, Dona Henriqueta broke the silence *"begging her guests' pardon for the flaws in the table service they were experiencing because of the servants' rebelliousness."* *"Under slavery, she continued, no house had better service than this one."* These words unchained a vociferous debate among those present about the best ways to deal with workers emerging from slavery. Sampaio, the hard line planter, flinging harsh criticism at the government for letting the freedmen *"vagabond about and insult their masters,"* congratulated himself for always having treated his slaves rigorously; for that reason, he said, *"they are almost all with me."* But later he finished: *"Just yesterday I gave a good beating to a guy I had put in the stocks."* The other planter, named Cândido, said that he believed it more convenient to treat his slaves in a less aggressive fashion, since he could not depend on the support of the government to protect him against them.[22]

In the scene she recounts, the novelist seems to suggest that ex-masters held a variety of opinions about the best strategies to follow in dealing with the ex-slaves. Travassos himself appears in one piece as the archetype of the *"good master,"* the one who treated his captives zealously and generously. But they were all affected by abolition and even Travassos was subject to the *"ingratitude"* of his former captives. Dona Henriqueta, Letícia's aunt, represented the white chatelaine of a plantation house who suddenly saw herself deprived of enslaved workers, especially the domestic servants who cooked and waited at table. In one piece of conversation, Dona Henriqueta deplored being obliged to prepare the meal: *"What alternative do I have but to take care of everything!"* Eurico, Letícia's husband, observes ironically that he can't complain about abolition; he doesn't miss the slaves. *"'That's because you're not in my place!' retorted Dona Henriqueta. 'It's not just their absence; it's the audacity, the insults!'"* Further along she continued: *"who wouldn't feel their ingratitude? I raised many of them; I treated them more like a mother than a mistress."*[23]

---

[21] Bittencourt, 1908, p. 69.
[22] Bittencourt, 1908, p. 94.
[23] Bittencourt, 1908, p. 95.

Against her husband's wishes, Letícia decided to remain on the plantation to care for her father, principally because:

> *"We are going through a terrible crisis, especially the ex-masters who live in the countryside. A bit of skill and tactical thinking is what is necessary to get work out of the ex-slaves. That is what my aunt [Dona Henriqueta] lacks. If they stay here a few more days, they will see that they need my help in the most insignificant aspects of running the house. Poor thing! She cries, she despairs, they [the ex-slaves] play the worst tricks on her. (...) I am proud to say that I still have some moral force with these people; they will see how they obey me."*[24]

Despite Letícia's efforts, the plantation did not return to the production of the period prior to abolition and it collapsed as a result of the crisis that hit the sugar industry because of the labor problems. The loss of his enslaved property shocked Travassos and the author suggests that was the principal cause of the illness that led to his death shortly after the proclamation of the Republic.

We can underscore that, whether in fiction or in the discourse of the ex-masters, the initiatives of the freedmen appear as unpremeditated acts, a simple refusal to work or the rejection of seigniorial authority that did not reach the level of *"skills and tactics."* This was one more of the inconveniences of the law that the ex-owners identified, as it abruptly elevated to the condition of free people, those supposedly unprepared for a life of liberty. Even so, the seigniorial discourse poorly hid planter fears that the freedmen's behavior threatened the social order. Rarely in the history of Bahia had the practices and symbols of power and planter command been challenged in such a profound manner.

In a story entitled "The Mysterious Case of Pouco Ponto," published in 1943, João da Silva Campos revealed the horrors that populated the planters' nightmares shortly after May 13th. He related that, one morning in May three or four days after abolition, a total stranger appeared at the gate house of the Pouco Ponto Plantation near the city of Santo Amaro. After dismounting from his horse, he climbed the staircase to the big house and, unceremoniously, entered the dining room where the owner and his family were dining. The stranger pulled up a chair, sat down and began to talk. He said that he had been sent by God to take revenge for all of the cruelties, injustices, and crimes of the past. Sometimes he seemed to talk to himself, and then he demanded food and voraciously consumed everything brought to him. Finally satisfied, he went down the stairs, mounted his horse and took off down the road. No one on the plantation recognized the man. Silva Campos suggested two explanations for the mysterious apparition: either he was simply some *"crazy guy,"* or he was someone who had *"gone crazy as a result of the new Law of the 13th of May."*[25]

---

[24] Bittencourt, 1908, pp. 83–84.
[25] da Silva Campos, 1942, pp. 159–160.

Aside from allowing us to think about the fears of the planters in the days following abolition, this story helps us identify some of the symbols of the social order under threat. The ghost – Silva Campos insinuates that we are dealing with a slaveowner who has lost his mind – came into the home of Pouco Ponto's owner, and, breaking with all of the rituals of respect and deference practiced on the plantations, made himself comfortable at the dining room table. The ghost identified himself as a messenger of God who was there to make amends for all of the injustices and *"crimes of the past,"* in an allusion to slavery, by then abolished. The story then reflected the crisis of conscience that haunted those who had previously owned slaves. Not by accident, the chronicler tried to raise the profile of planter Garcia Pires, the Pouco Ponto owner, identifying him as an abolitionist of conviction who, before abolition, had already freed all of his slaves.

In slaveowner memoirs, novels and stories, abolition appears as a decisive break in the patterns of etiquette and values established by the slaveocracy. The planters had both a political and an ideological interest in conceiving of abolition in these terms. The concept of abolition as a serious rupture served as the basis of an important political statement that the master class had been treated unjustly and then abandoned by the imperial government that had abolished slavery. Central to that position was the reality that abolition had not been preceded either by indemnification or by complementary laws that guaranteed planters some level of control over the freedmen. In the 1890s, the sugar planters raised these complaints as a way to explain the decadence of the sugar industry and as a major argument for extracting credit, loans at low interest and financial assistance in modernizing the sugar mills from the new republican government. Therefore, it was expedient for them to be able to show that abolition had broken a lifestyle constructed on a solid hierarchical foundation, as though the world of slavery had not been subject to constant tension.

Reading between the lines of the seigniorial discourse, it is possible to see that the ex-slaves had reached their own conclusions about the period in which they were living. The plans for freedom and the efforts that they made to distance themselves from the past were based on the experiences of struggles fought against slavery itself. This was an important aspect of the clashes that followed abolition and that the seigniorial discourse silenced.

A *"badly managed freedom"*

The letters and newspaper articles written by the authorities and ex-slaveowners provide an opportunity to reflect on what they thought about the changes in attitude on the part of the population coming out of slavery. Obviously the planters were interested in demonstrating that the social order was seriously threatened by the "*disobedience*" and the disorder growing out of the way in which the question of the "*servile element*" had been handled. Read against the grain, these sources reveal important clues about the expectations the freedmen held about the end of captivity, since a great deal of the discomfort on the part of the masters grew out of initiatives on the part of the ex-slaves who rejected the old practices or behaviors reigning under slavery. Beyond this, the expectations of the freedmen included long held aspirations, among which were access to land and distancing themselves from the forms of "*subjugation*" inherent in the enslaved condition. It is from this perspective that we can analyze letters that a prominent Recôncavo planter sent to the governor.

Six days after the 13th of May, Egas Moniz Barreto de Aragão, the Baron Moniz Aragão, town council president of São Francisco do Conde and the owner of several Recôncavo sugar plantations detailed the events that took place there after abolition in a long letter to the governor. He acknowledged having received the announcement from the Ministry of Agriculture, ordering the publication of the Golden Law [the Abolition Law], and wrote that he had not managed to call a meeting of the councilmen because of the harsh winter and because they were on their properties "*in an effort to take care of their individual interests.*" We should not be surprised that, in the face of abolition, personal interest took precedence over obligations to the municipality.[26]

Moniz Aragão also informed the governor that before the news that the bill for the definitive abolition of slavery had been presented to the legislature, almost all of the slaveowners in the community had unconditionally freed their slaves and children born free under the 1871 Law of the Free Womb – known as *ingenuos* – in an attempt to avoid a "*mass flight*" to the provincial capital. They were trying to anticipate the law in order to prevent slaves from abandoning plantations. According to him, only a few planters remained firmly in possession of their slaves until May 13th and he tried to give evidence of his statements by revealing that, on May 7th, his son's birthday, he had liberated 346 adult slaves and another 143 *ingenuos* from his Cassarangongo, Mataripe and Maragangalha plantations.

Certainly the granting of freedom was more a way to contain the disorder and insubordination than an act of generosity on the part of our baron. Since March, the slaves on Moniz Aragão had not appeared when called to the canefields, something that had been happening on the other plantations in the region as well. The freedmen clearly knew about the parliamentary debates and the pressure to end slavery on the part of the abolitionist movement. Possibly, the refusal to work was a way of forcing the baron to award freedom, something that masters had been doing as a way to contain the flights and the

---

[26] APEB, Câmara, 1436 (1881–89), Baron of Moniz Aragão and Captain Francisco Norberto Teles de Menezes to the governor, 19 May 1888.

total paralysis of the plantation activity as the cane harvest approached. The actions of slaves and of freedmen did not grow out of delirium, as the masters thought and the memorialists later argued.

Moniz Aragão stated that on the *"more ordered plantations, among which I count my own, there is something that I call respectful inertia."* He wrote:

> *"In the last two weeks none of them has done any work, none of them understands what is good for them, nor do any of them know what to do. Here there is no delirious joy at being liberated; here there is simply a disposition to live from what falls from heaven, in the form of meat and cassava flour, without working, and from what they can steal from their neighbor."*

What Moniz Aragão meant by *"respectful inertia"* remains, unfortunately, unclear but it might mean that the freedmen on his property strategically continued to mix deference with a firm refusal to bend their backs in the cane fields. Yet the Baron remained concerned about disobedience on the part of these freedmen.[27]

According to Moniz Aragão, the freedmen threw themselves into *"vagrancy"* and *"audacious"* theft of the herds in the pastures. According to him, the planters had been preparing *"appropriate proposals [to resolve the situation]; but everything is in suspense and speeches; only by wandering around can you see the naked and cruel truth of the horrible and dangerous state into which this community has fallen"*. Everything indicates that, after the 13th of May, refusing to work acquired a different meaning for the freedmen. Possibly they refused to work on the old terms of slavery and they saw doing so as a *"continuation of captivity."*

The correspondence from Moniz Aragão demonstrates that the freedmen in the region had expectations that went far beyond the rupture of the ties of slavery. For that reason he feared the return of those who had banded together to go to Salvador in the days just before abolition, supposing that they would demand *"to remain on the property, without working or paying rent or any other arrangement with the plantation owner, simply because abolition had been promised and taking advantage of liberation."* Possibly he supposed that, after contact with the agitation in Salvador in the days following abolition, the freedmen would return imbued with the urge to occupy the land without providing any services to the former master. As a result, the baron deplored the absence of measures on the part of the authorities to repress such *"intrusions"* or *"rebellion"* on the part of the freedmen. But, according to what he said, we can infer that his greatest worry concerned the freedmen who remained on the properties and refused to work. As he stated, a few planters were able to take advantage

---

[27] The attitudes of the ex-slaves approach what James Scott labels a hidden transcript, in other words, a *"hidden discourse"* invented by subalterns unable to openly criticize their superiors, through which they questioned those superiors without exposing themselves to repercussions; see Scott, 1990, pp. 1–5.

of some *"moral force,"* but aside from this *"paradigm"* there was no way to contain the *"vagrancy and the crime."*

In the eyes of the baron, the way in which the freedmen advanced on the cattle in the pastures and their expectation of access to land represented not only a threat to the social order, but also a fundamental challenge to the right to private property. The *"theft"* of animals and of land indicated that ex-slaves were fighting for what they considered *"justly"* belonging to them as free men. The *"respectful inertia"* that Moniz Aragão described on his properties could mean that some planters still had some moral authority over the freedmen, but that this was not sufficient to make the plantations function.

In a letter dated July 10, 1888, Moniz Aragão once again reported that he had not been able to hold a meeting of the local councilmen, because of what he called the *"disorganization of society and of labor"* to which the community had been subjected since the beginning of the year. According to him, the councilmen, most of whom were plantation owners, were unable to leave their properties because they felt threatened by the *"base instincts of the vagabonds who in their delirious joy were taking advantage of this badly managed freedom..."* From his statements, we can deduce that the presence of the planter councilmen on their properties was not sufficient to maintain order and that the *"respectful inertia"* and the *"absence of excitement"* were perilously giving way to *"delirious joy."* Like the Baron of Vila Viçosa, he preferred to believe that the initiatives of the freedmen were the product of the irrationality of *"base instincts"* or of *"delirious joy"* that grew out of plans and dreams which freedmen held as slaves.[28]

On the same day, Moniz Aragão clarified his worries and fears in another letter to the governor, this one marked confidential. He reported that, after receiving the circular from the Ministry of Agriculture proclaiming the approval of the Law of May 13, he had ordered the legislative decision published in a public notice. But after this

> *"to our unhappiness, the great majority of the recently-freed men in the community have not shown themselves deserving of the title of citizen which has been conferred on them; everyone knows that in this Recôncavo one found the best treated and best behaved members of the 'Servile Element of the Province;' even so it is impossible to reorganize service, either in agriculture or in the house; everything is disorganized and in appalling confusion."*[29]

He advised the governor that the refusal to work in the cane fields threatened sugar production, since, if there were fresh canes to be collected and

---

[28] APEB, Câmara, 1436 (1881–89) Baron of Moniz Aragão, president of the town council of São Francisco, to the governor, 10 July 1888.

[29] APEB, Câmara, 1436, Moniz Aragão, president of the town council of São Francisco to the governor, 10 July 1888; the document is marked "confidential."

transformed into sugar and molasses for this harvest, there would only be old cane available to the next one. After that, he avowed that the mills could close their doors, because no one had been planting new cane or preparing the fields for any other kind of crop. He predicted that 1889 and 1890 would be years of destitution and hunger.

Here he returned to what he defined as a *"poorly managed freedom"* and *"delirious joy."* According to Moniz Aragão, the freedmen sought compliance with a supposed "Order of the Court" that instructed owners to turn land over to them. In his view, they misunderstood the circular from the Ministry of Agriculture that ordered the announcement of the law of the 13th of May. For our baron, the *"miserable freedman"* read *"communism"* in the document in question, especially from the passage stating that *"on becoming the pride of the nation, the land no longer represented for him forced and unpaid labor, but the common good."* Moniz Aragão underestimated the freedmen's capacity for comprehension, since, from his perspective, the desire to own land could only be the fruit of a huge misunderstanding or of a *"badly managed freedom."*

Moniz Aragão's worry also had to do with the way in which ex-slaves tried to disconnect access to their own farm plots from their former obligation of working the land of their former owners. Still it is possible that, in those early days after the declaration of abolition, rumors that the freedmen had the right to land were circulating in the slave cabins of the region's sugar plantations.

The nervous tone of the letters from Moniz Aragão and the other provincial authorities reveals the fear of the owners at the unpredictable twists and turns of the process of abolition. The most worrisome aspect of abolition, for them, was that the former captive demonstrated expectations for freedom that went well beyond the ties that had bound them in captivity. The desire to own land and the other meanings that they had given to the idea of freedom convinced many masters that order was under serious threat.

The Delights of Freedom

A more detailed analysis of the conflicts that occurred after the proclamation of the Law of May 13th, demonstrates that, in various ways, the freedmen not only staved off seigniorial attempts to continue to interfere in their daily lives, to control their movements, to castigate and punish them, to dictate the rhythm of work, but they also dedicated themselves to assuring and amplifying privileges acquired during the period of slavery. In this way, for the ex-slaves of the sugar plantations, the plans for freedom included the maintenance of customary rights, among which was the opportunity to

The Abolition of Slavery and Plans for Freedom

continue to occupy their provision grounds, known as *roças* in the Recôncavo.[30] Without a doubt, the defense of access to *roças* was part of the freedmen's struggle to amplify the possibilities of survival alternatives to labor in the cane fields.[31]

Many freed persons remained in the localities in which they had been born or had lived as slaves in order to be allowed to continue to cultivate their small farms. Days after abolition, Moniz Aragão tried to transfer freedmen from his Maracangalha Plantation to another plantation called Cassarangongo, from which he intended to coordinate what he called the *"transition"* to free labor in his dominions. But his plans were frustrated because the freedmen refused to leave the plantation where they had been enslaved. When the master/baron, in retaliation, opened the plantation corrals and let the cattle out to graze in the provision grounds, the freedmen began to beat the animals who invaded their fields. They also became involved in conflicts with the plantation manager when they refused to obey him.

We can observe that, in addition to the maintenance of customary rights to the *roças* the freed men were searching for a way to make survival in freedom possible through free access to local markets. They also wanted to be able to put whatever price they wanted on what they cultivated in their fields. One ex-slave from Maracangalha stated that for four or five months after abolition they accepted food supplies furnished by the ex-owner, but *"in the end we didn't want to do anything else and even rejected rations."* He clarified that it had nothing to do with the poor quality of the food and that

> *"[...] we were completely enchanted and our heads were spinning; that everybody could make money from the cassava on the plantation and practically everyone said that they didn't need to work for the plantation, because we didn't want to be subjected to anybody anymore and we didn't want to go and get our rations from the plantation store and if the cashier wanted to sent the rations to the house he could do it, and if he didn't want to, he could keep them."*[32]

The abolition of slavery appears in the freedman's statement as a decisive moment in his personal development and in that of his companions in the slave cabins. The references to *"enchantment"* and *"heads spinning"* revealed that they had decided to create conditions of survival in which they no longer needed to live under *"subjugation."* To have a *roça* was to dream of the

---
[30] The confrontations between masters and ex-slaves after emancipation have been detected in other parts of the Americas. See Tomich, 1995, p. 241. See too, Litwack, 1980, p. 142; Scott, 2005, pp. 61–128.
[31] On the ways in which custom can become a field of change and dispute, see Thompson, 1993, pp. 16–17.
[32] APEB, Processos crimes, 15/538/2 (1889), fl. 26.

possibility of distancing themselves from an enslaved past and to create some personal space in the world of the sugar plantations. For those freedmen, continuing to accept the rations furnished by the masters meant having to continue to provide service in the cane fields, something that they were not disposed to do on the terms proposed by the ex-owners.

For them, the viability of freedom depended upon the increase of the production of the crops cultivated on their *roças* and free access to local markets. Deep down, the incidents involving freedmen and ex-owners were a manifestation of different and conflicting plans in relation to the definition of the material conditions of survival within plantation agriculture. While the ex-masters concerned themselves with guaranteeing the basis of the sugar industry, simply reabsorbing the ex-slaves as dependent workers, the freedmen saw planting crops and access to local markets as guarantees of their ability to subsist independent from seigniorial control. Their behavior suggests that the master's ideas that the ex-slaves were unprepared for freedom had no foundation.

Throughout the years of 1888 and 1889, freedmen occupied public lands or simply invaded lands that had been abandoned by their former owners. On June 16, 1888, the sheriff of the town of São Francisco informed the chief of police that *"vagrants, vagabonds and disorderly persons"* were getting together on the Bomba and São Paulo Plantations and in the surrounding areas. The sheriff accused those individuals of shocking the residents of those districts and advised that the number of them would tend to grow *"in view of the large quantity of freedmen who, not wishing to subject themselves to labor, are abandoning the plantations."* He finished by alerting the chief of police that there had been an outbreak of small problems with order as a result of the accumulation of *"vagrant freed persons who devote themselves to noisy sambas at night."*[33]

These encampments of freedmen lasted for months before the region's sugar planters broke them up. On April 6, 1889, an announcement appeared in the Diário da Bahia newspaper, signed by "The Victims," accusing the Barons of Rio de Contas and Moniz Aragão of not fencing their properties and letting the cattle invade neighboring properties, ruining crops. The accusers said that the workers of the Bomba Plantation suffered the most injury, since the Barons were trying to oblige them to abandon their fields to make way for the cattle. The informant referred to an episode that occurred on the night of March 16th, when armed men invaded the property, surrounding the homes of the workers, breaking down doors and tying up the residents whom they managed to capture. After that, they set fire to the houses and took possession of all of the objects and cash that they found.

---

[33] APEB, Policia-delegados, 3003 91887–89), sheriff of the town of São Francisco, Luís de Oliveira Mendes, to the chief of police, 16 June 1888.

The Abolition of Slavery and Plans for Freedom

According to the accusation, the captured workers were taken to the Mataripe and Tanque Plantations, belonging to the Barons Moniz Aragão and Rio de Contas, respectively. On those properties they were put in the stocks and beaten until Captain Francisco Ribeiro Lopes, *"proprietor and ex-master,"* requested their release. Among the things taken from the freedmen were pigs, chickens, agricultural tools and the equipment for making cassava flour.[34] The list of things stolen demonstrates that the domestic economy of the ex-slaves included the raising of animals, the planting of cassava and the processing of cassava flour. Therefore, the attack on them was one designed to break up small nuclei of freedmen, among whom were probably found the ex-slaves of the masters who ordered the destruction of the houses.

The author of the announcement, probably Captain Ribeiro Lopes himself, tried to connect those events to what he called the *"consequences brought about"* by the Law that abolished slavery. According to him, *"The nobleman deprived of living off the sweat of the miserable black, has become his declared enemy to the point of not allowing him any peace anywhere: jail or working for free – that's the choice."* He further denounced the overseers and the cashiers of the plantations for acting as though they were the police. For him, the freedmen were not criminals or vagabonds: *"they're just victims of a ferocious persecution for having been an obstacle to those who would like to to turn other people's plantations into pastures for the cattle of certain feudal lords."*[35] Hear the informant revealed that the freedmen's *roças* could be obstacles to the ex-owners efforts to amplify the area devoted to cattle pasture on sugar plantations in decline.

Conclusion

Without a doubt, throughout 1888 and 1889, the social situation in the Recôncavo was potentially explosive. Serious conflicts occurred in various parts of the region. Beginning in December of 1888, the region's authorities began to report large numbers of fires and thefts on the sugar plantations. Most of these incidents were attributed to the ex-slaves. On January 6, 1889, *"A correspondent"* from the town of São Francisco reported that fires, principally involving fences and cane fields, were breaking out all over the plantations. According to him, many of the fires were *"intentionally set by freedmen given over to vagrancy."*[36] On January 14, 1889, a report published in the *Diário da Bahia*

---

[34] APEB; "Um crime monstruoso", Diário da Bhaia, 6 April, 1889, p. 2.
[35] APEB; 'Um crime monstruoso', Diário da Bhaia, 6 April, 1889. The informant defined that event as an action against freedom and the right to property; he also affirmed that the authorities did not investigate the crime, because the deputy sheriff had ordered it and the sheriff was a relative of another one of the men behind it.
[36] BPEBa; 'Villa de São Francisco', Diário da Bahia, 6 January 1889, p. 1.

entitled "Desperate Crisis" claimed that the intentional torching of cane fields, fences and pastures was being carried out by *"vagabonds"* who were attempting to take advantage of the situation to steal cattle from the plantations.[37] The author of the story, certainly an ex-slaveowner, established a connection between the fires and thefts of cattle, both ingredients of what he called the *"insubordination"* of the freedmen.

The fires can, in part, be credited to the conflicts that were taking place on the plantations. The lists of damages published in the newspapers show that the flames principally involved fences, cane fields, wooded areas and pastures belonging to the masters. Under slavery, slaves had commonly used the burning of cane fields or wooded areas in order to sabotage the plantations. They may have done so after abolition was declared as well: certainly the destruction of the *roças* by the cattle and the repression of those who refused to work in the cane fields created an atmosphere of resentment and contributed to elevating social tension to a dangerously explosive level.

It is also evident that the plantation owners were searching for a way to gain political advantage from these episodes. The shocking notices sent to the press were an opportunity, once again, to demand from the national and regional government's assistance for plantation agriculture in the form of agricultural credit and, principally, repressive measures to reestablish planter control over their ex-slaves. Therefore, the notices demanded the repression of vagrancy, of the fires and of the cattle and crops. Throughout 1888, the sugar plantation owners asked the provincial police for permission to act freely in the repression of insubordinate freedmen or those who refused to work in the cane fields. They attempted to reestablish forced recruitment to the armed forces, ignoring the restrictions that the law imposed on the imprisonment of free citizens. The pressure on the local authorities from plantation owners generated consequences for the freedmen's day-to-day existence.

The sugar plantation owners and the authorities of the rural parishes also tried to expel from the district anyone who would not submit to discipline or who refused to work in the cane fields. All through 1888 and 1889, the sheriffs of the Recôncavo's cities remanded individuals accused of vagabondage or vagrancy to the custody of officials in the provincial. On December 11, 1888, for example, the sheriff of Santo Amaro sent Malaquias Ferreira, *"a vagabond of the worst sort,"* José dos Santos, who *"voluntarily"* wanted to enlist and José Nunes dos Santos, a vagabond who *"has no way to make a living and does not seek to have any"* to his superiors in Salvador as military recruits.

Truthfully, the powerful frequently used the repression of vagrancy to expel from their distincts individuals considered *"insubordinate"* or who would not

---

[37] BPEBa, 'Villa de São Francisco', Diário da Bahia, 6 January 1889, p. 1.

submit to seigniorial authority.[38] The ex-masters feared the loss of control over the freedmen, especially if the latter decided that they no longer wanted to work in the cane fields or in any other service traditionally reserved to them. It was not by accident that the sugar plantation owners began to demand of the government more rigorous measures against vagrancy and vagabondage. In this way, ex-masters attempted to limit the ability of those who were emerging from slavery to search for alternative methods of survival.

Without a doubt, in 1888 and 1889, the violence against freedmen in the Recôncavo escalated. Many planters began to act on their own, seizing people, inflicting corporal punishments on them and placing people accused of setting fires and other offences against property in the stocks. Some contracted armed men to guard the fields, and to intimidate or expel from the plantations anyone who refused to work in the sugar industry.

The provincial authorities tried to intervene in the conflicts occurring in the Recôncavo. There are indications that, in December 1889, eight companies of Police Guards were sent to the interior of Bahia and instructed to apprehend "*rural guards*" in service to the planters and assist the town councils in the formation of settlements "*designed to provide work to the vagabonds and lazy guys that have been sent from neighboring towns; obliging them to sign a promise of good behavior.*"[39] We lack reports about the way these police forces behaved on the plantations, but the government's measure demonstrates that it was trying to disarm seigniorial militias and establish rigid control over the population emerging from slavery.

The evidence shows that once the tensest period of 1888–1889 had past, the authorities became convinced that antivagrancy laws made no sense. The plantations needed temporary laborers and that implied periodically allowing people to move from the Bahian interior to the coastal sugar districts, something that such laws made more complicated.

We can observe, therefore, that after those early tense days, the ex-slaves and their descendents continued to struggle to amplify their activities independent of sugar plantation agriculture, to cultivate subsistence crops in their *roças* and to sell the surplus in the local markets, to slow the pace of work, to negotiate better remuneration, in short, to create conditions that would distance them from a past in slavery. Their battle was complicated and difficult, perhaps more subject to retreats than to advances, since land and access to public resources continued to be concentrated in the hands of their former owners. Abolition did not imply changes in the socio-racial hierarchy built over the course of long centuries of slavery. Even so, the ex-slaves and their

---

[38] APEB, Polícia-delegados, 6227 (1885–89), Sheriff of Santo Amaro, Antônio Lourenço de Araújo to the Chief of Police, 11 December 1888.
[39] APEB, Polícia-assuntos, 6507 (1888–1889)

descendents did not forget or discount the implications and the meanings of abolition in their lives. It is enough to say that the 13th of May was well celebrated by rural workers many years after slavery had been abolished.

On the other hand, the Republican governments that followed the end of the Empire in 1889 tried to strip the 13th of May of its meaning. By the end of the 1890s, the celebration had lost a great deal of the brilliance of the early years. Elites had political reasons to encourage people to forget that date and the events that culminated in abolition. One of them was certainly an effort on the part of republican politicians to denigrate something that had been identified as one of the Brazilian monarchy's great accomplishments. The other, perhaps more veiled, was the foal of silencing conflicts and demands that had been born in the course of the struggles against slavery and for citizenship.

Bibliography

Alves, I. (1967), *Matas do sertão de baixo*, Bahia.
Bittencourt, A. R. G. (1908), *Letícia*, Bahia.
Brito, J. (1996), *A abolição na Bahia: uma história política, 1870–1888*, Bahia.
Foner, E. (1988), 'O significado da liberdade', *Revista Brasileira de História*, 12, São Paulo.
Garcia, A. (1989), *O Sul: caminho do roçado: estratégias de reprodução camponesa e transformação social*, São Paulo.
Kraay, H. (1999), 'Between Brazil and Bahia: Celebrating Dois de Julho in nineteenth-century Salvador', *Journal of Latin American Studies*, 31.1, pp. 255–286.
Litwack, Leon F (1980), *Been in the storm so long: the aftermath of slavery*, Nova York.
Matta, R. (1988), *Carnivals, Rogues and Heroes*, South Bend.
Regeneração, J. C. G. (1892), *Agrícola do Estado da Bahia*, Bahia.
Scott, J. (1990), *Domination and the Arts of Resistance*, New Haven.
Scott, Rebecca J. (2005), *Degrees of Freedom: Louisiana and Cuba after slavery*, Cambridge/Massachusetts.
Schwartz, S. B. (1985), *Sugar Plantations in the Formation of Brazilian Society: Bahia, 1550–1825*, New York.
da Silva Campos, J. (1942), *Tempo antigo, Tempo antigo, crônicas d'antanho, marcos do passado, histórias do Recôncavo*, Bahia.
Thompson, E. P. (1993), *Customs in Common: Studies in Traditional Popular Culture*, London.
Tomich, D. (1995), 'Houses provisions grounds and the reconstitution of labour in post-emancipation Martinique', in M. Turner (ed.), *From Chattel Slaves to Wage Slaves: The Dynamics of Labour bargaining in the Americas*, Bloomington, pp. 241–260.
Viotti da Costa, E. (2000), *The Brazilian Empire: Myths and Histories*, 2nd ed., Chapel Hill.

INDEX

Abolition 12, 14–15, 84, 97–98
   Brazil, May 13th 147–148
   Concerns 148
   Expectations 157
   Impact 91, 149–163
Activists 115–116
Administration,
   Of Greek city states 23
   Of Macedonia 23
Adoption 43
Aemilius Paulus 27, 31
Affection 65
Africa
   South 4
   West 41, 44
Alliances 44, 47, 49, 52
Ancilla 61–64, 65
Anti-Slavery Movement 148, 157
Apophora 124
Aptheker, Herbert 103–104, 115
Archaeological material 10–11, 59–60, 67
   Settefinestre 59
Aristotle 123–124
Armies 99–100
Armilla 11, 60–61, 63–64

Banking 124, 128
Behavior 91, 149–151, 153
Biographies 115
Bithynia 123
Bloch, Marc 3–4
Borders 49
Bradley, Keith 6, 28, 96, 98–99
Brazil 11, 15, 147–166
   Ilheus, Bahia 71–91
   Salvador 158
Buildings 60–62
Bush, Michael L. 8
Business, slave operated 126

Cacao 73–76, 79–84, 88
Captives 9, 42, 53
Capture 41, 47
Caribbean 43
Carthage 30
Cartledge, Paul 125
Cattle 162
Census 86–87
Children 73, 75–76, 77–78, 80, 81, 86, 91
   Ingenuos 75, 76, 81, 157
   Of slaves 132
Christianity 10, 54
   African Methodist Episcopal Church 107, 108, 109, 112–113
Class 5
Cohen, Edward 128, 137
Coinage 34
Colonization 41, 43
Commerce 142
   Prohibition of 33
Communities 132, 159
   Maroon 98–99
   Urban 125
Comparative approaches 3–9, 10, 15–16
Conflict 162–164, 165, 166
Conspiracy 108, 111, 112, 114, 116
Contempt 131
Costabile, Felice 64–65
Courts
   Athenian commercial 131, 141
   Athenian law 127–128
   Roman 66
   Charleston, South Carolina 110–111, 114
Cynoscephalae, battle of 23

d'Iberville, Pierre Le Moyne 45, 48
Debt 52, 53
   Bondage 9, 36, 37
   Crisis 23

Index

Depopulation 27
Deportation 54
Diodorus 100
Disease 47
Dutch West Indies Company 30

Economy
  Greek 26
  Internal economy of slavery 79, 82
  Macedonian 34, 37
  Measures 37
  Roman 9, 34
Egypt 62
Elderly 38
Elites 6
  Brazilian 148–149, 166
  Greek 23, 31
    Thessalian 23
  Macedonian 33, 34, 37
  Pompeian 61
  Thracian 23
Emancipation 83
  Fund 73, 90
English colonists 9, 43, 46, 48–53
English Royal African Company 30
Enslavement 9, 27–28, 37, 41, 42, 48, 49, 53, 54
Entrepreneurs
  Roman 33
    Publicani 34
Equality 150
Escaped Slaves 79
Estates 27
  Haciendas 43
  Management of 23
Eunuchs 123
Ex-slaves 74, 155, 156, 157–158, 160–163
  Control of 156
  Freedmen 81, 82–84, 125, 127, 136
  Hermias 123
  Lavradores 84, 88–89
  Obligations 139, 141, 151, 161

Family 72, 73–84, 91
Famines 31
Fear
  Of local tribes 52, 54
  Of ex-slaves 148–149, 151, 155, 159
Finley, Moses 6

French colonists 9, 43, 45–46, 48
Freedom 12, 72, 79–84, 126, 140, 149, 159–162
Freehling, William W. 109
Fredrickson, George 4–5

Gender 72, 91
Genocide 29
Greece
  Achaea 21
  Aetolian 21, 23, 26
  City States
    Athens 124–143
    Abdera 25
    Chalcis 25
    Haliartus 25
    Messene 101
    Oreus 25
    Sparta 100–102
    Thebes 25
  Epirus 27
  Monetary capacity 32
Gruen 33
Government 82, 84, 88, 156
Guns 44, 45, 47, 50
Guzzo, Pier Giovanni 61–64

Hannibal 21, 29
Harris, William 28
Helots 100–102
Hellenistic kingdoms 21
  Antigonids 35
Hopkins, Keith 6, 27
Hostility 131, 132
Households 10, 66, 74, 126
Husbands 63

Illyria 27
Independents 14, 117, 124, 126, 142
Inheritance 77, 80–81
Inscriptions
  Greek 36, 97, 139
  Latin 11, 61, 63, 64, 65
Italy 27–28

Jagunços 89
Jewellery 63–64
Johnson, Michael P. 109, 111, 115
Jordan, Winthrop D. 116

Index

Kolchin, Peter 4–5
Labour force 6, 9
   Of Macedonia 26
   Shortage 5
Land 165
   Acquisition of 33, 84, 160
   Availability of 5
   Clearance 88
   Conflict over 88–89, 162–163
   Occupation of 158, 161–162
   Royal 33, 35
Laws 43
   Of the Free Womb 12, 75, 76, 81, 157
Leadership 101
Leasing 33
Leticia 153–156
Livy 22
Lofton, John 108
Lucretius Gallus, Gaius 25

Macedonia 32–33
Macedonian Wars
   First 21, 23, 26
   Second 21, 23
   Third 21, 22, 31
Manumission 14, 124, 125, 127, 134, 136, 138, 139, 141
Markets 79
Marriage 65, 74, 127
   Jus conubii 32, 37
Marxism 62
Massacre 24–26
Master 61, 65, 91
Men 76, 78, 81, 82, 86, 91
Metics 125, 130, 137
Migration 85–86, 91
Military Practices 30
   Roman
      Direptio 24
Mines 33, 34–35
Missions 44
Morality 67, 151–152
Morgan, Philip 116–118
Motivation 126

Native Americans 9, 28–29, 41, 47–48, 54
   Confederations 49
   Involuntary labour 43
   Slaves 29, 45

Trade with 43
Tribes
   Arkansas 50
   Alabama 45, 48, 49, 50, 53
   Apalachee 48–49, 51, 53
   Cherokee 50, 53
   Chickasaw 48, 50, 53
   Chitimachas 45
   Choctaw 48
   Creek 44, 50
   Guale 43, 44
   Timucua 43, 44
   Tuscarora 53
   Westo 44, 47
   Yamasee 44, 50, 53, 54
North America 4, 41
   Carolinas 13, 47, 48, 49–50, 51, 53, 54
   Charleston 107–118
   Colonial southeast 42
   Florida 43, 44, 49, 51, 52, 53
      St Augustine 43, 50
   Louisiana 47, 51
   Mississippi River 45
   Virginia 47, 53

Order 149, 155–156
Owners, Slave 5, 76–77, 81, 90
   Ex- 85, 88, 148–156, 164

Passivity 117
Paternalism 5, 153–154
Patterson, Orlando 6, 28–29, 104, 125
Perceptions 67, 153–154
Pergamum 96–97
Perioikoi 102
Perseus of Macedon 21, 30, 31
Philip V of Macedon 21, 22
Piccinin, Pierre 95, 100
Pillaging 24, 25, 26
   Destruction of Crops 30
   Looting 35
Place 152
Plantations 5, 9
   Sugar Plantations 147, 149, 151
   Cacao Plantations 75–76
Police 164
Polybius 22
Pompeii
   Cellae meretriciae 62

169

Index

Pompeii (*cont.*)
  Frescoes 61
  House of the Vettii 61, 63
  Moregine 60, 63
  Suburban baths 63
Poor 95–96
Power 33, 149
Prejudice 132, 143
Prisoners 29
Profits
  Of property 31
  Of war 32
Property 12, 33
Prostitution 11, 61–67, 90
Public slaves 133
Punic Wars 28
Punishment 89, 90, 134
  Hanging 111
  Whipping 111
Pydna, battle of 21, 31, 32, 36

Queen Annes's War 42, 48

Race 87–88
Racism 10, 43
Raids, 46, 49, 51–52, 53
Ransoming 29
  Profits 29
Rebelliousness 115, 116, 125
Refusal to work 149–150, 157–160, 164
Relations
  Master and slave 65–67, 71, 72, 101
  Patron and client 88
  Slave and slave 71, 74
Relatives, of slaves 29
Religious superiority 43
Relocation 51, 76–78
Reproduction 62, 65, 73
Resistance 116, 118
Revolts 12, 43, 95–105
  American 103–104, 115
  Of Aristonicus 96
  Saint Domingue 98
  Sicilian 95–96, 103
Rights 14, 134, 137, 141, 149, 159, 160–161, 166
Roças 79–83
Roles of Slaves
  Agents 124, 128
  Agriculture 46, 140

Concubines 45
Craftsmen 46, 124
Domestics 45, 46, 127, 140
Hunters 45
Guides 45
Managers 124, 128
Retail 140
Rowers 127
Traders 140
Woolworkers 140
Rome
  Colonies 27
  Italy
    Sicily 95–96, 103
  In the East 21, 32
Runaways 52

Sacrifice 24–25
Sale
  Of captives 41
  Of slaves 76–78
Salt 33
Samnite Wars 28
Satyricon 64
Scarano Usani, Vincenzo 61–64
Schiedel, Walter 6, 28, 59
Separation 76–78
Sex 61–62, 67
Sexual exploitation 63, 64, 65
Shaw, Brent, 6, 97
Shipbuilding 34
Ship owning 124, 127, 130
Skins 46, 54
Skocpol, Theda 4
Slave Trade 41, 46, 49
  Export 46, 49
  Traders 29, 50, 52, 53
  West African 54
Socialism 104
Soldiers
  Roman
    Attitude 37
  Spanish 44
Somers, Margaret 4
Spanish colonists 9, 43–44, 48–49
Spartacus 95–96, 100, 103
Starvation 37
Status 75, 128, 131, 134
  Citizenship 136

Sugar 75, 85, 88, 147, 155, 159–160, 162
Systems, Slave 5–9, 42–43, 62
   American 5
   Chattel slavery 43
   Indebtedness 43
   Roman 9
Serfdom 5

Talbert, Richard 101–102
Taxes 35
   Tributum 36
Theft 158, 163
Thrace 22
Timber 33–34, 37
Tinkler, Robert S. 113–114
Torture 89, 118, 129
Trade 32, 44–45, 47
   Ban 36
   Overseas 130
Transportation 28–30, 111
   Logistics 29
Tuscarora Wars 53

Uprisings see revolts
Urban environments 108

Usner, Daniel 47

Van Hoek, Stephen 48
Vesey, Denmark 107–108
Violence 89, 91
   Against masters 100–101
Vogt, Joseph 96

Wade, Richard C. 108–109, 116
Warfare
   Ancient 22, 30, 41
   Captives 27
   Native American 48
Wealth
   Accumulation of 32, 135
   From warfare 36
Weber, Max 3
Whitby, Michael 102
White, Richard 47
Wiedemann, Thomas 96–97
Women 11, 38, 60–61, 72, 73, 75–76, 78, 80, 81, 86, 90, 91, 116, 127, 140
Worship 113

Yavetz, Zvi 96

Leicester Archaeology Monographs

This series was established in 1993 to publish work related to the research interests and activities of the School of Archaeology & Ancient History, including the work of the University of Leicester Archaeological Service (ULAS). The most recently published titles are listed below, while more information can be found at:
http//www.le.ac.uk/archaeology/research/pubs/catalogue.html

Monument, Memory and Myth, Use and re-use of three Bronze Age barrows at Cossington, Leicestershire (2008) John Thomas ISBN 978 0 9538914 8 1

The Archaeology of the East Midlands (2006) ed. Nicholas Cooper
ISBN 0 9538914 7 X

Coins, cult and cultural identity (2005) Eberhard Sauer ISBN 0 9538914 4 5

Ethnography and Archaeology in Upland Mediterranean Spain (2004) by N. Christie, P. Beavitt, J. G. Santonja, J. Segui & M. V. Gil Senis ISBN 0 9538914 6 1

Re-searching the Iron Age (2003) ed. Jodie Humphrey ISBN 0 9538914 5 3

The Prehistory of the East Midlands Claylands (2002) Patrick Clay
ISBN 0 9538914 3 7

Researching Material Culture (2000) ed. Sue Pearce ISBN 0 9538914 2 9

The Archaeology of Rutland Water (2000) Nicholas Cooper ISBN 0 9538914 0 2

Roman and Medieval Occupation in Causeway Lane, Leicester (1999) Aileen Conner and Richard Buckley ISBN 0 9510377 8 1

For further information, please contact:
Leicester Archaeology Monographs c/o School of Archaeology & Ancient History, University of Leicester, University Road, Leicester LE1 7RH, UK
Tel: +44 (0)116 252 2611; Fax: +44 (0)116 252 5005; arch-anchist@le.ac.uk